Who's Who in Dickens

Who's Who in Dickens

JOHN GREAVES

TAPLINGER PUBLISHING COMPANY
NEW YORK

823
DIC

First published in the United States in 1973 by
TAPLINGER PUBLISHING CO., INC.
New York, New York

Copyright © 1972 by John Greaves
All rights reserved
Printed in Great Britain

Library of Congress Catalog Card Number: 73–5335

ISBN 0–8008–8266–0

c.1

Contents

Foreword

The world Charles Dickens created is so teeming with life, so densely populated, as to be alarming to all but the possessors of prodigious memories. (John Greaves, fortunate man, is one of these.) Dickens characters have a vitality, a theatrical one if you like but none the less irrepressible, that raises them like bubbles of oxygen in the mind on all sorts of occasions—in conversation, in reading some unrelated subject, glimpsing a face in the street that is like Wemmick's, hearing someone mention spontaneous combustion and then at once there is Mr. Krook. . . .

And then, their names. So innumerable, so mysteriously apt, almost always telling us something *about* the character in the most unidentifiable way, by a secret route of subconscious links and suggestions. Dickens attached great importance to names; his working memoranda are full of scribbled attempts, suggestions, rejections. Those immortal solicitors, for example, Messrs. Spenlow and Jorkins, began life as Aiguille and Tanguille, went on a stage as Tranguille and Jorker, and then, across the page and doubly underlined—'No. *Spenlow & Jorkins*'—from which point they are part of our language. Miss Mowcher, too (perfect name for that *louche* little oddity), had her shaky beginnings. 'Miss Croodledey, Miss Croodledy, Miss Croodlejeux . . .' and then as before, with absolute decision, 'No. Miss Mowcher.'

The characters proliferate, the names have an incantatory importance—but how do we remember them all? Who was Mr. Mallard, what was Miss Petowker's Christian name, in which novel did we laugh at Grandfather Smallweed?

The first persons to provide a guide to the enchanted labyrinth were two single-minded Americans called Pierce and Wheeler, whose *Dickens Dictionary*, a monumental work, was published in the United States two years after Dickens's death, and in England by Chapman and Hall six years later, in 1878. It has long, long been out of print; old copies are hungrily sought for by Dickens addicts. It is copious, contains much small print and is of formidable accuracy. (John Greaves has discovered one minor error, but I doubt if anyone else has.)

Other less monumental (and it must be admitted, less accurate) guides or encyclopedias appeared in 1908 and 1924, a charming (but less complete) 'Companion' in 1965. Nothing, till now, to provide us with an up-to-date, manageable volume which gives us everything we need.

John Greaves, as many thousands of readers already know, is the perfect man to undertake the task. Devoted from childhood to the works of Dickens, immersed in Dickensiana for the past twenty-five years as Honorary Secretary of the Dickens Fellowship, and as lecturer, reader and amateur performer in nearly 2,000 recitals in many parts of the world, he knows the details of the master's work and characters as it is given to few men to know them. Over the years he has put me right on innumerable points and settled innumerable questions.

Only once has he failed me, and that was in my anxiety to know what were the 'stacks of biffins' at Mrs. Todgers's boarding-house party. Naturally, if they had been people he would have known them at once, and their addresses; but this is one of those moments when Dickens's zest for domesticity, for cooking, for everything homely and appetizing, is in the ascendant. Biffins, in short, are not characters, but apples. Red Norfolk apples, roasted or toasted at the fire, pressed into a flattened shape and served as part of the dessert, with nuts and raisins.

MARGARET LANE

A

AARON: Nickname given to Mr. Riah—*see* Riah, Mr.

ABBEY, MISS: Short for Abigail—*see* Potterson, Miss Abbey

ADAMS: Head boy at Dr. Strong's School at Canterbury during David Copperfield's early days there. *David Copperfield*

ADAMS, CAPTAIN: One of the seconds in the duel at Ham between Sir Mulberry Hawk and Lord Verisopht, in which the latter is killed. Captain Adams arranges for the removal of the body, then escapes to safety. *Nicholas Nickleby*

ADAMS, JACK: A man in an anecdote told by Cousin Feenix at the Dombey dinner. Jack's brother Joe also features in the story. *Dombey and Son*

AFFERY: *see* Flintwinch, Mrs. Affery

AFRICAN KNIFE SWALLOWER: A member of the Theatrical Company of Mr. Vincent Crummles, who looks and speaks remarkably like an Irishman. *Nicholas Nickleby*

AGED, THE: *see* Wemmick, Senior

AGNES: *see* Wickfield, Agnes

AKERMAN, MR.: Head jailor and Governor of Newgate Prison, who defends it unsuccessfully against the Gordon Rioters. This character was named after a real person in office at Newgate, a friend of James Boswell. *Barnaby Rudge*

AKERSHEM, SOPHRONIA: Daughter of Horatio Akershem of Yorkshire. An acquaintance of the Veneerings, and an adventuress, who marries Alfred Lammle, adventurer. They deceive each other and finally agree to prey on society together. 'A mature young lady; raven locks, and complexion that lights up well when well powdered—as it is . . .' *Our Mutual Friend*

ALICE: Youngest of the Five Sisters working a pattern of embroidery, which is said to have been represented in the famous 'Five Sisters' window in York Minster. *Nicholas Nickleby*

ALLEN, ARABELLA: Sister of Benjamin Allen, a medical student of Guy's Hospital. She secretly marries Mr. Winkle, one of the Pickwickians, who met her first at Manor Farm, Dingley Dell. 'A black eyed young lady in a very nice pair of boots with fur round the top.' *Pickwick Papers*

ALLEN, BENJAMIN: Friend of Bob Sawyer, a fellow medical student at Guy's. He has plans for Bob Sawyer to marry his sister, Arabella. He is 'a coarse, stout, thick set young man, with black hair cut rather short, and a white face cut rather long—embellished with spectacles'. *Pickwick Papers*

ALPHONSE: Mrs. Wititterly's diminutive page boy. 'If ever an Alphonse carried plain Bill in his face, that page was the boy.' *Nicholas Nickleby*

AMELIA: Wife of Bill, a criminal who is being defended by Mr. Jaggers. When Pip calls at Mr. Jaggers' office in Little Britain, he sees her, and hears Mr. Jaggers threaten to drop the case if she persists in worrying him. *Great Expectations*

AMELIA: *see* 'Melia

ANALYTICAL CHEMIST, THE: Mr. Veneering's famous butler—like a gloomy analytical chemist, who at dinner seemed to say, 'Chablis, sir?—you wouldn't if you knew what it's made of.' *Our Mutual Friend*

ANNE: One of Mr. Dombey's housemaids, who, when the House of Dombey crashes, marries Towlinson, the butler of the household. They settle in Oxford Market, in the general greengrocery and herb and leech line. *Dombey and Son*

ANNIE: *see* Strong, Mrs. Annie

ANNY: The old pauper woman in Oliver's workhouse, who summons Mrs. Corney, the matron to witness the death of another old pauper, Sally—instrumental in unravelling the mystery surrounding Oliver Twist's parentage. *Oliver Twist*

ARTFUL DODGER: *see* Dawkins, Jack

AUGUSTA: *see* Guster

AUNT OF BENJAMIN ALLEN: Benjamin's sister Arabella stays with this aunt in Bristol where, thanks to Sam Weller, Mr. Winkle discovers her, renews his attentions and finally marries her. When the aunt visits her nephew in Bristol, she faints in his shop and Sam Weller announces, 'Here's a wenerable old lady a lyin' on the carpet waitin' for dissection or galwinism, or some other rewivin' and scientific invention!' *Pickwick Papers*

AUNT, MISS PANKEY'S: Lives at Rottingdean where Miss Pankey, one of the unfortunate pupils at Mrs. Pipchin's Establishment, visits her at weekends. *Dombey and Son*

AUNT, MR. F'S: Part of the legacy left to Flora Finching by her late husband, she has the habit of offering remarks in a deep warning voice, which have nothing to do with the subject under discussion, and which 'confounded and terrified the mind'. She takes a great dislike to Arthur Clennam, the hero of the story, who is terrified of her. *Little Dorrit*

AVENGER, THE: *see* Pepper

AYRESLEIGH, MR.: A debtor whom Mr. Pickwick meets in Namby's sponging house. *Pickwick Papers*

B

BABLEY, RICHARD: *see* Dick, Mr.

BACHELOR, THE: A kindly old gentleman who lives in the parsonage of the village where Little Nell and her grandfather finally conclude their wanderings, and where the little girl dies. He is the brother of Mr. Garland and it is as a result of a letter from the Bachelor to Mr. Garland that the whereabouts of the wanderers are discovered. *The Old Curiosity Shop*

BADGER, BAYHAM: A Chelsea doctor to whom Richard Carstone is articled; a cousin of Mr. Kenge (lawyer) and third husband of Mrs. Bayham Badger. He is 'a pink, fresh-faced, crisp looking gentleman, with a weak voice, white teeth, and surprised eyes'. *Bleak House*

BADGER, MRS. BAYHAM (LAURA): Wife of the doctor and widow of Captain Swosser of the Royal Navy and of Professor Dingo. She frequently talks of her late husbands, especially of the Captain of the 'Crippler'. *Bleak House*

BAGMAN, THE ONE-EYED: A traveller Mr. Pickwick meets at the Peacock at Eatanswill and at the Bush Inn at Bristol. He relates two stories, The Bagman's Story and The Story of the Bagman's Uncle. *Pickwick Papers*

BAGMAN'S UNCLE: *see* Martin, Jack

BAGNET, MALTA: Elder daughter of the Bagnets. She was so named because of the place of her birth, where her father was stationed in the army. *Bleak House*

BAGNET, MATTHEW: Ex-artilleryman and proprietor of a musical instrument shop near the Elephant and Castle—nicknamed Lignum Vitae. He is the friend of George Rouncewell, also an ex-army man, for whom he stands guarantor in a loan. His voice is deep and resonant, not at all unlike the tones of the instrument to which he is devoted, the bassoon. *Bleak House*

BAGNET, MRS.: Wife of Matthew, whom she calls Mat. Her husband leaves the control of everything to her and he calls her 'the old girl'. She always seems to be washing greens. When their friend George Rouncewell is arrested in connection with the murder of Mr. Tulkinghorn, the lawyer, she brings George and his mother, from whom he has been separated, together. *Bleak House*

BAGNET, QUEBEC: Youngest daughter of the Bagnets, also named after her place of birth. *Bleak House*

BAGNET, WOOLWICH: Son of the Bagnets named after his place of birth. He plays the fife in the same theatre orchestra as his father. *Bleak House*

BAGSTOCK, MAJOR JOSEPH: A retired army man who lives opposite Miss Tox in Princess's Place and who introduces Mr. Dombey to his second wife, Edith Granger. He often refers to himself as old Joe Bagstock, Old Joey Bagstock, Old J. Bagstock, Josh or Joey B. *Dombey and Son*

BAILEY, BENJAMIN or BAILEY JUNIOR: The young boots at Mrs. Todgers' Commercial Boarding Establishment, near the Monument. He is given innumerable nicknames by the boarders including Uncle Ben, Uncle Barnwell, Mr. Pitt, Young Brownrigg, Collars etc. After leaving Mrs. Todgers he becomes groom to Tigg Montague and is severely injured in a carriage accident. *Martin Chuzzlewit*

BAILEY, CAPTAIN: A rival admirer of David Copperfield's first love, the eldest Miss Larkins. *David Copperfield*

BAILLIE, MAC: He lived in Edinburgh and the bagman's uncle sups at his house on kippered salmon, Finnon haddocks, a lamb's head and a haggis, plus plenty of drink, which no doubt provoked the peculiar dream of the bagman's uncle. *Pickwick Papers*

BALDWIN, ROBERT: *see* Boffin, N.

BAMBER, JACK: An old man who was never heard to talk of anything but the Inns of Court where he lived until he was half crazy. In the Magpie and Stump he relates The Old Man's Tale about a Queer Client to Mr. Pickwick. *Pickwick Papers*

BANGHAM, MRS: Charwoman and messenger who acts as nurse to Mrs. Dorrit in her confinement at the Marshalsea Prison, when Amy Dorrit is born. She was not a prisoner, though she had been one, but was a popular medium of communication with the world outside the prison. *Little Dorrit*

BANTAM, ANGELO CYRUS: Master of Ceremonies at Bath and friend of Mr. Dowler, who welcomes Mr. Pickwick and his friends when they visit Bath. *Pickwick Papers*

BAPS, MR.: Dancing master at Dr. Blimber's School at Brighton, attended by Paul Dombey. His invariable question was what were you to do with your raw materials. The only reply that Toots, a senior boarder, could think of was, 'Cook 'em.' *Dombey and Son*

BAPS, MRS.: Wife of the dancing master at Dr. Blimber's School. *Dombey and Son*

BAR: *see* Merdle, Mr.

BARBARA: Little servant at Mr. and Mrs. Garland's— very tidy, modest and demure. Kit Nubbles gets to know her when Mr. Garland takes him on to look after the pony. Kit eventually marries Barbara. They have several children, including Barbara, Abel, Dick and Jacob. *The Old Curiosity Shop*

BARBARA'S MOTHER: She and Kit's mother, Mrs. Nubbles, become very friendly. They both thoroughly enjoy exchanging stories of their children's various ailments. *The Old Curiosity Shop*

6

BARBARY, MISS: She lived in Windsor and was the sister of Lady Dedlock, and godmother and aunt of Esther Summerson, Lady Dedlock's illegitimate daughter. She was a good woman; went to church three times every Sunday, but never smiled. *Bleak House*

BARBARY, CAPTAIN: He is a plaintiff in the case against Tip Dorrit, William Dorrit's scapegrace son. MRS. CAPTAIN BARBARY of Cheltenham parted with her horse for twenty pounds. *Little Dorrit*

BARCLAY AND PERKINS: Brewers, mentioned by Mrs. Micawber. *David Copperfield*

BARDELL, MRS. MARTHA: Mr. Pickwick's landlady in Goswell Street, and plaintiff in the Bardell *v* Pickwick case, the relict and sole executrix of a deceased custom-house officer. Although she wins the court case she finishes up in a Debtors' Prison, from which she is released when Mr. Pickwick pays her debt. *Pickwick Papers*

BARDELL, MASTER THOMAS: The only son of Mrs. Bardell, used in the court case to attract sympathy. He was 'clad in a tight suit of corduroy, spangled with brass buttons of a very considerable size'. *Pickwick Papers*

BARKER, PHIL: A drunken criminal in the Three Cripples public house. *Oliver Twist*

BARKIS, MRS.: *see* Peggotty, Clara

BARKIS, MR.: The carrier who used to drive his cart between Blunderstone and Yarmouth. He sends his famous proposal of marriage—'Barkis is willin''—' by David Copperfield to David's nurse Clara Peggotty. He later marries her and leaves her all his money and possessions, which he kept in a box under the bed referred to by him as 'old clothes'. *David Copperfield*

BARLEY, MISS CLARA: She is engaged to Herbert Pocket and nurses her father, Old Bill Barley, an irritable old invalid nicknamed by Herbert, 'Old Gruffandgrim'. Herbert and Clara get married when her father eventually dies. *Great Expectations*

BARLEY, OLD BILL: 'Gruffandgrim'—Clara's father, a bedridden purser who is nursed by his daughter. He doles out the day's rations to her and summons her to his room by banging on the floor with his walking stick. *Great Expectations*

BARNACLE, CLARENCE: Barnacle Junior. Tite Barnacle's son employed in the Circumlocution Office. He is very disturbed by Arthur Clennam presenting himself in his office and demanding an answer. He has an eyeglass, which keeps falling from his eye, much to his discomfort. *Little Dorrit*

BARNACLE, FERDINAND: Private Secretary to Lord Decimus Tite Barnacle. *Little Dorrit*

BARNACLE, JOHN: Another member of the famous family of Barnacles. 'If John Barnacle had but abandoned his most unfortunate idea of conciliating the mob, the country would have been preserved.' *Little Dorrit*

BARNACLE, LORD DECIMUS TITE: Uncle of Mr. Tite Barnacle and head of the Circumlocution Office. *Little Dorrit*

BARNACLE, TITE: A high official in the Circumlocution Office who lives in state in Mews Street, near Grosvenor Square. 'He wound and wound folds of white cravat round his neck, as he wound and wound folds of tape and paper round the neck of the country.' *Little Dorrit*

BARNACLE, WILLIAM: A Parliamentary Barnacle, who made the famous coalition with Tudor Stiltstalking, a member of the aristocracy. Also Tom, Dick and Harry Barnacle. *Little Dorrit*

BARNEY: One of Fagin's Jewish confederates, who was waiter at the Three Cripples, Little Saffron Hill in London, a public house frequented by criminals. He assists Bill Sikes in the attempted burglary at Chertsey. *Oliver Twist*

BARRONEAU, HENRI: Innkeeper of the Cross of Gold in Marseilles who, according to Monsieur Rigaud, 'Had the misfortune to die.' *Little Dorrit*

BARRONEAU, MADAME: Henri Barroneau's widow. She marries one of her lodgers, Monsieur Rigaud, after her husband dies and is apparently murdered by Rigaud for her money. *Little Dorrit*

BARSAD, JOHN: *see* Pross, Solomon

BATES, CHARLEY: One of the boy pickpockets in Fagin's gang. He turns against Bill Sikes, after the murder of Nancy. At the end of the story he repents his life of crime and becomes 'the merriest young grazier in Northamptonshire'. *Oliver Twist*

BAYTON, MRS.: Hers is the first funeral attended by Oliver Twist in his new job as mute. *Oliver Twist*

BAZZARD, MR.: Confidential clerk to Mr. Grewgious, possessed of some strange power over Mr. Grewgious, his employer. If the story had been finished he may have had a significant part to play in the plot. *The Mystery of Edwin Drood*

BEADLE, HARRIET: *see* Tattycoram

BECKY: Barmaid at the public house at Hampton, where Bill Sikes and Oliver Twist stop to have a cold meal before going on to the burglary at Chertsey. *Oliver Twist*

BEDWIN, MRS.: Mr. Brownlow's housekeeper, who mothers Oliver Twist and nurses him through his illness. She has great faith in his honesty even when it is in doubt. *Oliver Twist*

BEGS, MRS. RIDGER: Mr. Micawber's daughter, who gets married after the family have emigrated to Australia. *David Copperfield*

BELINDA: *see* Pocket, Mrs. Matthew

BELLA: *see* Wilfer, Bella

BELLA: Baby daughter of Mr. and Mrs. John Rokesmith (Harmon), named after her mother—Bella Wilfer. She was nicknamed 'The Inexhaustible' because she was dressed and undressed so many times in the day without it appearing to tire her. *Our Mutual Friend*

BELLE: A comely matron in Scrooge's dream, who was once his old sweetheart. Although engaged to him she returned his ring on finding that his only love was for gold. *A Christmas Carol*

BELLER, HENRY: A drunken toastmaster, who drinks a great deal of foreign wine. He is converted to teetotalism and is mentioned in the secretary's annual report to the Brick Lane Branch of the United Grand Junction Ebenezer Temperance Association. *Pickwick Papers*

BELLING, MASTER: A natural child from Taunton, one of Mr. Squeers' pupils at Dotheboys Hall. He is first seen on a trunk in The Saracen's Head, in Snow Hill, London, when Mr. Squeers has collected him. *Nicholas Nickleby*

BELLOWS: *see* Dorrit, W.

BELLOWS, BROTHER: *see* Merdle, Mr.

BELVAWNEY, MISS: Member of the Vincent Crummles Theatrical Company. She 'seldom aspired to speaking parts, and usually went on as a page, in white silk hose, to stand with one leg bent, and contemplate the audience'. *Nicholas Nickleby*

BEN: Guard of the mail coach waiting at the Post Office at Hatfield whom Bill Sikes overhears talking about the murder of Nancy in London. *Oliver Twist*

BENCH: *see* Merdle, Mr.

BENJAMIN: One of the Prentice Knights, whose captain is Sim Tappertit. He carried the glass when the captain entered the cellar. *Barnaby Rudge*

BENJAMIN, THOMAS: A suitor in a divorce suit. The husband whose name was Thomas Benjamin married under the name of Thomas only. Later he disclosed his full name, and claimed therefore that he was not legally married. The Court in Doctors Commons upheld this. *David Copperfield*

BERENTHIA or BERRY: Miss Pipchin's niece who also acts as her servant in her establishment at Brighton. She enjoyed romping with the children as much as they did. *Dombey and Son*

BERTHA: *see* Plummer, Bertha

BET or BETSY: Nancy's friend and one of Fagin's female thieves. Having to identify Nancy's body after the murder, the horror of the scene drives her mad. She is very friendly with a member of the gang, Tom Chitling. *Oliver Twist*

BETSEY: Maid at The Nutmeg Grater, a public house owned by Mr. and Mrs. Benjamin Britain. *The Battle of Life*

BETSEY JANE: Mrs. Wickham's uncle's child. Mrs. Wickham was Paul Dombey's nurse. *Dombey and Son*

BETSEY: Mrs. Raddle's maid who attended on Bob Sawyer at a party given to the Pickwickians at his lodgings in Lant Street. *Pickwick Papers*

BEVAN, MR.: An American from Massachusetts boarding at the Pawkins' establishment in New York. He befriends Martin Chuzzlewit and Mark Tapley in America and lends them money to return home to England. *Martin Chuzzlewit*

BIB, MR. JULIUS WASHINGTON MERRYWEATHER: An American in the deputation waiting to welcome Mr. Elijah Pogram. *Martin Chuzzlewit*

BIDDY: Mr. Wopsle's great-aunt's grand-daughter. She tended the little general shop in the village and looked after Mr. Wopsle's great-aunt's school. She later went to look after Pip's sister after her attack by Orlick, and finally becomes Joe Gargery's second wife when Pip's sister died. They have a girl and a boy, the latter named Pip. *Great Expectations*

BIFFIN, MISS: She was recalled by Mrs. Nickleby as having been very proud of her toes. *Nicholas Nickleby*

BILBERRY, LADY JEMIMA: Daughter of the fifteenth Earl of Stiltstalking and wife of Lord Decimus Tite Barnacle. *Little Dorrit*

BILER: *see* Toodle, Robin

BILL: The former turnkey at the Fleet Prison who allowed the little prisoner called Number Twenty out into the street after serving seventeen years in prison. *Pickwick Papers*

BILL: The gravedigger at the burial of the pauper, Mrs. Bayton. The grave was so full that the uppermost coffin was within a few feet of the surface. *Oliver Twist*

BILL, MY: A criminal whose case is in the hands of Mr. Jaggers, who threatens to let the case slip through his fingers if he is worried by Bill's wife. *Great Expectations*

BILL, BLACK: A criminal in Newgate, seen by Wemmick. *Great Expectations*

BILLICKIN, MRS.: Keeper of a lodging house in Southampton Street, Bloomsbury Square. Mr. Grewgious, lawyer, arranges for his ward, Rosa Bud to take rooms with her. She and Miss Twinkleton are sworn enemies. *The Mystery of Edwin Drood*

BILSON AND SLUM: Cateaton Street, City, for whom Tom Smart was traveller. The Bagman's Story Interpolated story told by the one-eyed bagman in the Peacock at Eatanswill. *Pickwick Papers*

BISHOP: *see* Merdle, Mr.

BISHOP, MRS.: *see* Merdle, Mr.

BITHERSTONE, BILL: Father of Master Bitherstone, who asked Major Bagstock to call on his son if he ever went to Brighton. This gave Major Bagstock an excuse to meet Mr. Dombey at Brighton. *Dombey and Son*

BITHERSTONE, MASTER: A pupil and boarder at Mrs. Pipchin's Establishment. His father was in India. He later attends Dr. Blimber's School. *Dombey and Son*

BITZER: A pupil in Gradgrind's school in Coketown. He later obtains a job at Bounderby's Bank and almost succeeds in capturing Gradgrind's son, Tom, after the robbery at the Bank, thereby obtaining promotion for himself. *Hard Times*

'BLACK LION': The landlord of the inn where Joe Willet met the recruiting sergeant. *Barnaby Rudge*

BLACKBOY, MR.: The fictitious name on the lid of a box carried by Mr. Barkis, which contained his possessions. It was labelled 'Mr. Blackboy, to be left with Barkis till called for'. *David Copperfield*

BLACKPOOL, STEPHEN: A hand in Mr. Bounderby's mill in Coketown. He is married to a woman who is a drunkard, and is unable to afford a divorce although he wants to marry another mill hand, Rachel. *Hard Times*

BLACKPOOL, MRS. STEPHEN: The drunken wife of Stephen. *Hard Times*

BLADUD, PRINCE: According to the fable read by Mr. Pickwick, he was the founder of the Baths in Bath. *Pickwick Papers*

BLANDOIS, MONSIEUR: *see* Rigaud, M.

BLANK BLANK, THE REVEREND: Of St. James's Church, Piccadilly, who married the Lammle's. *Our Mutual Friend*

BLATHERS: The Bow Street detective who investigates the burglary at Mrs. Maylie's house at Chertsey. *Oliver Twist*

BLAZE AND SPARKLE: Society jewellers who deal with Lady Dedlock. *Bleak House*

BLAZES: *see* Tuckle, Mr.

BLAZO, SIR THOMAS: Jingle's opponent in the cricket match played in the West Indies, which Jingle won after everyone had collapsed from the heat. *Pickwick Papers*

BLIGHT, YOUNG: The office boy who looks after Mortimer Lightwood's office in the Temple, He makes up names in the Appointments Book to impress callers—Mr. Aggs, Mr. Baggs, Mr. Caggs, Mr. Daggs, Mr. Faggs, Mr. Gaggs, Mr. Alley, Mr. Balley, etc. *Our Mutual Friend*

BLIMBER, DR.: He runs an educational establishment for boys at Brighton, which young Paul Dombey attends, and where the pupils are forced like hot-house plants. *Dombey and Son*

BLIMBER, MISS CORNELIUS: Daughter of the Dr. Blimber in whose school she teaches. She marries the assistant master, B. A. Feeder. She was dry and sandy with working in the graves of deceased languages. *Dombey and Son*

BLIMBER, MRS.: Wife of the Doctor. She is not learned herself, but she pretends to be, and that does quite as well. She said at evening parties, that if she could have known Cicero, she thought she would have died contented. *Dombey and Son*

BLINDER, MRS.: A good-natured old woman with a dropsy or an asthma or perhaps both. She took care of the Neckett children, when their father, a bailiff's man, died. *Bleak House*

BLOCKITT, MRS.: Nurse to the first Mrs. Dombey, when Paul was born. 'A simpering piece of faded gentility, who did not presume to state her name as a fact, but merely offered it as a mild suggestion.' *Dombey and Son*

BLOCKSON, MRS.: Charwoman employed by Miss Knag, assistant to Madame Mantalini. She gives notice on account of having too much work and too little pay, and being criticized for working in her bonnet. *Nicholas Nickleby*

BLOGG, MR.: The beadle of the Poorhouse who allows Betty Higden to adopt Sloppy to help her with the mangling she took in. *Our Mutual Friend*

BLOSSOM, LITTLE: *see* Spenlow, Dora

BLOTTON, MR.: A haberdasher of Aldgate, and member of the Pickwick Club, who calls Mr. Pickwick a humbug, but qualifies it as having been said in a Pickwickian sense. He tries to discredit Mr. Pickwick's discovery of the ancient stone at Cobham. *Pickwick Papers*

BLOWERS, MR.: A barrister and eminent silk gown. He said that a certain thing might happen 'when the sky rained potatoes'. The Lord Chancellor corrected him by saying 'or when we get through Jarndyce and Jarndyce'. *Bleak House*

BLUFFY: *see* Rouncewell, Mr. George

BLUNDERBORE: A legendary and ferocious giant who was in the habit of expressing his opinion that it was time to lay the cloth. *Pickwick Papers*

BOB: Turnkey at the Marshalsea Debtors' Prison and godfather of Little Dorrit who was born in the prison. Mr. Dorrit having become rich and left the prison has a breakdown and whilst addressing a rich assembly at a dinner in Italy suddenly calls for Bob, who by that time had died. *Little Dorrit*

BOBBY, LORD: He has a dispute over a bottle of champagne with Lord Mizzler. *The Old Curiosity Shop*

BOBSTER, CECILIA: The girl that Newman Noggs traces in mistake for Madeline Bray. She grants a secret interview with Nicholas Nickleby and they are surprised by the sudden return of her father. *Nicholas Nickleby*

BOBSTER, MR.: Father of the young lady Newman Noggs mistakes for Madeline Bray. *Nicholas Nickleby*

BOCKER, TOM: The orphan whom the Rev. Frank Milvey suggests that Mr. and Mrs. Boffin should adopt. He turns out to be nineteen and the driver of a water-cart. *Our Mutual Friend*

BODGERS, MR. AND MRS.: A couple in Blunderstone. There was a tablet to Mr. Bodgers in the church: 'Affliction sore long time he bore.' *David Copperfield*

BOFFER, MR.: A bankrupt expelled from the Exchange; a friend of Wilkins Flasher, stockbroker. *Pickwick Papers*

BOFFIN, MRS. HENRIETTY: Wife of Nicodemus Boffin, the Golden Dustman. Her father's name was Henry and her mother's Hetty—hence her own name. She was servant to old Harmon, the dust contractor. *Our Mutual Friend*

BOFFIN, NICODEMUS (Nick or Noddy Boffin): Harmon's servant, who inherits his fortune, the son having been presumably murdered. He hires an old rascal, Silas Wegg to read to him, and pretends to be a scraping old miser to teach a lesson to a young girl he has adopted—Bella Wilfer. *Our Mutual Friend*

BOGSBY, JAMES GEORGE: Landlord of the Sols' Arms, where two inquests are held of characters dying in the adjoining court—Captain Hawdon and Krook. Of an evening the Harmonic Assemblies are held in this public house. *Bleak House*

BOGUEY, OLD: *see* Krook

BOKUM, MRS.: A widow who is bridesmaid to Mrs. Mac-Stinger at her marriage to Captain Bunsby, Captain Cuttle's friend. *Dombey and Son*

BOLDER: One of the pupils at Dotheboys Hall. He is caned by Squeers the schoolmaster because his father's payments were £2. 10s. short. *Nicholas Nickleby*

BOLDWIG, CAPTAIN: Sir Geoffrey Manning's neighbour, on whose property Mr. Pickwick was innocently trespassing, when he was found asleep in a wheelbarrow, after drinking too much cold punch at the picnic. He ordered Mr. Pickwick to be wheeled into the pound. *Pickwick Papers*

BOLO, MISS: One of the whist party in the Assembly Rooms at Bath and Mr. Pickwick's partner in the rubber. After losing at the card game, Miss Bolo rose from the table considerably agitated and 'went straight home, in a flood of tears, and a sedan-chair'. *Pickwick Papers*

BOLTER, MORRIS: *see* Claypole, Noah

BONNEY, MR.: Promoter of the United Metropolitan Improved Hot Muffin and Crumpet and Punctual Delivery Company. His white hat was so full of papers that it would scarcely stick upon his head. Ralph Nickleby was a shareholder in this company. *Nicholas Nickleby*

BOODLE, LORD: A distinguished guest of Sir Leicester Dedlock's at Chesney Wold. Of considerable reputation with his party . . . and who tells Sir Leicester Dedlock with much gravity after dinner, that he really does not see to what the present age is tending. He supposes that if the present government was overthrown, the choice of the Crown would lie between Lord Coodle and Sir Thomas Doodle if it was impossible for the Duke of Foodle to act with Goodle, in view of the breach arising out of the affair with Hoodle, and so on. *Bleak House*

BOOTS: He and Brewer are two toadies who always attend the Veneering dinners and parties and act as a sort of chorus to Society. *Our Mutual Friend*

BORRIOBOOLA-GHA, KING OF: King of the neighbour-hood on the left bank of the River Niger, where Mrs. Jellyby proposed sending families to cultivate coffee and educate the natives. The king upset these plans by wanting to sell everybody. *Bleak House*

BORUM, MR. & MRS.: Patrons of the Crummles Theatrical Company at Portsmouth, who take a private box for them-selves, and two of their six children, for Miss Snevellicci's benefit. When Nicholas Nickleby and Miss Snevellicci call upon them to ask for their support, Augustus Borum amuses himself by pinching the Infant Phenomenon, Mr. Crummles' daughter. Two of the other Borum children are named Charlotte and Emma. *Nicholas Nickleby*

BOUNDERBY, JOSIAH: A banker and millowner in Coke-town, who marries Louisa Gradgrind, daughter of his friend. He boasts of his supposed humble beginnings. *Hard Times*

BOUNDERBY'S GRANDMOTHER: According to Mr. Bounderby she was 'the wickedest and the worst old woman that ever lived'. She actually died before he was born. *Hard Times*

BOUNDERBY'S MOTHER: *see* Pegler, Mrs.

BOUNDERBY, MRS. LOUISA (Loo): *see* Gradgrind, Louisa

BOWLEY, LADY: A stately lady in a bonnet, who was much younger than her husband. She introduced pinking and eyelot-holing among the men and boys in the village as a nice evening's employment, which was naturally not appreciated. *The Chimes*

BOWLEY, MASTER: Twelve-year-old son of Sir Joseph who Alderman Cute predicted would go into Parliament. *The Chimes*

BOWLEY, SIR JOSEPH: 'I am the Poor Man's Friend. As such I may be taunted. As such I have been taunted. But I ask no other title.' So says Sir Joseph to Trotty Veck, the old ticket porter bringing him a letter from Alderman Cute. *The Chimes*

BOYTHORN, LAWRENCE: Schoolfellow and boisterous friend of John Jarndyce, residing in a house adjoining Chesney Wold. He has a dispute with Sir Leicester Dedlock regarding a right of way beside his house. *Bleak House*

BRANDLEY, MISS: Daughter of Mrs. Brandley. Her complexion was yellow and she set up for theology. *Great Expectations*

BRANDLEY, MRS.: A widow and an old friend of Miss Havisham, who lived in an old house on the Green at Richmond. Estella stays with her to complete her education and to meet people. Her complexion was pink and she set up for frivolity. *Great Expectations*

BRASS, MR. (Senior): Called by his friends 'Foxey', he was the father of Sampson and Sally Brass. He was disappointed that his daughter could not take out an attorney's certificate. *The Old Curiosity Shop*

BRASS, SALLY: Sister to Sampson Brass and a much stronger character than her brother. When her brother turns Queen's evidence against Quilp, she stands out to the last. She bore a striking resemblance to her brother and carried upon her upper lip certain reddish demonstrations, which might have been mistaken for a beard. In complexion Miss Brass was sallow—rather a dirty sallow, relieved by the healthy glow which mantled in the extreme tip of her laughing nose. *The Old Curiosity Shop*

BRASS, SAMPSON: A lawyer in league with Quilp and concerned in shady business with the help of his sister. 'A tall, meagre man, with a nose like a wen, a protruding forehead, retreating eyes, and hair of deep red ... a cringing manner, but a very harsh voice.' Among other things he gets Kit Nubbles falsely accused of theft after planting a five pound note in the boy's hat. *The Old Curiosity Shop*

BRAVASSA, MISS: A member of the Theatrical Company of Vincent Crummles. She had once had her likeness taken in character—of which impressions were hung up for sale, whenever the announcement bills came out for her annual night. *Nicholas Nickleby*

BRAY, MADELINE: One of the heroines of the story, with whom Nicholas Nickleby falls in love. She is nearly married to a very old moneylender, Arthur Gride, but is rescued by Nicholas who eventually marries her himself. She was the daughter of someone with whom Charles Cheeryble was once in love, but who married Walter Bray. *Nicholas Nickleby*

BRAY, WALTER: Madeline's father and a debtor who is confined to the Rules of the King's Bench Prison. He is prepared to force his daughter to marry Arthur Gride, an ancient old moneylender, to get himself out of debt, but dies before this can come about. *Nicholas Nickleby*

BREWER: A toadying guest of the Veneerings, who, with his colleague Boots, always attended the dinners and parties given by them. *Our Mutual Friend*

BRICK: *see* Dorrit, W.

BRICK, JEFFERSON: War correspondent of the *Rowdy Journal*, a New York newspaper, who meets Martin Chuzzlewit on his arrival in America. 'A small young gentleman of very juvenile appearance, and unwholesomely pale in the face; partly, perhaps, from the excessive use of tobacco, which he was at that moment chewing vigorously.' *Martin Chuzzlewit*

BRICK, MRS. JEFFERSON: Wife of Jefferson Brick, referred to as a 'matron in blue', but, according to Martin Chuzzlewit, 'a sickly little girl with tight round eyes' who attended lectures nearly every night in the week. She has two young children. *Martin Chuzzlewit*

BRICK, THE: *see* Jo

BRIGGS: Stony-faced pupil of Dr. Blimber's at Brighton, the school attended by Paul Dombey. *Dombey and Son*

BRITAIN, BENJAMIN: Manservant of Dr. Jeddler who marries Clemency Newcome, another domestic in the family. They become owners of the Nutmeg Grater, a small public house. He is known as 'Little Britain'. *The Battle of Life*

BRITTLES: One of Mrs. Maylie's servants at Chertsey. He 'assisted' a fellow servant, Giles, in capturing Oliver Twist after the burglary. He was treated as a promising young boy still, though he was something past thirty. *Oliver Twist*

BROBITY, ETHELINDA: *see* Sapsea, Mrs. Ethelinda

BROGLEY, MR.: Broker and appraiser of Bishopsgate Street Without, where he keeps a second-hand furniture shop. Walter Gay stayed with him on returning from abroad, because Florence Dombey was occupying his room at the Little Wooden Midshipman. *Dombey and Son*

BROOKER, MR.: A former clerk of Ralph Nickleby, who had left Ralph's only child at a Yorkshire school, where he is known as Smike, and from which he is rescued by Nicholas Nickleby, without knowing about the relationship. He is eventually instrumental in identifying Smike as Ralph's son. *Nicholas Nickleby*

BROOKS: One of the pupils at Dotheboys Hall. With him in his bed were Jennings, little Bolder, Graymarsh, and 'what's his name', which made Squeers decide that 'Brooks is full.' *Nicholas Nickleby*

BROOKS: A pieman and friend of Sam Weller, with whom he lodged. He kept a number of tabby kittens which he made into beefsteak, veal, or kidney pies, according to demand. *Pickwick Papers*

BROOKS OF SHEFFIELD: This is the name by which Mr. Murdstone refers to David Copperfield at Lowestoft to prevent his knowing to whom they are alluding, as they are talking about his mother. They drink a toast in which David joins, 'Confusion to Brooks of Sheffield'. *David Copperfield*

BROWDIE, JOHN: A good-natured Yorkshire corn factor who befriends Nicholas when he runs away from Dotheboys Hall. He is greatly amused to hear that Nicholas has 'beatten' Mr. Squeers. He marries Matilda Price, a friend of Fanny Squeers, and goes to London on his honeymoon. *Nicholas Nickleby*

BROWN, ALICE: Alias Alice Marwood. Daughter of 'Good Mrs. Brown', first cousin of Edith Granger, and discarded mistress of James Carker. 'A solitary woman of some thirty years of age; tall; well-formed; handsome; miserably dressed.' She is helped against her wish by Harriet, Carker's sister. *Dombey and Son*

BROWN, CAPTAIN JOHN: Of Deptford. Captain of the *Polyphemus*, private West India trader. *Dombey and Son*

BROWN, CONVERSATION: An acquaintance of Cousin Feenix—'a four-bottle man at the Treasury Board'. *Dombey and Son*

BROWN, CORPORAL: A corporal in the East Indies, known to Mrs. Nubbles. He was suggested by her as a reference for Kit, when Mr. Garland thought of offering him a job. *The Old Curiosity Shop*

BROWN, 'GOOD' MRS.: Rag-and-bone vendor, mother of Alice, who stole Florence Dombey's clothes when she found her lost in the streets. 'A very ugly old woman, with red rims round her eyes, and a mouth which mumbled and chattered of itself when she was not speaking.' *Dombey and Son*

BROWN OF MUGGLETON: The maker of the shoes cleaned by Sam Weller, at the White Hart, in the Borough, by which Mr. Wardle was able to identify his sister, Rachael, who had run away with Mr. Jingle. *Pickwick Papers*

BROWNDOCK, MISS: According to Mrs. Nickleby, she was Kate Nickleby's father's cousin's sister-in-law, who was taken into partnership by a lady who kept a school at Hammersmith, and won ten thousand pounds in a lottery. *Nicholas Nickleby*

BROWNLOW, MR.: After Oliver Twist has been wrongly accused of picking Mr. Brownlow's pocket, the old gentleman takes pity on him and adopts him. Although Fagin gets Oliver back, the boy is finally rescued and lives once more with Mr. Brownlow. *Oliver Twist*

BROWNRIGG: *see* Bailey, Benjamin

BUCKET, MR.: A detective who investigates the murder of Mr. Tulkinghorn, and traces Lady Dedlock on her flight. His father was first a page, then a footman, then a butler, then a steward, then an innkeeper. His brother is in service and his brother in law. His aunt of ninety lived in Chelsea, next door but two to the original Bun House. *Bleak House*

BUCKET, MRS.: Wife of Inspector Bucket. She helps her husband with his work, in keeping a close eye on Mlle. Hortense, the murderess of Mr. Tulkinghorn. *Bleak House*

BUD, ROSA: The pet pupil of Miss Twinkleton's Seminary for Young Ladies, in Nun's House, Cloisterham, and heroine of the story. Edwin Drood has been chosen as her husband by their parents, but they decide to break off the engagement. She is called Little Miss Impudence by Edwin. Her mother 'a pretty little creature' was brought home in her father's arms, drowned. Her father died brokenhearted on the first anniversary of the accidental drowning of his wife. *The Mystery of Edwin Drood*

BUDGER, MRS.: She attends the Charity Ball, held in the Bull Inn at Rochester. Dr. Slammer of the 97th was paying his addresses to her, but was cut out by Mr. Jingle, who was wearing Mr. Winkle's blue dress coat. This culminated in a challenge to Mr. Winkle to fight a duel with Dr. Slammer. *Pickwick Papers*

BUFFERS, TWO OTHER STUFFED: Guests at the Veneering's dinner party. *Our Mutual Friend*

BUFFUM, OSCAR: One of the spokesmen in the deputation that waited on Elijah Pogram at the National Hotel in America. A levée was arranged and held in honour of Pogram. *Martin Chuzzlewit*

BUFFY, THE RT. HON.: He attends the dinner at Sir Leicester Dedlock's at Chesney Wold and attributes the shipwreck of the country to Cuffy. He also expresses the opinion that if you had prevented him from going over to Duffy, you would have got him into an alliance with Fuffy, and so on. *Bleak House*

BULDER, COLONEL: Head of the Garrison at Rochester, who attends the Charity Ball at the Bull Inn. *Pickwick Papers*

BULDER, MISS: Daughter of Colonel and Mrs. Bulder, who was warmly welcomed by the Miss Clubbers at the Charity Ball at Rochester. *Pickwick Papers*

BULDER, MRS. COLONEL: Wife of the Colonel, who also attends the Charity Ball and whose greeting with Lady Clubber was one of the most affectionate description. *Pickwick Papers*

BULLAMY: Porter of the Anglo-Bengalee Disinterested Loan and Life Assurance Company, run by Tigg Montague, a plausible rascal. 'A wonderful creature in a vast red waistcoat, and a short-tailed pepper-and-salt coat.' *Martin Chuzzlewit*

BULLDOGS, THE UNITED: The name assumed by the Society of Prentice Knights. They were led by Simon Tappertit, and took part in the Gordon Riots. *Barnaby Rudge*

BULLMAN: The plaintiff in a case undertaken by Dodson and Fogg, against Ramsey. *Pickwick Papers*

BULLOCK: Churchwarden and defendant in a case heard in Doctors' Commons, dealt with by David Copperfield when he worked for Mr. Spenlow. *David Copperfield*

BULPH: A pilot, at whose house in Portsmouth Vincent Crummles and his family had lodgings. *Nicholas Nickleby*

BUMBLE, MR.: Beadle of the workhouse where Oliver Twist was born. He gave Oliver his name. He married Mrs. Corney, matron of the workhouse, as he said later 'for six tea-spoons, a pair of sugar-tongs, and a milk-pot, with a small quantity of second-hand furniture, and twenty pound in money'. For plotting against Oliver Twist he is deprived of his office by Mr. Brownlow. *Oliver Twist*

BUNKIN, MRS.: A friend of Mrs. Sanders and Mrs. Bardell, who is mentioned in the Bardell *v.* Pickwick case. *Pickwick Papers*

BUNSBY, CAPTAIN JACK: Skipper of the *Cautious Clara* and friend of Captain Cuttle. In rescuing his friend Cuttle from Mrs. MacStinger, he becomes involved himself and eventually she marries him. Captain Cuttle has a great respect for his wisdom. *Dombey and Son*

BURGESS AND CO.: Tailors to Mr. Toots. As he used to say —'Fash'nable but very dear'. *Dombey and Son*

BURTON, THOMAS: Purveyor of cat's meat to the Lord Mayor and sheriffs and several members of the Common Council. Converted to teetotalism as stated in the Annual Report of the Secretary to the Brick Lane Branch of the United Grand Junction Ebenezer Temperance Association. *Pickwick Papers*

BUTTON, WILLIAM: A tailor of Tooley Street—a character sustained by Signor Jupe in Sleary's Circus. *Hard Times*

BUZFUZ, SERJEANT: Barrister for the plaintiff, Mrs. Bardell, in the Bardell *v.* Pickwick breach of promise case. He was successful in obtaining an award of £750 damages, which Mr. Pickwick refused to pay. *Pickwick Papers*

C

CABBERY: One of Mrs. Nickleby's many suitors. *Nicholas Nickleby*

CAMILLA, MRS.: A sister of Matthew Pocket and wife of Cousin Raymond, one of Miss Havisham's toadying relatives. Pip thought it was a mercy she had any features at all, so very blank and high was the dead wall of her face. *Great Expectations*

CAMILLA, RAYMOND: Husband of Mrs. Camilla, usually referred to as Cousin Raymond, a relative of Miss Havisham. *Great Expectations*

CAMPBELL, MR.: *see* Magwitch, Abel

CANKABY, LADY: Name by which Doctor Parker Peps referred to Mrs. Dombey by mistake, to point to his many distinguished patients. *Dombey and Son*

CARKER, HARRIET: Sister of James and John Carker. She befriends Alice Brown or Marwood, her brother James's discarded mistress and marries Mr. Morfin, a member of Mr. Dombey's office staff. *Dombey and Son*

CARKER, JAMES: Manager of the office of Dombey and Son in the City and Mr. Dombey's confidential assistant. He elopes with Mr. Dombey's second wife Edith and is killed by an express train when escaping from Mr.

Dombey's vengeance. 'A gentleman thirty-eight or forty years old, of a florid complexion, and with two unbroken rows of glistening teeth.' *Dombey and Son*

CARKER, JOHN: Brother of James and Harriet Carker, who is also employed in the office of Dombey and Son. In his youth he robbed the firm and has been kept on in a junior position under sufferance. *Dombey and Son*

CAROLINE: A mother whose husband is a debtor of Scrooge, and who is one of the people relieved to hear of his death. *A Christmas Carol*

CARROTS: *see* Jo

CARSTONE, MRS. ADA: *see* Clare, Ada

CARSTONE, RICHARD: A ward in Chancery and distant cousin of Ada Clare, another ward, whom he marries and by whom he has a son, Richard. The delay and disappointments of the Chancery case, Jarndyce and Jarndyce, to which he is a party and which has such a morbid attraction for him, eventually causes his early death. *Bleak House*

CARTON, SYDNEY: A dissolute barrister, who acts as Stryver's 'jackal'. He is in love with Lucie Manette, the heroine of the story. He gives his life to save that of her husband, Charles Darnay and is guillotined in his place. *A Tale of Two Cities*

CASBY, CHRISTOPHER: Landlord of properties in Bleeding Heart Yard and other slum buildings, former town agent of Lord Decimus Tite Barnacle, and father of Flora Finching. He used his agent Pancks to extort money from his tenants. Old ladies spoke of him as 'The Last of the Patriarchs', because of his shining bald head, which looked so large, because it shone so much; long grey hair at its sides and back, like floss silk, or spun glass, which looked so benevolent. Pancks eventually cuts his long hair and destroys his patriarchal appearance. *Little Dorrit*

CASSIM: A clerk in whom Eugene Wrayburn has a quarter interest in his shared office in chambers. Short nickname for Cassim Baba, who was quartered by the robbers in the story of Ali Baba—hence his name. *Our Mutual Friend*

CAVALLETTO, SIGNOR JOHN BAPTIST: A fellow prisoner with Rigaud in the jail in Marseilles. Later employed in England by Arthur Clennam, in his office, he helps to trace Rigaud. *Little Dorrit*

CHADBAND, MR.: A canting hypocrite in the ministry of no named denomination. He is concerned in the attempt to blackmail Sir Leicester Dedlock, but is frustrated by Inspector Bucket. A large yellow man, with a fat smile, and a general appearance of having a good deal of train-oil in his system. *Bleak House*

CHADBAND, MRS.: Wife of Mr. Chadband and formerly Mrs. Rachael, servant of Esther Summerson's aunt, Miss Barbary. *Bleak House*

CHANCELLOR, THE LORD HIGH: He presided in Lincoln's Inn Hall on the Jarndyce *v.* Jarndyce case. *Bleak House*

CHANCERY PRISONER, THE: A debtor in the Fleet Prison, from whom Mr. Pickwick rents a room. *Pickwick Papers*

CHARITABLE GRINDERS: A charitable institution to which Polly Toodles' eldest son was sent at Mr. Dombey's instigation. *Dombey and Son*

CHARLEY: *see* Neckett, Charlotte

Son of Mrs. Blockson, charwoman to Miss Knag. *Nicholas Nickleby*

Potboy at the Magpie and Stump, a public house visited by Mr. Pickwick. *Pickwick Papers*

Chatham marine store dealer who bought David Copperfield's coat for 1s. 4d. *David Copperfield*

CHARLOTTE: Servant to Mrs. Sowerberry, the undertaker's wife, who robs the till and runs away to London with Noah Claypole. They join Fagin's gang and later become informers. *Oliver Twist*

Deceased sister of Herbert Pocket. *Great Expectations*

Schoolfellow of Miss Wade, whom Miss Wade regards as her enemy. *Little Dorrit*

CHEERYBLE, CHARLES: The younger one of twin brothers who befriended Nicholas Nickleby, gave him work, and helped him to prosperity. 'A sturdy old fellow in a broad-skirted blue coat, made pretty large to fit easily.' *Nicholas Nickleby*

CHEERYBLE, FRANK: Nephew of the Cheeryble Brothers, who marries Kate Nickleby, sister of Nicholas, the hero of the story. *Nicholas Nickleby*

CHEERYBLE, NED: The elder twin brother of Charles, who also helped Nicholas to prosperity. 'Another old gentleman the very type and model of Mr. Charles.' *Nicholas Nickleby*

CHEGGS, ALICK: A market gardener and rival of Dick Swiveller for the hand of Sophy Wackles to whom he is finally married, when Swiveller gives her up. *The Old Curiosity Shop*

CHEGGS, MISS: Sister of Alick Cheggs. She helps her brother in his suit with Sophy Wackles and to cut out Dick Swiveller. *The Old Curiosity Shop*

CHERRY: *see* Pecksniff, Miss Charity

CHERUB, THE: *see* Wilfer, Rumty

CHESTER, EDWARD: Son of Sir John Chester, cast off by his father. He marries Emma Haredale. They have two children, Edward and Emma. *Barnaby Rudge*

CHESTER, SIR JOHN: A cynical, courtly, unprincipled rogue, determined to prevent a match between his son Edward and Emma Haredale, a Roman Catholic and daughter of his sworn enemy, Geoffrey Haredale. He is killed in a duel with Haredale. *Barnaby Rudge*

CHESTLE, MR.: The elderly hop-grower, from the neighbourhood of Ashford, who married the eldest Miss Larkins, one of David Copperfield's first loves. *David Copperfield*

CHICK OR CHICKWEED: *see* Smallweed, Young Bartholomew

CHICK, MR. JOHN: Husband of Mr. Dombey's sister, Louisa, who appears on various social occasions at Mr. Dombey's house, 'A stout old gentleman, who had a tendency to whistle and hum tunes.' *Dombey and Son*

CHICK, MRS. LOUISA: Sister of Mr. Dombey and wife of John Chick. She advises Mr. Dombey on the bringing up of little Paul, when Paul's mother dies in giving birth to him. She has two children, George and Frederick. *Dombey and Son*

CHICKENSTALKER, MRS. ANNE: A stout lady who kept a little general shop and was one of the creditors of Trotty Veck. She married Tugby, Sir Joseph Bowley's porter. *The Chimes*

CHICKSEY, VENEERING AND STOBBLES: Dealers in drugs and chemicals of Mincing Lane. *Our Mutual Friend*

CHICKWEED, CONKEY: A publican in Battle Bridge, who commits a fake burglary, detected by Jem Spyers, the Bow Street runner. *Oliver Twist*

CHIGGLE: The immortal sculptor who 'carved the Pogram statter in marble which rose so much con-test and pre-judice in Europe'. *Martin Chuzzlewit*

CHILDERS, E. W. B.: A member of Sleary's Circus who spoke his mind when Mr. Gradgrind was considering adopting Cissy Jupe. He later helps Gradgrind by smuggling his son Tom away to Liverpool to save his arrest for robbery. He marries Sleary's daughter Josephine, and they have a little boy who becomes known as The Little Wonder of Scholastic Equitation. *Hard Times*

CHILDERS, MRS. E. W. B.: *see* Sleary, Josephine

CHILLIP, DR.: The mild little doctor, who attended Mrs. Copperfield when David was born, and who was so nervous of Miss Betsey Trotwood, David's great-aunt. Later, on marrying his second wife, he went to live at Bury St. Edmunds. *David Copperfield*

CHILLIP, MRS.: Dr. Chillip's second wife. A tall, raw-boned, high-nosed wife. *David Copperfield*

CHILLIP'S BABY: Dr. Chillip's child by his second wife. *David Copperfield*

CHINAMAN, JACK: Keeper of the opium den run in opposition to that run by the old woman, Princess Puffer. *The Mystery of Edwin Drood*

CHISEL, YOUNG: *see* Jo

CHITLING, TOM: A member of Fagin's gang who, after coming out of prison, takes up with Betsy, Nancy's friend. *Oliver Twist*

CHIVERY, MR.: A non-resident turnkey at the Marshalsea Debtors' Prison, and father of young John. There was a native delicacy in Mr. Chivery—true politeness towards Mr. Dorrit. *Little Dorrit*

CHIVERY, MRS.: Wife of the turnkey and mother of young John. She kept a small tobacco shop in Horsemonger Lane, near to the Marshalsea Debtors' Prison. *Little Dorrit*

CHIVERY, YOUNG JOHN: Son of Mr. and Mrs. Chivery, who was in love with Little Dorrit. He helps Pancks to establish Mr. Dorrit's claim to a fortune. 'Of small stature, with weak legs and very weak, light hair.' *Little Dorrit*

CHIZZLE, MR.: A solicitor who had been given imaginary appointments by his office boy to keep suitors at bay. *Bleak House*

CHOKE, GENERAL CYRUS: An American militia gentleman and member of the Eden Land Corporation, who recommends Martin Chuzzlewit to purchase a plot of land at Eden, the useless swamp on the banks of the river. *Martin Chuzzlewit*

CHOLLOP, MAJOR HANNIBAL: A lawless and boastful American who calls unbidden on Martin Chuzzlewit, when he is ill with the fever at Eden. Chollop is a great advocate of violence. He was described by his friends as 'a splendid sample of our na-tive raw material, Sir'. *Martin Chuzzlewit*

CHOWLEY: *See* MacStinger, Charles

CHOWSER, COLONEL: A white-headed gentleman of the militia and the racecourse, who was one of the shady guests at Ralph Nickleby's dinner party, arranged principally to get business from Lord Verisopht. *Nicholas Nickleby*

CHRISTINA, DONNA: Only daughter of Don Bolaro Fizzgig, one of Jingle's imaginary Spanish conquests. She died after a stomach pump had been used on her to save her from being poisoned. In Jingle's own words—'Splendid creature —loved me to distraction—jealous father—high-souled daughter . . . ' *Pickwick Papers*

CHUCKSTER, MR.: Clerk to Mr. Witherden, the notary, and friend of Dick Swiveller; both were members of the club called the 'Glorious Apollers'. *The Old Curiosity Shop*

CHUFFEY, MR.: Anthony Chuzzlewit's old clerk, a faithful, half-crazy old man, who worships his old master. 'A little blear-eyed, weazen-faced, ancient man. He looked as if he had been put away and forgotten . . . and somebody had just found him in a lumber-closet.' *Martin Chuzzlewit*

CHUZZLEWIT, ANTHONY: Brother of old Martin Chuzzlewit and father of Jonas. A grasping old miser whose son turns on him. His face was so sharpened by the wariness and cunning of his life, that it seemed to cut him a passage through the crowded room. *Martin Chuzzlewit*

CHUZZLEWIT AND CO.: Martin Chuzzlewit and Mark Tapley at Eden in America. Mark Tapley insisted upon being called the 'Co.' *Martin Chuzzlewit*

CHUZZLEWIT AND SON: Anthony Chuzzlewit and his son Jonas, traded under this name in a narrow street in London, behind the Post Office. *Martin Chuzzlewit*

CHUZZLEWIT, DIGGORY: A remote ancestor of the Chuzzlewits, who makes constant reference to an 'uncle.' *Martin Chuzzlewit*

CHUZZLEWIT FAMILY: There were a number of other members of this family, including a grand-nephew of old Martin, 'very dark and very hairy,' Mrs. Spottletoe, once his favourite niece, Chevy Slyme, a dissolute nephew, and a cousin, who was remarkable for nothing but being very deaf, living by herself, and always having the toothache. *See* Spottletoe, Slyme. *Martin Chuzzlewit*

CHUZZLEWIT, GEORGE: A gay bachelor cousin of old Martin Chuzzlewit. He had such an obvious disposition of pimples, that the bright spots on his cravat, the rich pattern on his waistcoat, and even his glittering trinkets, seemed to have broken out upon him. *Martin Chuzzlewit*

CHUZZLEWIT, JONAS: Only son of Anthony Chuzzlewit, who marries Mercy Pecksniff, purely to break her spirit.

He murders Tigg Montague, a business associate and commits suicide on being arrested. *Martin Chuzzlewit*

CHUZZLEWIT, MARTIN (THE ELDER): Cousin to Mr. Pecksniff and grandfather of young Martin. He is suspicious of all friends and relations because he thinks they are after his wealth. He quarrels with his grandson and turns him out, but later becomes reconciled to him. *Martin Chuzzlewit*

CHUZZLEWIT, MRS. JONAS: *see* Pecksniff, Mercy

CHUZZLEWIT, MRS. NED: Widow of a deceased brother of old Martin and mother of three daughters. She had a dreary face, and a bony figure, a masculine voice, and was a strong-minded woman. *Martin Chuzzlewit*

CHUZZLEWIT, TOBY: One of the Chuzzlewit family, who when asked upon his deathbed who his grandfather was, replied, 'The Lord No-Zoo'. *Martin Chuzzlewit*

CHUZZLEWIT, YOUNG MARTIN: Grandson of old Martin, and hero of the story. After being turned out by his grandfather he goes to America to try to make his fortune, but does not succeed. He learns humility, however, and on his return is eventually reconciled to his grandfather, and marries the old man's companion, Mary Graham. *Martin Chuzzlewit*

CICERO: Emancipated negro slave who had bought his freedom because his strength had nearly gone. Mark Tapley hires him to carry the luggage in New York. *Martin Chuzzlewit*

CLARE, MISS ADA: A ward in Chancery, who marries her cousin, Richard Carstone, also a ward in Chancery. She has a son by Richard who dies before the baby is born. *Bleak House*

CLARISSA: *see* Spenlow, The Misses

CLARK, MR.: Employed by Dombey and Son, in their wharfinger's office. When Florence Dombey was lost and came to the wharf for help, Walter Gay from the City Office happened to be there. Mr. Clark, a stout man, gave her into Walter Gay's charge and Walter took her back home. *Dombey and Son*

CLARK, MRS.: Madeline Bray was sent to Mrs. Clark for a job. *Nicholas Nickleby*

CLARKE, SUSAN: *see* Weller, Mrs. Tony

CLARRIKER: A shipping broker introduced to Pip by Wemmick. Pip purchases a partnership in the firm for his friend Herbert Pocket. Later when Pip loses his money he is employed by the firm of Clarrikers. *Great Expectations*

CLAYPOLE, NOAH: Alias Morris Bolter, under which name he joins Fagin's gang. He is a charity boy employed by Mr. Sowerberry, the undertaker. He runs away with the servant Charlotte and comes to London where he falls in with Fagin. He spies on Nancy, which results in her murder by Bill Sikes. Later he becomes an informer. His mother was a washerwoman and his father a drunken soldier. *Oliver Twist*

CLEAVER, FANNY: A doll's dressmaker and cripple, usually known as Jenny Wren, who becomes a friend of Lizzie Hexam, a girl who helps her father make his living by the river. Jenny Wren keeps her drunken father—known as Mr. Dolls—with the money she makes selling dolls. *Our Mutual Friend*

CLEAVER, MR.: Jenny Wren's drunken father, usually known as Mr. Dolls. He lives to get his three penn'orths of rum, and often spends his money before his daughter can get it from him. He is finally knocked down in the street and dies in a chemist's shop to which he is taken. *Our Mutual Friend*

CLEMENCY or CLEMMY: *see* Newcome, Clemency

CLENNAM, ARTHUR: Adopted son of Mrs. Clennam, and hero of the story. He is actually the son of Mr. Clennam and another woman, before he married Mrs. Clennam. For a time Arthur is in love with a young daughter of his friend Pet Meagles, who, however, marries someone else. He eventually marries Little Dorrit, whom he has long looked upon almost as his daughter. *Little Dorrit*

CLENNAM, GILBERT: Uncle to Arthur Clennam's father. He proposed the marriage of Arthur Clennam's father to Mrs. Clennam. *Little Dorrit*

CLENNAM, MR.: Arthur's father, who went to China to look after the business, and died there. *Little Dorrit*

CLENNAM, MRS.: Arthur's widowed and adopted mother. When she finds that her husband, before his marriage to her has a son by another woman, she adopts the boy and brings him up as her own son in an atmosphere of austerity. For many years she is confined to her room by a malady of the legs, and spends her time reading her large family Bible out loud. *Little Dorrit*

CLEOPATRA: *see* Skewton, Mrs.

CLERGYMAN, THE: The very kind clergyman of the village where Little Nell and her grandfather end their journey, who agrees that Nell shall be custodian of the old church. *The Old Curiosity Shop*

CLERGYMAN, THE OLD: He recites The Ivy Green when Mr. Pickwick and his friends visit Manor Farm, Dingley Dell for the first time. *Pickwick Papers*

CLICKETT: An orphan girl from St. Luke's Workhouse, and servant of the Micawbers. A dark-complexioned young woman, with a habit of snorting. She told David Copperfield that she was an 'Orfling'. *David Copperfield*

CLIVE, MR.: A clerk in the Circumlocution Office to whom Arthur Clennam was referred in his enquiries about Mr. Dorrit's affairs. *Little Dorrit*

CLUBBER, LADY: Wife of Sir Thomas Clubber, who accompanies him to the Charity Ball and meets with the other local celebrities. A large lady in blue satin. *Pickwick Papers*

CLUBBER, THE MISSES: Daughters of Sir Thomas and Lady Clubber, also present at the Charity Ball. Two large young ladies in fashionably-made dresses of blue satin. *Pickwick Papers*

CLUBBER, SIR THOMAS: Head of the dockyard at Chatham, who attends the Charity Ball, at the Bull Inn, Rochester, at which Jingle and Mr. Tupman are present. *Pickwick Papers*

CLUPPINS, MRS. ELIZABETH: One of Mrs. Bardell's intimate friends and sister of Mrs. Raddle. She is called as a witness in the Bardell *v.* Pickwick breach of promise case. She was in the back room when Mr. Pickwick had his conversation with Mrs. Bardell. A little, brisk, busy-looking woman—mother of eight and, as she informs the Court, expecting a ninth. *Pickwick Papers*

CLY, ROGER: Former servant to Charles Darnay, who gives evidence against his master at the Old Bailey. He escapes from the mob by means of a fake funeral. *A Tale of Two Cities*

CO., MR.: *see* Tapley, Mark, and Chuzzlewit and Co.

COAVINSES: *see* Neckett, Mr.

COBB, TOM: General chandler and post office keeper at Chigwell. One of old John Willet's cronies in the chimney corner at the Maypole Inn, and beyond all question the dullest dog in the party. *Barnaby Rudge*

COBBEY: One of the pupils at Dotheboys Hall. His sister sent him eighteenpence which Mr. Squeers confiscated to pay for a broken window. His sister also sent him the news that his grandmother was dead and his Uncle John had taken to drink. *Nicholas Nickleby*

COBBLER, THE: A prisoner in the Fleet Prison from whom Sam Weller hires a bed. He sleeps under the table in lieu of a four-poster bedstead. *Pickwick Papers*

COBWEB: *see* Summerson, Esther

CODGER, MISS: A literary lady presented to Elijah Pogram at his levée in the National Hotel in America. Stuck on her forehead by invisible means was a massive cameo, in size and shape like a raspberry tart. *Martin Chuzzlewit*

CODLIN, THOMAS: Punch and Judy man, and partner of Harris or Short. He carried the booth when they were travelling and stood in front of the public when the performance was given. He had a surly grumbling manner and an air of always counting up what money they hadn't made. He and his partner are met by Little Nell and the grandfather on their wanderings. *The Old Curiosity Shop*

COILER, MRS.: A widow lady and neighbour of Mr. Matthew Pocket at Hammersmith. *Great Expectations*

COLE, KING: Likened to King Lud, whose son, Prince Bladud, was said to have founded Bath. Interpolated story —The True Legend of Prince Bladud. *Pickwick Papers*

COLONEL: *see* Jo

COMPEYSON: A swindler who deceived and robbed Miss Havisham and promised to marry her. Later he is a convict on the prison hulks with Magwitch. When he escapes Magwitch is instrumental in his recapture, having a grudge against him. When Magwitch returns to this country from Australia he becomes liable to the death penalty. Compeyson betrays him to the police. Magwitch and Compeyson fight in the river and Compeyson is drowned. *Great Expectations*

COMPEYSON, MRS. SALLY: Wife of Compeyson, who took pity on Arthur Havisham, Miss Havisham's brother. *Great Expectations*

CONKEY, CHICKWEED: *see* Chickweed

CONWAY, GENERAL: A member of Parliament and opponent of Lord George Gordon. *Barnaby Rudge*

COPPERFIELD, DAVID: The hero of the story who marries Dora Spenlow, a flighty young girl, and after her death, Agnes Wickfield, his childhood's friend. They have several children, the eldest Agnes, also a Betsey Trotwood, a Dora, and several boys. He has a very unhappy childhood when his mother marries a second time. After being put out to work he runs away and is brought up by his great aunt, Betsey Trotwood, who calls him Trotwood Copperfield. *David Copperfield*

COPPERFIELD, DAVID, THE ELDER: David's father who died before his son was born. *David Copperfield*

COPPERFIELD, MRS. CLARA: David Copperfield's mother, a widow, who married a second time—Mr. Murdstone, and died after giving birth to another boy. She was very unhappy in her second marriage. *David Copperfield*

COPPERFIELD, MRS. DAVID: *see* Spenlow, Dora, and Wickfield, Agnes

COPPERFULL, MR.: Name given to David Copperfield by his landlady Mrs. Crupp. *See* Copperfield, David

CORNEY, MR.: Deceased husband of Mrs. Corney, matron of the workhouse. *Oliver Twist*

CORNEY, MRS.: Widow and workhouse matron, who marries Mr. Bumble. She is concerned in a plot to withhold information that would establish the parentage of Oliver Twist, who was born in the workhouse. When found out, she and Mr. Bumble are deprived of their offices. *Oliver Twist*

COUSIN JOHN: *see* Jarndyce, John

39

CRACKIT, TOBY: A housebreaker, confederate of Fagin and Bill Sikes, with whom he is concerned in the attempted burglary at Chertsey. It was in his house on Jacob's Island that Bill Sikes was brought to bay. *Oliver Twist*

CRADDOCK, MRS.: Mr. Pickwick's landlady in the Royal Crescent at Bath, where Mr. Winkle had his unfortunate experience by being shut out in the street in his night clothes. *Pickwick Papers*

CRAGGS, MRS.: Wife of Mr. Craggs, who was on principle suspicious of his partner, Mr. Snitchey. *The Battle of Life*

CRAGGS, THOMAS: Partner of Snitchey and Craggs, solicitors to Dr. Jeddler. He usually left his partner Snitchey to speak for him. *The Battle of Life*

CRATCHIT, BOB: Scrooge's clerk who was paid fifteen shillings a week by his miserly employer. He lived with his family, Mrs. Cratchit, Peter, Martha, Belinda and two younger Cratchits and Tiny Tim the cripple in a small house in Camden Town. *A Christmas Carol*

CRATCHIT, MISS BELINDA: Second daughter of Mr. and Mrs. Cratchit, who was 'also brave in ribbons'. *A Christmas Carol*

CRATCHIT, MISS MARTHA: The Cratchit's eldest daughter who was a poor apprentice at a milliner's, and had the day off for Christmas. *A Christmas Carol*

CRATCHIT, MRS.: Bob's wife, and mother of the family. For the occasion she was 'dressed out but poorly in a twice-turned gown, but brave in ribbons, which are cheap and make a goodly show for sixpence'. They have six children altogether. *A Christmas Carol*

CRATCHIT, PETER: Eldest son of the Cratchits, who is shortly to start out to work. He is described as getting the corners of his monstrous shirt collar, which he wears in honour of Christmas Day, into his mouth. *A Christmas Carol*

CRATCHIT, TIM: *see* Tiny Tim

CRAWLEY, MR. (THE YOUNGEST): He attends the ball at the Assembly Rooms at Bath. His father had £800 a year that died with him, and consequently the son was not considered an eligible young man by mamas with marriageable daughters. *Pickwick Papers*

CREAKLE, MISS: Mr. and Mrs. Creakle's daughter. *David Copperfield*

CREAKLE, MR.: Headmaster of Salem House Academy, a school attended by David Copperfield as a boarder. Creakle loved caning the boys, especially the chubby ones, and called himself a Tartar. 'Mr. Creakle's face was fiery; he had no voice, but spoke in a whisper . . .' For that reason he was always followed by a wooden-legged man named Tungay, who used to repeat what he had said in a loud voice. *David Copperfield*

CREAKLE, MRS.: Wife of the headmaster, who was kind to David and broke the news to him of his mother's death in a kindly way. *David Copperfield*

CREEVY, MISS LA: *see* La Creevy, Miss

CREWLER, MRS.: Sophy's mother, who when she heard of her daughter's engagement to Traddles, gave a scream and became insensible. *David Copperfield*

CREWLER, THE REV. HORACE: Sophy's father. A poor Devonshire clergyman. The Crewlers have ten daughters— Caroline (called Beauty), Louisa, Sophy, Lucy, Margaret, Sarah, and four others. *David Copperfield*

CREWLER, SARAH: Second daughter of the Crewlers, who has something wrong with her spine. When she hears of Sophy's engagement, 'she clenched both her hands, shut her eyes; turned lead colour, became perfectly stiff; and took nothing for two days but toast and water, administered with a tea-spoon'. *David Copperfield*

CREWLER, SOPHY: Fourth daughter of Mr. and Mrs. Crewler, whom Traddles describes as 'the dearest girl in the world'. She looks after most of the family, even after she is married to Traddles. *David Copperfield*

CRIMPLE, DAVID: Secretary and Director of the Anglo-Bengalee Disinterested Loan and Life Assurance Company, a fraudulent company founded by Tigg Montague. He was originally David Crimp, 'tapster at the Lombard's Arms', in other words, a pawnbroker. *Martin Chuzzlewit*

CRIPPLES, MASTER: Son of Mr. Cripples, who gives evening tuition at his Academy. 'A little white-faced boy, with a slice of bread and butter and a battledore.' *Little Dorrit*

CRIPPLES, MR.: Proprietor of the Academy in the house where old Frederick Dorrit and his niece, Fanny Dorrit, lodge. *Little Dorrit*

CRIPPS, TOM: Bob Sawyer's boy at his surgery in Bristol— 'Sawyer, late Nockemorf.' Tom leaves bottles of medicine at wrong houses and calls Bob Sawyer out of church on Sunday mornings to impress people with the large practice that Sawyer must have. *Pickwick Papers*

CRISPARKLE, MRS.: Mother of the Rev. Septimus who lives with him in Minor Canon Corner, Cloisterham (Rochester). 'What is prettier than an old lady, except a young lady—when her dress is as the dress of a china shepherdess, so dainty in its colour?' *The Mystery of Edwin Drood*

CRISPARKLE, SISTER OF MRS.: A childless widow who is another piece of Dresden china, matching her sister so neatly that they would have made a delightful pair of ornaments for the two ends of any old-fashioned chimney-piece. *The Mystery of Edwin Drood*

CRISPARKLE, THE REV. SEPTIMUS: Minor Canon at Cloisterham; fair and rosy and perpetually pitching himself head-foremost into all the deep running water in the surrounding country. He becomes tutor to Neville Landless. *The Mystery of Edwin Drood*

CROOKEY: Namby's waiter at his sponging-house, in Bell Yard, to which Mr. Pickwick is taken on his way to the Fleet Prison. *Pickwick Papers*

CROPLEY, MISS: Mrs. Nickleby's friend at Exeter, whose brother was said to have a place at Court. *Nicholas Nickleby*

CROWL, MR.: Fellow lodger of Newman Noggs, who is incredibly selfish and sponges on Newman. *Nicholas Nickleby*

CRUMLINWALLINER: A bard whose name sounded like that, who according to Mrs. Woodcourt had sounded the praises of her ancestor, Morgan ap-Kerrig, in a piece called 'Mewlinnwillinwodd'. *Bleak House*

CRUMMLES, MASTER: Elder son of Mr. Vincent Crummles, who was a member of the Theatrical Company. He and his brother fight a very convincing stage duel with swords. *Nicholas Nickleby*

CRUMMLES, MRS.: Wife of Mr. Vincent Crummles and member of the Theatrical Company. 'A stout portly female, apparently between forty and fifty, in a tarnished silk cloak, and her hair (of which she had a great quantity) braided in a large festoon over each temple.' Always very theatrical in her manner. *Nicholas Nickleby*

CRUMMLES, NINETTA: Daughter of Mr. Crummles, and a dancer, known as The Infant Phenomenon. She danced, among other items, the ballet of the Savage and the Maiden, and was said by her father to be no more than ten years old, an age she had sustained for at least five years. 'A little girl in a dirty white frock, with tucks up to the knees, short trousers, sandelled shoes, white spencer,

43

pink gauze-bonnet, green veil, and curl-papers.' *Nicholas Nickleby*

CRUMMLES, PERCY: Younger son of Mr. Vincent Crummles, also a member of the Theatrical Company. *Nicholas Nickleby*

CRUMMLES, VINCENT: A good-hearted manager of a travelling Theatrical Company, with whom Nicholas Nickleby obtains a job, under the name of Mr. Johnson. Nicholas meets Mr. Crummles on his way with Smike to Portsmouth, with the idea of going to sea in mind. Mr. Crummles eventually takes his family to America. *Nicholas Nickleby*

CRUNCHER, JEREMIAH (JERRY): Odd-job-man and general messenger for Tellson's Bank during the day, and Resurrectionist by night. His body-snatching work helps to clear up the identity of a spy in France later in the story. 'He had eyes much too near together—as if they were afraid of being found out in something singly, if they kept too far apart . . . Except on the crown, which was raggedly bald, he had stiff, black hair, standing jaggedly all over it.' *A Tale of Two Cities*

CRUNCHER, MRS.: Wife of Jerry Cruncher and much worried about his body-snatching, hence her inclination to pray for him, which he terms 'flopping'. *A Tale of Two Cities*

CRUNCHER, YOUNG JERRY: Son of Jerry Cruncher, who sometimes took his father's place as messenger outside the Bank, when his father had been sent on an errand. He was much interested in his father's night activities, which were always referred to as 'fishing'. Young Jerry was puzzled because his father's hands always seemed to be covered with rust when he came home from these expeditions. This he got, of course, from the iron railings round the cemeteries and tombs. *A Tale of Two Cities*

CRUPP, MRS.: David Copperfield's landlady in Buckingham Street, Adelphi. She was martyr to a peculiar disorder which she called 'spazzums', which could be cured only with tincture of cardamums or, failing that, brandy. She makes quite a good thing out of her young lodger, until his great-aunt, Betsey Trotwood moves in, when things are somewhat different. *David Copperfield*

CRUSHTON, THE HON. MR.: Lord Mutanhed's friend, who was with him at Bath and acted as a sort of 'chorus'. *Pickwick Papers*

CUMMINS, TOM: He took the chair at the social evening attended by one of the clerks from Dodson and Fogg's office. *Pickwick Papers*

CUPID: *see* Kidderminster

CURDLE, MR.: A literary man and patron of the Crummles Theatrical Company at Portsmouth. He was most anxious to know, when Nicholas called upon him to solicit his support, if the unities had been preserved. He had written a pamphlet of sixty-four pages, post octavo, on the character of the nurse's deceased husband in Romeo and Juliet. *Nicholas Nickleby*

CURDLE, MRS.: Wife of Mr. Curdle and also a patron of the Crummles Company. 'Dressed in a morning wrapper, with a little cap stuck upon the top of her head.' *Nicholas Nickleby*

CURZON, MISS: Daughter of Thomas Curzon. She is loved by the apprentice, Mark Gilbert, but she does not return his love. *Barnaby Rudge*

CURZON, THOMAS: Hosier, Golden Fleece, Aldgate. Master of Mark Gilbert, apprentice. He is denounced by the Prentice Knights. *Barnaby Rudge*

CUTAWAY: *see* Dorrit, W.

CUTE, ALDERMAN: A magistrate who stated that he would 'put down' any nonsense on the part of the poor people, such as talks about want or starvation and in particular any suggestion of suicide. *The Chimes*

CUTLER, MR. AND MRS.: A newly-married couple who visited Mr. and Mrs. Kenwigs in their courtship, and are asked to the party to meet Uncle Lillyvick. *Nicholas Nickleby*

CUTTLE, CAPTAIN EDWARD (NED): Nautical friend and later partner of Solomon Gills, nautical instrument dealer at the Little Wooden Midshipman, in the City. He befriends and takes care of Florence Dombey, when she is turned out of her home by her father. He had a hook attached to his right wrist in place of a hand. His well-known saying when referring to the Bible was: 'When found, make a note on.' *Dombey and Son*

D

DABBER, SIR DINGLEBY: A poet who Mrs. Nickleby imagined might publish some lines on contemplating the portrait of Lady Mulberry Hawk, her daughter, if she got married to Sir Mulberry. *Nicholas Nickleby*

DAISY: Steerforth's nickname for David Copperfield. 'My dear young Daisy, you are a very Daisy. The Daisy in the field at sunrise is not fresher than you are.' *See* Copperfield, David

DAISY, SOLOMON: Parish clerk and bell-ringer at Chigwell, and one of John Willet's cronies round the boiler in the Maypole Inn. He thinks that he sees the ghost of a murdered man in the churchyard but in reality is seeing the murderer. 'A little man—had round, black, shiny eyes like beads—wore at the knees of his rusty black breeches, and on his rusty black coat, and all down his long-flapped waistcoat, queer little buttons like nothing except his eyes. He seemed all eyes from head to foot.' *Barnaby Rudge*

DAME DURDEN: *see* Summerson, Miss Esther

DANCER, DANIEL: *see* Boffin, N.

DARBY: A police constable, who accompanied Inspector Bucket and Mr. Snagsby when they were searching for Jo, the crossing-sweeper, in the slums of Tom-all-Alones. *Bleak House*

DARNAY, CHARLES: His real name is Charles St. Evrémonde, nephew of the Marquis St. Evrémonde. Disagreeing with the way the poor people are treated in France he relinquishes his estate when he inherits it by the death of the Marquis, and becomes a teacher of French in England. He marries Lucie Manette, the daughter of a French doctor. He is drawn back to France to save one of his employees from the revolutionaries, and is himself arrested and imprisoned as an emigrant aristocrat. He is saved from the guillotine by Sydney Carton, who, resembling him in looks, takes his place. His name is adapted from that of his mother—D'Aulnais. *A Tale of Two Cities*

DARNAY, MISS LUCIE: Daughter of Charles Darnay, who also escapes from France with her father and mother. *A Tale of Two Cities*

DARNAY, MRS.: *see* Manette, Lucie

DARTLE, ROSA: Companion to Mrs. Steerforth and in love with her son, who, however, does not treat her seriously. She never asks anything directly, but hints at it. She was a little dilapidated—like a house—with having been so long to let. The scar on her lip had been caused by Steerforth who, when he was young, had thrown something at her. Whenever she was agitated this scar showed up very plainly. *David Copperfield*

47

DASH, THE REVEREND DASH: He assisted the Rev. Mr. Blank at the marriage of Mr. and Mrs. Lammle at St. James's Church, Piccadilly. *Our Mutual Friend*

DATCHERY, DICK: The mysterious stranger who arrives in Cloisterham and starts making enquiries into the disappearance of Edwin Drood. Obviously someone disguised, but never revealed because the book was unfinished when the author died. 'This gentleman's white head was unusually large, and his shock of white hair was unusually thick and ample.' (This seems to be purposely pointing to the fact that he wore a wig.) *The Mystery of Edwin Drood*

D'AULNAIS: The name of Charles Darnay's mother, from which he forms the name he adopts in England. *See* Darnay, Charles. *A Tale of Two Cities*

DAVID: An old retainer and butler to the Cheeryble Brothers, who produced a bottle from behind his back with the corkscrew already inserted, uncorked it at a jerk and placed the magnum and the cork before his master. *Nicholas Nickleby*

DAVID: The pawnbroker where Martin Chuzzlewit pawns his gold watch to get money to enable him to live in London, after he has been turned out of home by his grandfather and before he goes to America. *Martin Chuzzlewit*

DAVID, OLD: He carries out the sexton's duty in the parish church in the village where the grandfather and Little Nell finally end their journey and their lives. *The Old Curiosity Shop*

DAWES, MARY: She was a nurse in a poor nobleman's family, where Miss Wade was the governess. A rosy-faced woman always comparing her own cheerfulness with Miss Wade's ill-humour. *Little Dorrit*

DAWKINS, JACK: Better known as The Artful Dodger. He is the leading member of Fagin's gang of pickpockets. He met Oliver north of London, probably at Barnet, and brought him into London to become one of Fagin's gang. Dawkins is finally caught for the theft of a snuff-box and is sentenced to transportation for life. *Oliver Twist*

DAWS, MARY: Kitchenmaid in Mr. Dombey's household— of inferior rank, in black stockings. She rather disgraces herself in the eyes of the domestic staff, when Mr. Dombey becomes bankrupt, by sitting with her mouth open for a long time, and then suddenly saying words to the effect: 'Suppose the wages shouldn't be paid!' *Dombey and Son*

DEAN, MR.: Dean of Cloisterham Cathedral. With a pleasant air of patronage, the Dean as nearly cocks his quaint hat as a Dean in good spirits may, and directs his comely gaiters towards the ruddy dining-room of the snug old red-brick house where he is at present in residence, with his wife, Mrs. Dean, and daughter. *The Mystery of Edwin Drood*

DEDLOCK, LADY: Wife of Sir Morbury Dedlock, whose ghost was said to have haunted the Ghost's Walk at Chesney Wold. She was lame and her halting footsteps were always said to be heard whenever disgrace or disaster threatened the Dedlock family. *Bleak House*

DEDLOCK, LADY HONORIA: Wife of Sir Leicester Dedlock. Mother of Esther Summerson by Captain Hawdon, before being married to Sir Leicester. She thereby brings disgrace on the great Dedlock family name, and runs away. Sir Leicester forgives her and employs Inspector Bucket to pursue her and bring her back. Bucket finds her too late, however, and she dies at the gateway to the paupers' cemetery in which her lover was buried. *Bleak House*

DEDLOCK, SIR LEICESTER, BART.: Typical of the great country families, he is the owner of Chesney Wold. Although he appears formal and distant, he is very much in love with, besides being proud of, Lady Dedlock, and forgives her when she brings disgrace on the family name. *Bleak House*

DEDLOCK, SIR MORBURY: Ancestor of Sir Leicester Dedlock, whose crippled wife originated the haunting of the Ghost's Walk at Chesney Wold. *Bleak House*

DEDLOCK, VOLUMNIA: Cousin of Sir Leicester Dedlock. One of the great family's 'hangers-on'. She was doubly highly related, having the honour to be the poor relation, on her mother's side to another great family. She lives on an annual present from Sir Leicester and makes occasional appearances in the country houses of her cousins. *Bleak House*

DEEDLES: A banker, high in office in the Goldsmiths' Company, and a friend of Alderman Cute and Sir Joseph Bowley. He commits suicide in his own banking house. When the news is received by Alderman Cute, he forgets his vow to 'put down' suicide on the part of the poor people. *The Chimes*

DEFARGE, ERNEST: Keeper of a wine shop in the suburb of Saint Antoine, in Paris. Servant at one time of Dr. Manette, he looks after his old master when he is rescued from the Bastille Prison, until Manette's daughter comes to take her father to England. Defarge is the leader of the revolutionaries and his wine shop becomes one of their headquarters. *A Tale of Two Cities*

DEFARGE, MADAME THÉRÈSE: Wife of Ernest Defarge and fierce leader of the women revolutionaries. Nearly always seen to be knitting. She is killed in a fight with Miss Pross, Lucie Manette's companion. *A Tale of Two Cities*

DEMPLE, GEORGE: One of David Copperfield's schoolfellows at Salem House Academy; his father was a doctor. *David Copperfield*

DENHAM, EDMUND: *see* Longford, Edmund

DENNIS, NED: The hangman at Newgate, who joins the Gordon Rioters. He was very proud of his profession, but is terrified when he comes to be hanged himself. 'A squat, thick-set personage, with a low, retreating forehead, a coarse shock of red hair, and eyes so small and near together that his broken nose alone seemed to prevent their meeting and fusing into one of the usual size. A dingy handkerchief, twisted like a cord about his neck—his dress was of threadbare velveteen—a faded, rusty, whitened black, like the ashes of a pipe . . . ' *Barnaby Rudge*

DEPUTY: Boy at the Traveller's Twopenny, known also as Winks. He is paid by Durdles, a stonemason, to stone him home if he sees him out after ten o'clock at night. He might possibly have been of great importance in solving the mystery of the disappearance of the hero, Edwin Drood, if the book had been finished. *The Mystery of Edwin Drood*

DIBABS, JANE: An acquaintance of Mrs. Nickleby, who according to that lady, *would* marry a man a great deal older than herself. *Nicholas Nickleby*

DIBDIN, THE LATE MR.: A poet, who had written a temperance song called 'The Jolly Young Waterman'. *Pickwick Papers*

DICK: An orphan playmate of Oliver Twist, in the orphanage. *Oliver Twist*

The guard of the coach taking Nicholas Nickleby and Squeers and the boys to Yorkshire. *Nicholas Nickleby*

The hostler at the tavern in Salisbury where Tom Pinch used to stay. *Martin Chuzzlewit*

Youngest apprentice to Joram, who is assistant to Mr. Omer, the undertaker. *David Copperfield*

DICK, MR.: His real name is Richard Babley; a mild lunatic cared for by Miss Betsey Trotwood, in her cottage at Dover. He was occupied in memorializing the Lord Chancellor, but never got far with his writing, without introducing the subject of King Charles the First's head. He often flew a great kite which was covered all over with writing, this being his way of spreading the facts. 'Mr. Dick was grey-headed and florid. His grey eyes prominent and large, with a strange kind of watery brightness in them . . . He could cut oranges into such devices as none of us had an idea of. He could make a boat out of anything, from a skewer upwards. He could turn crampbones into chessmen; fashion Roman chariots from old court cards; make spoked wheels out of cotton reels, and bird cages of old wire. But he was greatest of all, perhaps, in the articles of string and straw.' Mr. Micawber calls him Mr. Dixon. *David Copperfield*

DIGBY, MR.: *see* Smike

DILBER, MRS.: The laundress in Scrooge's dream, who sells his belongings after his death, to a rag-shop man. She produced sheets and towels, a little wearing apparel, two old-fashioned silver tea-spoons, a pair of sugar-tongs, and a few boots. *A Christmas Carol*

DINGO, PROFESSOR: Botanist, and second husband of Mrs. Bayham Badger. *Bleak House*

DIRTY DICK: A nickname. *See* Dorrit, Frederick

DISMAL JEMMY: The nickname of the strolling player, Jem Hutley, and brother of Job Trotter, Jingle's friend. He relates The Stroller's Tale to the Pickwickians at the Bull Inn, Rochester. *Pickwick Papers*

DIVER, COLONEL: Editor of the New York *Rowdy Journal*, who meets Martin Chuzzlewit on his arrival at New York. He finds Martin somewhere to stay, at the Pawkins' Boarding House. *Martin Chuzzlewit*

DIXON, MR.: The name by which Mr. Micawber calls Mr. Dick. *See* Dick, Mr.

DODGER, THE ARTFUL: *see* Dawkins, Jack

DODSON, MR.: Partner in the firm of Dodson and Fogg, the rascally lawyers who took up Mrs. Bardell's breach of promise case against Mr. Pickwick, on the chance of getting their costs out of the gentleman. Failing that, Mrs. Bardell committed herself to pay them, and consequently lands up in the Fleet Prison. *Pickwick Papers*

DOE, JOHN: A name used with that of Richard Roe to create fictional leases. *Bleak House*

DOG'S MEAT MAN: *see* Dorrit, W.

DOLLOBY, MR.: A dealer in second-hand clothes in the Kent Road, London, to whom David Copperfield sold his waistcoat for ninepence, to get money to take him on his walk to find his aunt in Dover. *David Copperfield*

DOLLS, MR.: *see* Cleaver, Mr.

DOLPH: *see* Tetterby, 'dolphus

DOMBEY, FLORENCE: Mr. Dombey's only daughter, who was neglected by him, although she loved him very dearly. She is turned away from home by her father, when his second wife leaves him, and she goes to the Little Wooden Midshipman, where Captain Cuttle looks after her. She eventually marries Walter Gay, old Sol Gills's nephew, and has two children, Paul and Florence. She later becomes reconciled to her father. *Dombey and Son*

DOMBEY, MRS. EDITH: *see* Granger, Edith

DOMBEY, MRS. FANNY: Mr. Dombey's first wife, and mother of Paul and Florence. In giving birth to Paul, according to Mrs. Chick, Mr. Dombey's sister, she did not make an effort and consequently died. *Dombey and Son*

DOMBEY, PAUL (Little Paul): Mr. Dombey's only son, of whom he has great hopes, but the boy is ill and weakly and dies very young. He adores his sister Florence. He had a strange, old-fashioned way. *Dombey and Son*

DOMBEY, PAUL: Head of the firm of Dombey and Son, City Merchants, and father of Little Paul and Florence. After the death of his first wife, he marries Edith Granger, a proud widow who is not very well off. Having lost his son, he turns against his daughter, and his second wife leaves him. He is finally ruined and is on the point of suicide when his daughter finds him and he is reconciled to her and her family. *Dombey and Son*

DONNYS, THE MISS: Twin sisters and proprietresses of Greenleaf, the girls' boarding school where Esther Summerson was a pupil and later a pupil teacher, and from which she went in time to be Mr. John Jarndyce's companion and housekeeper. *Bleak House*

DORA: *see* Spenlow, Dora

DORKER: Former pupil at Dotheboys Hall, for whom Ralph Nickleby paid the account on behalf of his parents, and who died at the school. *Nicholas Nickleby*

DORRIT, AMY: Known as Little Dorrit, the heroine of the story. Her father was William Dorrit and she was born in the Marshalsea Debtors' Prison. She marries Arthur Clennam, the hero of the story, at St. George's Church, where she was also christened. She was taught sewing by a milliner who was a prisoner, and Little Dorrit hires herself out to do sewing, which is how Arthur Clennam meets her at his mother's. *Little Dorrit*

DORRIT, EDWARD: Known as Tip, he was the son of William Dorrit, and brother of Amy and Fanny. A ne'er-do-well, who is constantly in and out of jobs and getting into debt, from which Arthur Clennam rescues him. The shadow of the prison walls seems to walk with him, and he tires of everything he puts his hand to. *Little Dorrit*

DORRIT, FANNY: Elder daughter of William Dorrit, who was taught dancing by an insolvent dancing master in the

Marshalsea Prison. She became a dancer at the theatre and lodges outside the prison with her uncle Frederick. When her father comes into his fortune she marries Edmund Sparkler, son of Mr. Merdle, the banker and financier. *Little Dorrit*

DORRIT, FREDERICK: Brother of William Dorrit, who lodges over Mr. Cripples' Academy, whose boys nickname him Dirty Dick. He is clarinet-player in a theatre orchestra. 'He was dirtily and meanly dressed, in a threadbare coat, once blue, reaching to his ankles and buttoned to his chin, where it vanished in a pale ghost of a velvet collar—a confusion of grey hair and a rusty stock. A greasy hat it was and napless. His trousers were so long and loose, and his shoes so clumsy and large, that he shuffled like an elephant.' *Little Dorrit*

DORRIT, MRS: Wife of William Dorrit, she lived with him in the Marshalsea Prison. Mother of three children, Fanny, Edward and Amy, the last named being born in the prison. She goes on a visit to an old friend in the country and dies there. *Little Dorrit*

DORRIT, WILLIAM: A debtor who was a prisoner in the Marshalsea Debtors' Prison for twenty-five years. He became known as the Father of the Marshalsea, and rather proud of the title. Discharged debtors leave sums of money for him, which he terms 'testimonials'. They use pseudonyms—Bellows, Brick, Cutaway, Dog's Meat Man, Old Gooseberry, Mops, Snooks, Wideawake, etc., which he considers in bad taste. Later, he inherits a great fortune, and travels abroad with his family. He invests his fortune on the guidance of Mr. Merdle, a financier and banker, who turns out to be a common swindler. Mr. Dorrit loses all his money, but dies before he is aware of this. He is taken ill in Italy at a rich dinner and imagines that he is back again in the debtors' prison. *Little Dorrit*

DOT: *see* Peerybingle, Mrs.

DOWDLES, THE MISSES: They kept a school for twenty-five young ladies in Devonshire, which was attended by Kate Nickleby. *Nicholas Nickleby*

DOWLER, MR.: An officer in His Majesty's Service, who travels to Bath with the Pickwickians and lodges with them in the Royal Crescent. He appears to be very fierce, but it is all show and is in reality a bit of a coward. *Pickwick Papers*

DOWLER, MRS.: Wife of Mr. Dowler and of whom he is very jealous. She is concerned in an incident with Mr. Winkle, when he gets shut out of the house in the Royal Crescent in his night clothes. *Pickwick Papers*

DOYCE, DANIEL: Son of a North Country blacksmith. An engineer and an inventor, with whom Arthur Clennam becomes a partner. Frustrated by the Circumlocution Office in trying to obtain a patent for his invention, he eventually goes abroad. *Little Dorrit*

DRIZZLE: An ill-used man whose case would be looked into when Jarndyce and Jarndyce was concluded. In other words, there was little chance of anything being done. *Bleak House*

DROOD, EDWIN: Known also as Eddy or Ned (as the old opium woman said, 'a threatened name'). The hero of the story, nephew of John Jasper. Edwin mysteriously disappears, but whether he has been murdered or not or by whom is never disclosed, because Dickens died before he could finish the book. Edwin was engaged to Rosa Bud, but just before his disappearance they break off the engagement, which had been arranged by their parents. *The Mystery of Edwin Drood*

DRUM, THE: A private friend of Trotty Veck's who plays the drum in the local band. *The Chimes*

DRUMMLE, BENTLEY: A fellow pupil of Pip at Matthew Pocket's, and his rival for the hand of Estella, whom he marries. He is nicknamed the Spider by Mr. Jaggers, the criminal lawyer. *Great Expectations*

DUBBLEY: Officer of Justice who takes part in Mr. Pickwick's arrest at Ipswich. Miss Witherfield reports to the Mayor that Mr. Pickwick and Mr. Magnus are about to fight a duel, although they have no such intention. *Pickwick Papers*

DUFF: A Bow Street runner, concerned with Blathers in investigating the burglary by Bill Sikes of Mrs. Maylie's house at Chertsey. *Oliver Twist*

DUMKINS, MR.: One of the leading batsmen of the All Muggleton Cricket Club, who was caught out after a splendid innings. Following the match, he was Chairman at the Cricket Club Dinner, which was attended by the Pickwickians. *Pickwick Papers*

DUNKLE, DOCTOR GINERY: 'A shrill boy' and a gentleman of great poetical elements who was spokesman of the committee welcoming Mr. Elijah Pogram, at the National Hotel in America. *Martin Chuzzlewit*

DUNSTABLE: A village butcher, who is referred to by Uncle Pumblechook at the Christmas lunch at Joe Gargery's. *Great Expectations*

DURDLES: A stonemason in Cloisterham, who spends a great deal of his time tapping the walls of tombs, and deciding upon their contents. He was employed by Jasper to show him some of the secret places in the cathedral crypt. It is assumed that Jasper wants to put this knowledge to some nefarious purpose. Being a drunkard, Durdles pays the young boy Deputy to stone him home if he finds him out after ten o'clock at night. *The Mystery of Edwin Drood*

DUSTMAN, THE GOLDEN: *see* Boffin, Nicodemus

E

EDDY: *see* Drood, Edwin

EDMUNDS, JOHN: A robber, about whom the old clergyman at Manor Farm, Dingley Dell, tells a story. It also
concerns his father and mother, Mr. and Mrs. Edmunds.
Interpolated story—'The Convict's Return'. *Pickwick
Papers*

EDWARDS, MISS: A poor boarder at Miss Monflather's
Establishment, who pays no fees and is kept on as a teacher
more or less at the same rate. Little Nell is attracted by her.
The Old Curiosity Shop

EGBERT: *see* Pardiggle, Egbert

ELIZABETH, MISS: One of the imaginary inhabitants of the
corner house outside which Silas Wegg has his little stall.
Our Mutual Friend

ELWES, JOHN: *see* Boffin, N.

EM'LY, LITTLE: An orphan, and Dan'l Peggotty's niece,
she lives with him in the old boat house on the shore at
Great Yarmouth. She becomes engaged to her cousin Ham
Peggotty, but runs away with Steerforth, David Copper-
field's handsome friend. Steerforth discards her abroad, and
she returns to London, where she is found by her uncle
Dan'l, who emigrates with her to Australia. *David
Copperfield*

EMMA: *see* Micawber, Mrs. and Miss.

One of the maid-servants at Manor Farm, Dingley Dell.
Pickwick Papers

ENDELL, MARTHA: At one time worked at the shop of Mr.
Omer, undertaker in Great Yarmouth, sewing the mourning. She was friendly with Little Em'ly who also worked

there. After going on the streets, and going to London, she helps Dan'l Peggotty to find Little Em'ly. *David Copperfield*

ESTELLA: Daugher of Magwitch, the convict and Molly, Mr. Jaggers' housekeeper. She is adopted and brought up by Miss Havisham, the eccentric recluse, to take revenge on mankind. Pip, the hero of the story, falls in love with her, in spite of her warning that she has no heart, but she eventually marries Pip's rival, Bentley Drummle, who ill-treats her. Pip meets her years later and it is hinted that they may get married. *Great Expectations*

ETHELINDA: *see* Sapsea, Mrs.

EUSTACE, MR.: The classical scholar and traveller referred to by Mrs. General. *Little Dorrit*

EVANS, RICHARD: A pupil of Mr. Marton, schoolmaster in the village where the grandfather and Little Nell finally settle. *The Old Curiosity Shop*

F

F., MR.: Flora Finching's husband, whom she refers to as Mr. F. *Little Dorrit*

FAGIN: Head of a gang of thieves and pickpockets and a receiver of stolen property, into whose hands Oliver Twist falls. Monks, Oliver's half-brother pays Fagin to make the boy a thief, hence Fagin's anxiety to retain Oliver. He plays upon the ignorance and brutality of Bill Sikes. 'A very old, shrivelled Jew, whose villainous and repulsive face was obscured by a quantity of matted red hair. He was dressed in a greasy flannel gown, with his throat bare.' He is finally caught and hanged, and the gang is broken up. *Oliver Twist*

FAN, LITTLE: Scrooge's little sister, whom he sees in his dream. Mother of his nephew, Fred. *A Christmas Carol*

FANG, MR.: A bullying Police Magistrate, before whom Oliver Twist appeared, accused of stealing Mr. Brownlow's handkerchief. 'His face was stern and much flushed. If he were not really in the habit of drinking rather more than was exactly good for him, he might have brought an action against his countenance for libel, and have recovered heavy damages.' *Oliver Twist*

FAT BOY: *see* Joe

FATHER OF THE MARSHALSEA: *see* Dorrit, William

FEEDER, B. A., MR.: Dr. Blimber's assistant in the school at Brighton, which was attended by Paul Dombey. He marries Miss Blimber, and succeeds to the school. He was a kind of human barrel-organ, with a little list of tunes at which he was continually working, over and over again, without any variation. *Dombey and Son*

FEEDER, M.A., THE REV. ALFRED: Brother of B. A. Feeder, who officiated at his marriage with Cornelius Blimber. *Dombey and Son*

FEEDER, MRS. B. A.: *see* Blimber, Cornelius

FEENIX, LORD: Nephew of Mrs. Skewton and Edith Granger's cousin, who had been a man about town forty years ago. He gives Edith away at her marriage to Mr. Dombey, and gives shelter to her when she leaves her husband. *Dombey and Son*

FERDINAND, MISS: A high-spirited pupil at Miss Twinkleton's Academy, at the Nun's House, Cloisterham, who is given an imposition for being incorrigible. *The Mystery of Edwin Drood*

'FERGUSON': *see* Bonney, Mr.

FERN, LILIAN: Niece of Will Fern, and an orphan. Trotty Veck, the ticket porter has a terrible dream about her. *The Chimes*

FERN, WILL: A poor man, who comes to London with his niece, Lilian, seeking work. He is brought up as a vagrant before Alderman Cute. *The Chimes*

FEZZIWIG, MRS.: Wife of old Fezziwig, who attended the Christmas party for the workers in the warehouse, which was part of Scrooge's dream of his past. 'In came Mrs. Fezziwig—one vast substantial smile.' *A Christmas Carol*

FEZZIWIG, OLD: Scrooge's generous old employer, with whom he was an apprentice, and about whom he dreams. 'An old gentleman in a Welsh wig, sitting behind such a high desk, that if he had been two inches taller he must have knocked his head against the ceiling.' *A Christmas Carol*

FEZZIWIGS, THREE MISS: Daughters of old Fezziwig, who broke the hearts of the six young followers. *A Christmas Carol*

FIBBITSON, MRS.: An inmate of the almshouses where Mr. Mell the schoolmaster's mother lived. 'An old woman in a chair by the fire, who was such a bundle of clothes that I feel grateful to this hour for not having sat on her by mistake.' This occurs when Mr. Mell takes David Copperfield to see his mother. *David Copperfield*

FIELDING, MAY: Friend of Dot Peerybingle, who after a long absence of her lover, Edward Plummer, agrees to marry Mr. Tackleton, the owner of the toy factory. Edward returns in time to stop the wedding and to marry May himself. *The Cricket on the Hearth*

FIELDING, MRS.: Mother of May Fielding. 'A little querulous chip of an old lady with a peevish face.' *The Cricket on the Hearth*

FIELDING, SIR JOHN: A magistrate whose house is burned in the Gordon Riots. *Barnaby Rudge*

FIERY FACE: The name given to John Westlock's charwoman at his chambers in Furnival's Inn. She was rather put out by the appearance of Ruth Pinch, as she realized that she might soon lose her job, if John and Ruth got married. *Martin Chuzzlewit*

FILER, MR.: A friend of Alderman Cute, who was against the poor and was keen on quoting statistics against them. *The Chimes*

FILLETOVILLE, SON OF THE MARQUIS OF: A young gentleman in a powdered wig, and a sky-blue coat trimmed with silver. In the bagman's uncle's dream he is concerned with the abduction of a beautiful young lady, and is finally pinned to the wall by a sword. Interpolated story, told by the one-eyed bagman in The Bush at Bristol: 'The Story of the Bagman's Uncle'. *Pickwick Papers*

FINCHBURY, LADY JANE: According to Lord Feenix— a bit of an artist. 'The woman with tight stays.' *Dombey and Son*

FINCHES OF THE GROVE: A club whose quarrelsome members dined fortnightly in a Covent Garden Hotel. Pip, Herbert Pocket, Bentley Drummle, and Startop are members. *Great Expectations*

FINCHING, FLORA: A widow living with her father Christopher Casby. Once the object of Arthur Clennam's affections, but they were parted and she marries Mr. Finching (referred to as Mr. F.). Arthur Clennam went out to China, and many years later meets Flora when he returns to London. He is rather horrified at what he finds. Flora, who had been spoiled and artless long ago, is determined to be spoiled and artless now. *Little Dorrit*

FIPS, MR.: A solicitor of Austin Friars, who employed Tom Pinch, when he came to London, on behalf of old Martin Chuzzlewit, in a job in the Temple. *Martin Chuzzlewit*

FISH, MR.: Confidential secretary to Sir Joseph Bowley. 'A not very stately gentleman in black, who wrote from dictation.' *The Chimes*

FITZ-MARSHALL, CAPTAIN CHARLES: The name assumed by Jingle at Eatanswill and Ipswich. *See* Jingle, Alfred

FIZKIN, HORATIO: Of Fizkin Hall. The Buff candidate in the Eatanswill Election, who is defeated by the Blue candidate, the Hon. Samuel Slumkey. *Pickwick Papers*

FIZZGIG, DON BOLARO: The Spanish Grandee, father of Donna Christina, one of Jingle's conquests. He is found in the main pipe of the public fountain, in the great square, 'with a full confession in his right boot'. *Pickwick Papers*

FIZZGIG, DONNA CHRISTINA: Don Bolaro's daughter, in love with Jingle. On her father's forbidding the marriage, she took prussic acid and had to be revived by means of a stomach pump, a remedy she did not survive. *Pickwick Papers*

FLABELLA, LADY: Ficticious character in a fashionable novel read aloud by Kate Nickleby to Mrs. Wittitterley. *Nicholas Nickleby*

FLADDOCK, GENERAL: A first-class passenger on the *Screw* returning to America. A friend of the Norris family, he is very embarrassed when he finds that Martin Chuzzlewit, whom he meets at the Norton house, was a fellow passenger on the *Screw*, but in the steerage. *Martin Chuzzlewit*

FLASHER, WILKINS: A stockbroker who transferred the stock left by Mrs. Weller to her relict Tony Weller. His clerk and groom are also mentioned, the latter being on his way to the West End to deliver game. *Pickwick Papers*

FLEDGEBY, MR.: Father of 'Fascination Fledgeby' who had been a moneylender. *Our Mutual Friend*

FLEDGEBY, MRS.; Lord Snigsworth's cousin who offends her family by marrying Fledgeby. *Our Mutual Friend*

FLEDGEBY, YOUNG: 'Fascination Fledgeby' who runs a money-lending business known as Pubsey and Co. The business is ostensibly carried out by an old Jew, named Riah, behind whom Fledgeby hides. He is at last found out by one of his victims, Alfred Lammle, who savagely attacks him. *Our Mutual Friend*

FLEMING, AGNES: Oliver Twist's mother who had been seduced by Edwin Leeford, the father of Monks, Oliver's half-brother. Running away from home, she took refuge in a workhouse where she died in giving birth to Oliver. The baby was named Oliver Twist by Bumble the Beadle. *Oliver Twist*

FLEMING, ROSE: *see* Maylie, Rose

FLESTRIN, JUNIOR QUINBUS—or THE YOUNG MAN MOUNTAIN: *see* Sparkler, Edmund

FLINTWINCH, EPHRAIM: Twin brother of Jeremiah, who is keeper at a lunatic asylum, and has to leave the country. He plots with his brother and is spied on by Affery, who thinks she is dreaming when she sees the twin likeness of her husband. *Little Dorrit*

FLINTWINCH, JEREMIAH: Mrs. Clennam's confidential clerk and later her business partner, because her son, Arthur, is not interested in the business. He plots with his brother to suppress some papers and swindle Little Dorrit out of a legacy. 'An old man, bent and dried. His neck was so twisted, that the knotted ends of his white cravat usually dangled under one ear—he had a weird appearance of having hanged himself at one time—and having gone about ever since halter and all—as some timely hand had cut him down.' *Little Dorrit*

FLINTWINCH, MRS. AFFERY: The lady who was made to marry Jeremiah Flintwinch by Mrs. Clennam, her employer. Affery regarded Mrs. Clennam and her husband as 'the clever ones' and was in awe of them. She is always hearing noises in the old house, which are later explained when the house collapses in a cloud of dust and rubble. *Little Dorrit*

FLITE, MISS: A little mad old woman. One of the suitors in the case of Jarndyce and Jarndyce, who is always expecting a judgment. She keeps a number of caged birds all bearing names, and plans to release them when the case is settled. She lodges over the shop kept by Krook, the rag-and-bone dealer. *Bleak House*

FLOPSON: One of Mrs. Pocket's two nurse-maids who look after the children. *Great Expectations*

FLOWERS: Mrs. Skewton's maid, who knows all about the secrets of the old lady's complicated make-up, and who takes her to pieces when she goes to bed at night. *Dombey and Son*

FLUGGERS: An old actor who does the heavy business in the Vincent Crummles Theatrical Company. *Nicholas Nickleby*

FLYNTERYNGE, MYNHEER VON JEREMIAH: Foreign name assumed by Flintwinch. *See* Flintwinch, Jeremiah

FOGG, MR.: Partner of the rascally lawyers, Dodson and Fogg, who take up Mrs. Bardell's breach of promise case against Mr. Pickwick. 'An elderly, pimply-faced vegetable-diet sort of man.' *Pickwick Papers*

FOLAIR, MR.: Dancer and pantomimist in the Vincent Crummles Theatrical Company, who always has to dance with the Infant Phenomenon. He takes the part of the savage with her in the ballet, 'The Indian Savage and the Maiden.' *Nicholas Nickleby*

FOLEY: An acquaintance of Lord Feenix, who was riding a blood mare at Brighton. *Dombey and Son*

FOULON, OLD: He told the starving people in France that they could eat grass. During the French Revolution the mob caught him, and he was hanged on a lamp-post, after having grass stuffed into his mouth. *A Tale of Two Cities*

FRANÇOIS: Waiter at the Golden Head Restaurant, Dijon, where Carker arranges to meet Mrs. Edith Dombey. *Dombey and Son*

FRED: Scrooge's nephew, and son of his sister, Little Fan. He invited Scrooge to dinner on Christmas Day, but was met with a grumpy refusal. When Scrooge reformed after his dream the first place he goes to is his nephew's to ask if he can come to dinner. They are very pleased to welcome him, and he thoroughly enjoys the party. *A Christmas Carol*

FRED, MRS.: Fred's wife. 'A dimpled, surprised-looking, capital face; a ripe little mouth, that seemed made to be kissed—as no doubt it was.' *A Christmas Carol*

FRIAR OF SAINT BENEDICT: One of the order of the black monks to whom the five sisters paid yearly dues. Interpolated story: 'The Five Sisters of York.' *Nicholas Nickleby*

F'S AUNT, MR.: *See* Aunt, Mr. F's.

G

GABELLE, THÉOPHILE: Postmaster of the village on the St. Evrémonde estate in France. Charles Darnay returns to France to rescue him from the revolutionaries. *A Tale of Two Cities*

GAFFER: *see* Hexam

GAG, TOM: Someone to whom Jonas Chuzzlewit was likened by Mr. Wolf, the literary guest at Tigg Montague's dinner. *Martin Chuzzlewit*

GALLANBILE, MR.: An M.P. whose wife needed a cook. *Nicholas Nickleby*

GALLOWS: *see* Jo

GAME CHICKEN, THE: A pugilist who teaches Mr. Toots the noble art of boxing. He was always to be heard of at the bar of the Black Badger, wore a shaggy white greatcoat in the warmest weather and knocked Mr. Toots about the head three times a week, for the small consideration of ten and six a visit. *Dombey and Son*

GAMFIELD, MR.: A chimney-sweep, who applied for Oliver Twist at the workhouse, when Oliver was put up for sale. His villainous face was a regular stamped receipt for cruelty. *Oliver Twist*

GAMP, MR.: Deceased husband of Mrs. Gamp, who said, 'When Gamp was summoned to his long home, and I see him a lying in Guy's Hospital with a pennypiece on each eye, and his wooden leg under his left arm, I thought I should have fainted away. But I bore up.' *Martin Chuzzlewit*

GAMP, MRS. SARAH: Midwife and nurse who lived in Kingsgate Street, High Holborn, over Mr. Sweedlepipe the barber's shop. She claimed an imaginary friend, a Mrs. Harris, and always carried a large loosely-rolled umbrella, which has come to be known as a 'gamp'. 'A fat old woman with a husky voice, and a moist eye. Her face—the nose in particular—somewhat red and swollen.' Her favourite beverage was gin and it was difficult to enjoy her society without becoming conscious of a smell of spirits. Her rusty black gown was rather the worse for snuff. *Martin Chuzzlewit*

GANDER, MR.: Boarder at Mrs. Todgers' Establishment, who was of a witty turn. *Martin Chuzzlewit*

GARGERY, JOE: The blacksmith and husband of Pip's sister. A fair man with curls of flaxen hair on each side of his smooth face, and with eyes of such a very undecided blue that they seemed to have somehow got mixed with their own whites. *Great Expectations*

GARGERY, MRS. BIDDY: *see* Biddy

GARGERY, MRS. JOE: Joe Gargery's first wife and Pip's sister. She is attacked and severely injured by Orlick, Joe's assistant at the forge, and eventually dies as a result. She brought up Pip very strictly, with a cane called 'tickler'. She was tall and bony, and almost always wore a coarse apron, fastened over her figure behind with two loops, and having a square, impregnable bib in front, that was stuck full of pins and needles. *Great Expectations*

GARLAND, MR.: A kindly old gentleman, the father of Abel, who befriends and later employs Kit Nubbles. A little fat, placid-faced old gentleman. He had a club-foot like his son. *The Old Curiosity Shop*

GARLAND, MR. ABEL: Son of Mr. and Mrs. Garland, articled to Mr. Witherden, a notary, and eventually becoming his partner. He married 'the most bashful young lady that was ever seen'. He had a club-foot. *The Old Curiosity Shop*

GARLAND, MRS.: Wife of Mr. Garland, and mother of Abel. Beside the old gentleman sat a little old lady, plump and placid like himself. *The Old Curiosity Shop*

GASHFORD, MR.: Lord George Gordon's secretary, an unscrupulous villain, who urges his master on and secretly encourages the Gordon Rioters to violence. He commits suicide by poison. *Barnaby Rudge*

GASPARD: The Parisian whose child was run over and killed by the carriage of the Marquis de St. Evrémonde. He follows the Marquis to his château, and murders him, for which crime he is hung on a gallows forty feet high above the village. *A Tale of Two Cities*

GAY, WALTER: Nephew of Sol Gills, employed at the office of Dombey and Son. Sent abroad, because Mr. Dombey takes a dislike to him, he is shipwrecked and given up for lost. He returns to London, however, and is reunited with his uncle Sol Gills who has gone to search for him. He eventually marries Florence Dombey, and they have two children, Florence and Paul. *Dombey and Son*

GAZINGI, MISS: A member of the Vincent Crummles Theatrical Company. She has an imitation ermine boa tied in a loose knot round her neck. *Nicholas Nickleby*

GENERAL, MRS.: Daughter of a clerical dignitary. The chaperon engaged by Mr. Dorrit to educate his two daughters. She recommends 'Papa, potatoes, poultry, prunes and prisms' as good words to form the lips. She is much resented by Fanny Dorrit. Mr. Dorrit obviously contemplates asking her to marry him but dies before this can come about. 'Her countenance and hair had rather a floury appearance. If her eyes had no expression, it was probably because they had nothing to express.' *Little Dorrit*

GENTLEMAN IN THE SMALL CLOTHES: Mrs. Nickleby's next door neighbour, a lunatic, who makes love to her over the garden wall. He plies her with gifts of various vegetables which he throws over the wall—marrows, cucumbers, etc. He is at last restrained by his keeper. Mrs. Nickleby is flattered, however, and refuses to believe that the old gentleman is mad. *Nicholas Nickleby*

GENTLEMAN IN THE WHITE WAISTCOAT, THE: A member of the Workhouse Board, before whom Oliver Twist is taken by Bumble, the beadle, after he has had the temerity to ask for more food. This old gentleman insists that Oliver will come to be hanged, because of this very bad beginning. *Oliver Twist*

GENTLEMAN, THE YOUNGEST: *see* Moddle, Augustus

GENTLEMEN, TWO PORTLY: They call on Scrooge one Christmas Eve collecting for the poor and destitute, but Scrooge rebuffs them. After his dream, however, he seeks them out in the street and makes a handsome donation to their cause. *A Christmas Carol*

GEORGE: Mrs. Jarley's handyman who looks after the travelling waxworks—a man in a carter's frock, who eventually marries her. *The Old Curiosity Shop*

A friend of the Kenwigs family, who on one occasion dares to make fun of Mrs. Kenwigs' uncle, Mr. Lillyvick, the water-rate collector. His fun is taken in very bad part, as Mr. Lillyvick is a sacred name in the family. *Nicholas Nickleby*

Insolvent friend of Tony Weller. *Pickwick Papers*

The guard on the coach taking David from Great Yarmouth to London. *David Copperfield*

GEORGE, MASTER: The fictitious name given to one of the imaginary characters who, according to Silas Wegg, the wooden-legged stallholder, occupy the corner house, outside which he has his stall. Master George was his mythical patron, who used to send him on imaginary errands. *Our Mutual Friend*

GEORGE, MRS.: One of the guests at Mrs. Quilp's tea-party, which is interrupted by the unexpected appearance of Quilp himself. *The Old Curiosity Shop*

GEORGE, TROOPER: *see* Rouncewell, George

GEORGIANA: A cousin of Matthew Pocket, and one of Miss Havisham's fawning relatives. *Great Expectations*

GHOST OF CHRISTMAS PAST: The first of Scrooge's nocturnal visitors in his dream, who shows him his wasted past. 'It was a strange figure—like a child: yet not so much like a child as like an old man. It wore a tunic of the purest white and round its waist a lustrous belt . . . from the crown of its head there sprung a bright clear jet of light . . .' *A Christmas Carol*

GHOST OF CHRISTMAS PRESENT: The second of Scrooge's nocturnal visitors in his dream, who shows him what he is missing by his miserly shut-up life, and that even people without money can enjoy themselves. The ghost holds aloft a glowing torch shaped like Plenty's horn from which he drops sprinklings on people to restore their good humour. 'A jolly giant, glorious to see . . . clothed in a simple green robe or mantle, bordered with white fur.' *A Christmas Carol*

GHOST OF CHRISTMAS YET TO COME: The third and last visitor in Scrooge's dream, who shows him what the future holds if he does not mend his ways. He is dreaded by Scrooge more than the others. 'A solemn Phantom, draped and hooded . . . shrouded in a deep black garment.' *A Christmas Carol*

GHOST OF JACOB MARLEY: Scrooge's old partner in business, who visits him in a dream, and predicts the coming of the other three ghosts. He tells Scrooge that he has obtained this chance for him to avoid his partner's fate or worse. *A Christmas Carol*

GHOST, AN OLD: He appears in Scrooge's dream among the floating spirits, and was of someone he knew once in business. He was in a white waistcoat, with a monstrous iron safe attached to his ankle. *A Christmas Carol*

GIGGLES, MISS: A pupil at Miss Twinkleton's Academy at Nun's House, Cloisterham. She is very interested in Rosa Bud's fiancé, Edwin Drood, and his quarrel with Neville Landless. *The Mystery of Edwin Drood*

GILBERT, MARK: Apprentice to a hosier, Curzon, in love with Curzon's daughter. He joined the secret society, the Prentice Knights. *Barnaby Rudge*

GILES, MR.: Butler and steward to Mrs. Maylie. He gave the alarm at the attempted burglary by Bill Sikes, and shoots Oliver Twist when he is put through the window. *Oliver Twist*

GILL, MR.: The husband of one of Mrs. Gamp's patients, who would back his wife against Moore's *Almanack*, to name the very day and hour of her baby's birth, for ninepence farthing. *Martin Chuzzlewit*

GILL, MRS.: A mother of six, attended by Mrs. Gamp. As far as regularity was concerned, Mrs. Gamp had great confidence in her. *Martin Chuzzlewit*

GILLS, SOLOMON: The nautical-instrument dealer and proprietor of the little shop known as The Little Wooden Midshipman, on account of the sign outside. He is uncle to Walter Gay, and he goes in search of his nephew when he is reported lost at sea. He eventually returns to London, after leaving his shop in the charge of Captain Cuttle, and is reunited with his nephew, who has returned safely. *Dombey and Son*

GLAMOUR, BOB: A riverside character and one of the regular customers at the Six Jolly Fellowship Porters. He helps when Rogue Riderhood is nearly drowned after being run down by a steamer in the river. *Our Mutual Friend*

GLAVORMELLY, MR.: A former actor at the Coburg Theatre and friend of Mr. Snevellicci. *Nicholas Nickleby*

GLIDDERY, BOB: Pot-boy at the Six Jolly Fellowship Porters, at Limehouse, whose late mother used to accelerate his retirement to rest with a poker. *Our Mutual Friend*

'GLORIOUS APOLLERS': A select convivial circle of which Dick Swiveller had the honour to be 'Perpetual Grand'. *The Old Curiosity Shop*

GLUBB, OLD: The drawer of Little Paul Dombey's wheel-chair when he is taken ill at Brighton, to whom Paul becomes very attached. *Dombey and Son*

GOBLINS, KING OF THE: A strange unearthly figure who takes Gabriel Grub, gravedigger, down below to teach him a lesson, for digging graves on Christmas Eve and, worse still, drinking on his own. Interpolated story: 'The Story of the Goblins who Stole a Sexton'. Told by Mr. Wardle at Christmas. *Pickwick Papers*

GOLDEN DUSTMAN, THE: *see* Boffin, Nicodemus

GOODWIN: Mrs. Pott's maid, who sided with her mistress against Mr. Pott. *Pickwick Papers*

GOODY, OLD MRS.: The grandmother of the child the Rev. Milvery suggested that Mr. and Mrs. Boffin might consider adopting. *Our Mutual Friend*

GOOSEBERRY, OLD: *see* Dorrit, W.

GORDON, COLONEL: A near relative of Lord George Gordon. *Barnaby Rudge*

GORDON, EMMA: A dancer and member of Sleary's Circus. She danced on the tightrope, and looked after Cissy Jupe when she was younger. A cheesemonger who saw her perform fell in love with her, and they were married. *Hard Times*

GORDON, LORD GEORGE: He became president of the Protestant Association and in his name the Gordon Rioters sack the houses of Roman Catholics and their churches in London and on the outskirts. He later becomes a Jew, and, after escaping to Holland, returns to England, is imprisoned for a time, and finally dies in this country. *Barnaby Rudge*

GOWAN, HENRY: An artist with no particular aim in life; he took up painting for the want of something better and was quite content to live on his wife's allowance from her father. He marries Pet Meagles, rather against her parents' wish. *Little Dorrit*

GOWAN, MRS.: Henry Gowan's mother; a widow living on pension in the Grace and Favour apartments at Hampton Court Palace. She considered that her son married beneath him. *Little Dorrit*

GOWAN, MRS. M.: *see* Meagles, Minnie (Pet)

GRADGRIND, ADAM SMITH: One of the younger Gradgrinds, who was usually out at a lecture in custody. *Hard Times*

GRADGRIND, JANE: The youngest of the Gradgrind family. After manufacturing a good deal of moist pipe-clay on her face with slate-pencil and tears, had fallen asleep over vulgar fractions. *Hard Times*

GRADGRIND, LOUISA: Mr. Gradgrind's elder daughter who marries Josiah Bounderby, rich banker, merchant, and manufacturer, although she does not love him. She really marries to help her brother Thomas, who wants to get on in Bounderby's Bank. She later avoids being seduced by a man about town, James Harthouse, and returns home to her father. *Hard Times*

GRADGRIND, MALTHUS: Another of the younger Gradgrinds, who is brought up like the others on facts and figures. *Hard Times*

GRADGRIND, MRS.: Wife of Thomas Gradgrind, who was bewildered by the masses of facts talked about around her. 'A little, thin, white, pink-eyed bundle of shawls of surpassing feebleness, mental and bodily.' *Hard Times*

GRADGRIND, THOMAS: Of Stone Lodge, Coketown. A retired millowner, who is obsessed with the doctrine of facts and neglects the normal human feelings. He makes a failure of trying to bring his children up under this doctrine. *Hard Times*

GRADGRIND, THOMAS: 'The Whelp', son of Thomas Gradgrind, senior, who becomes a clerk in Bounderby's Bank, which he robs. He is eventually smuggled out of the country by the help of Sleary, the circus proprietor. *Hard Times*

GRAHAM, MARY: The companion of old Martin Chuzzlewit. After being pursued by Mr. Pecksniff, she eventually marries young Martin Chuzzlewit, which was a match that old Martin really desired. *Martin Chuzzlewit*

GRAINGER: Friend of Steerforth, who is a guest at David Copperfield's first bachelor dinner party in his lodgings in Buckingham Street. *David Copperfield*

GRANDFATHER, LITTLE NELL'S: *see* Trent, Grandfather

GRANGER, COLONEL: A deceased army friend of Major Bagstock. He was Edith Granger's first husband. *Dombey and Son*

GRANGER, EDITH: Widow of Colonel Granger and daughter of Mrs. Skewton. She marries Mr. Dombey and, although cold and proud to him, loves his daughter Florence. This turns Dombey against her and she eventually makes it appear that she has run away with Dombey's manager, James Carker. She is later looked after and given shelter by Lord Feenix, her cousin. *Dombey and Son*

GRANNETT, MR.: Workhouse overseer in the workhouse where Oliver Twist was born. He relieved a dying pauper with an offer of a pound of potatoes and half a pint of oatmeal. *Oliver Twist*

GRAYMARSH: One of the pupils at Dotheboys Hall. His maternal aunt said in a letter to him that she thought Mrs. Squeers must be an angel and Mr. Squeers too good for this world. *Nicholas Nickleby*

GRAYPER, MR. and MRS.: Neighbours of Mrs. Copperfield, David's mother. It was at their house that she met Mr. Murdstone, who became her second husband. The Graypers went to South America. *David Copperfield*

GREEN, MISS: She lodges in the two-pair back in the house occupied by the Kenwigs family. She made Mrs. Kenwigs' dress and gave up her bed to the baby, when the Kenwigses had a party, to which she was therefore invited. *Nicholas Nickleby*

GREEN, MRS.: She lodges near to Mrs. Nubbles, at the cheesemonger's round the corner. She is cited by Mrs. Nubbles as witness to Kit's various ailments during his young life, when Mr. and Mrs. Garland call to arrange for Kit's employment by them. *The Old Curiosity Shop*

GREEN, SON OF MRS.: A law writer, three months out at sea on the way to China. His name was given to the beadle asking for witnesses at the inquest on Captain Hawdon. This greatly confuses the already confused beadle. *Bleak House*

GREEN, TOM: *see* Willet, Joe

GREGORY: Foreman packer at Murdstone & Grinby's warehouse where David Copperfield works, washing and labelling bottles. *David Copperfield*

GREGSBURY, M.P., MR.: Nicholas Nickleby applies for the job of secretary to this M.P., for which he is offered fifteen shillings a week. In view of the work required Nicholas does not accept the post. *Nicholas Nickleby*

GREWGIOUS, HIRAM: Rosa Bud's guardian, who had chambers in Staple Inn. When frightened by John Jasper's violent declaration of love, Rosa goes to her guardian's chambers and he installs her in London. *The Mystery of Edwin Drood*

GRIDE, ARTHUR: An ancient money-lender and business accomplice of Ralph Nickleby. They plot to compel Madeline Bray, the daughter of a debtor to Gride, to marry the old man. Their scheme is frustrated by the sudden death of Madeline's father. *Nicholas Nickleby*

GRIDLEY, MR.: A victim of Chancery, known as the Man from Shropshire. He dies, worn out, in George's Shooting Gallery as Inspector Bucket comes to arrest him for some further contempt of Court. *Bleak House*

GRIDLEY, SENIOR, MR.: He left his farm and stock to his wife during her life and then to his sons. Gridley's brother started the Chancery case, which ruined the whole family. *Bleak House*

GRIGGS FAMILY, THE: A family at Ipswich, who were friendly with the Nupkins family and whose derision they feared. *Pickwick Papers*

GRIMBLE, SIR THOMAS: Of Grimbly Hall, with six grown-up daughters. The family is recalled by Mrs. Nickleby when she hears that Smike is from Yorkshire. *Nicholas Nickleby*

GRIMWIG, MR.: Lame in one leg, he is a lawyer and friend of Mr. Brownlow. He has no faith in Oliver's honesty, when Oliver is sent on an errand with a five pound note. His *bête noir* is orange peel on the ground, and he backs his violent assertions with an oath: 'Or I'll eat my head!' *Oliver Twist*

GRINDER: A travelling showman. His party consisted of a young lady and a young gentleman on stilts and Mr. Grinder himself, who carried a drum. They are referred to as 'Grinder's Lot'. *The Old Curiosity Shop*

GROFFIN, THOMAS: A chemist, who serves on the jury for the case of Bardell *v.* Pickwick. He wished to be excused because he had left his shop in the charge of an errand boy whose knowledge of drugs was limited. The Judge overruled his application to be excused. *Pickwick Papers*

GROMPUS: One of Mr. Podsnap's guests at his daughter Georgiana's birthday party; he danced with her, which scared her very much. *Our Mutual Friend*

GROPER, COLONEL: One of the deputation who welcomed Mr. Elijah Pogram in America at the National Hotel, where Martin Chuzzlewit and Mark Tapley stop on their way from Eden. *Martin Chuzzlewit*

GROVES, JAMES: Landlord of the Valiant Soldier, and a gambler. He is described as 'Honest Jem Groves . . . a man of unblemished character, and has a good dry skittle-ground'. He tempts the old grandfather to gamble away little Nell's money. *The Old Curiosity Shop*

GRUB, OLD GABRIEL: A drunken and bad-tempered sexton who is digging a grave on Christmas Eve and drinking Holland's gin by himself, when he is carried away by goblins—or dreams that he is. Interpolated story, told by Mr. Wardle: The Story of the Goblins who Stole a Sexton. *Pickwick Papers*

GRUBBLE, W.: Landlord of the Dedlock Arms in the village, near to Chesney Wold, the home of Sir Leicester and Lady Dedlock. *Bleak House*

GRUDDEN, MRS.: A member of the Vincent Crummles Theatrical Company, who performs various duties and parts under a variety of names. She sometimes lit the blue fire for the finale, when everyone else available was on stage, took money at the doors and dressed the ladies, and swept the house and held the prompt book. *Nicholas Nickleby*

GRUEBY, JOHN: Servant of Lord George Gordon, who tries to get his master to act rationally. A square-built, strong-made, bull-necked fellow of the true English breed. *Barnaby Rudge*

GRUFF AND GLUM: An old pensioner at Greenwich, with two wooden legs. He was present at the wedding of John Rokesmith to Bella Wilfer. *Our Mutual Friend*

GRUFFANDGRIM: *see* Barley, Old Bill

GRUFF AND TACKLETON: *see* Tackleton

GRUMMER, DANIEL: The constable at Ipswich who effected the arrest of Mr. Pickwick and his friends, and conveyed them to the magistrate in a sedan-chair. *Pickwick Papers*

GRUNDY, MR.: A law clerk who was often to be found at the Magpie and Stump. *Pickwick Papers*

'GUARDIAN': *see* Jarndyce, John

GULPIDGE, MR.: He had something to do with the law business of the Bank. He was a guest of Mr. Waterbrook, whose house was visited by David Copperfield, and with whom Agnes Wickfield stayed. *David Copperfield*

GULPIDGE, MRS.: Wife of Mr. Gulpidge, who is also present at the party at Mr. Waterbrook's. *David Copperfield*

GUMMIDGE, MRS.: Widow of Dan'l Peggotty's partner. She acts as housekeeper to Dan'l in the old boat house on the sands at Great Yarmouth. Subject to fits of depression, she would declare that she was a 'lone lorn creetur' and that everything went 'contrairy' with her. At these times Dan'l Peggotty would excuse her saying that she was thinking of 'the old 'un', meaning her husband. She became very helpful when Little Em'ly runs away, and keeps house for Ham while Dan'l is away looking for his little niece. She eventually emigrates to Australia with Dan'l and Little Em'ly. *David Copperfield*

GUNTER, MR.: Medical student guest at Bob Sawyer's party in Lant Street. He attends in a shirt emblazoned with pink anchors, and is very quarrelsome at the party. *Pickwick Papers*

GUPPY, MRS.: Mother of William Guppy. She becomes very unreasonable when her son's romance with Esther Summerson does not prosper. 'An old lady in a large cap, with rather a red nose, and rather an unsteady eye, but smiling all over . . .' *Bleak House*

GUPPY, WILLIAM: Kenge and Carboy's clerk who proposes to Esther Summerson, and is concerned with ferreting out her parentage. When she is disfigured with small-pox, he withdraws his proposal, but renews it on finding that her looks have improved. *Bleak House*

GUSHER, MR.: A missionary friend of Mrs. Pardiggle. *Bleak House*

GUSTER: Servant of the Snagsbys, supposed to have been christened Augusta. She is subject to fits. A lean young woman from the workhouse, at Tooting. *Bleak House*

GWYNN, MISS: The writing and ciphering governess at Westgate House, a school for young ladies at Bury St. Edmunds, who thought that Mr. Pickwick was a madman, when he was found in the grounds of the school at midnight. *Pickwick Papers*

H

HAGGAGE, DR.: A drunken doctor who was a debtor in the Marshalsea Debtors' Prison, and attended Mrs. Dorrit at the birth of Amy, 'Little Dorrit'. He had been a surgeon on a passenger ship. *Little Dorrit*

HANCOCK AND FLOBBY: The Dry Goods Store where Mr. Putnam Smif was to be found. *Martin Chuzzlewit*

HANDEL: *see* Pip (Herbert Pocket's nickname for him)

HANDFORD, JULIUS: The name adopted by John Harmon, alias John Rokesmith, when he went to view the body found in the river purported to be himself. (*See* Harmon, John; and Rokesmith, John.) *Our Mutual Friend*

HANNAH: Servant of Miss La Creevy, the portrait painter. Hannah had an uncommonly dirty face. *Nicholas Nickleby*

HAREDALE, EMMA: Niece of Geoffrey Haredale, and daughter of Reuben (who was murdered). She marries Edward Chester, son of Sir Edward Chester, and goes abroad with him. *Barnaby Rudge*

HAREDALE, GEOFFREY: A Roman Catholic and enemy of Sir John Chester whom he kills in a duel, after which he leaves the country and joins a monastery. He tries to prevent his niece's marriage to Edward Chester, son of his enemy, but eventually accepts him as a son-in-law. *Barnaby Rudge*

HAREDALE, REUBEN: Father of Emma and elder brother of Geoffrey Haredale. Murdered by Rudge, his steward, at the Warren, his house at Chigwell. *Barnaby Rudge*

HARMON, JOHN: Alias Julius Handford, alias John Rokesmith, son of the dust contractor, old John Harmon. Because he pleads his sister's cause he is also turned out of home by his father and is sent abroad. On returning to

England to claim his inheritance he escapes an attempt on his life on the ship. He hides under the assumption of his supposed murder, takes the name of Rokesmith and becomes secretary to his father's servant, who in his absence has inherited his father's fortune. This also gives him an opportunity of meeting the girl he is supposed to marry as part of the conditions of his father's will. He eventually marries the girl, Bella Wilfer, declares his true identity, and inherits his fortune. *Our Mutual Friend*

HARMON, MISS: Daughter of the dust contractor, who turned her out because she would not marry someone of his choice. *Our Mutual Friend*

HARMON, MRS.: Wife of old John Harmon and mother of young John Harmon and his sister. *Our Mutual Friend*

HARMON, MRS. B.: *see* Wilfer, Bella

HARMON, OLD JOHN: Deceased dust contractor who, having cursed and turned his wife and daughter out of doors, leaves a fortune to his son, providing he marries a girl of his choice, Bella Wilfer. Failing the fulfilment of that condition, the fortune goes to his old servant, Boffin. Harmon also turns his son out of his house. *Our Mutual Friend*

HARRIET: *see* Carker, Harriet

HARRIS: Greengrocer, who waits on the footmen at the 'swarry' in Bath, which is also attended by Sam Weller. He is termed by Mr. Tuckle, one of the footmen, 'a wulgar beast'. *Pickwick Papers*

HARRIS, LITTLE TOMMY: He called Mrs. Gamp his own Gammy. As he is supposed to be the son of Mrs. Harris, Mrs. Gamp's fictitious friend, he too could not have existed. *Martin Chuzzlewit*

HARRIS, MR.: The real name of Mr. Short or Short Trotters, a punch and judy man. He befriends Little Nell and her grandfather, but hopes to get some reward for restoring them to their friends. *The Old Curiosity Shop*

HARRIS, MR.: Husband of Mrs. Harris, who (according to Mrs. Gamp, the nurse) said of her ninth, that 'it was one too many, if not two'. It thrived, however, though bandy. *Martin Chuzzlewit*

HARRIS, MRS.: Mrs. Gamp's imaginary friend, whom she is always quoting. She is never seen, and when Mrs. Prig, Mrs. Gamp's nursing partner, declares that she doesn't believe that such a person exists, this causes the parting of the two friends. *Martin Chuzzlewit*

HARRISON, LITTLE: An orphan who squints, and was suggested by the Rev. Frank Milvey to Mrs. Boffin for adoption. *Our Mutual Friend*

HARRY: A pedlar in the Eight Bells at Hatfield, who offers to take the bloodstain out of the hat of Bill Sikes, after the murder of Nancy, with startling effect. *Oliver Twist*

Grandson of Dame West, and the old schoolmaster's favourite scholar, who becomes very ill and dies, to the schoolmaster's great grief. *The Old Curiosity Shop*

HARTHOUSE, JAMES: Political agent and man of the world who tries unsuccessfully to get Louisa Bounderby to run away with him. *Hard Times*

HAUNTED MAN, THE: *see* Redlaw, Mr.

HAVISHAM, ARTHUR (JUNIOR): Son of Mr. Havisham and half-brother to Miss Havisham, who gets her involved with Compeyson, a swindler. *Great Expectations*

HAVISHAM, MISS: Pip's benefactress. An eccentric old lady who has shut herself up in Satis House, after being deserted on her wedding day. She has retained the wedding breakfast, stopped the clocks at twenty to nine, and wears her faded wedding dress. She dies as a result of burns when her dress catches fire. *Great Expectations*

HAVISHAM, MR.: Deceased father of Miss Havisham. A brewer. *Great Expectations*

HAVISHAM, MRS.: Miss Havisham's mother, who died when Miss Havisham was a baby. *Great Expectations*

HAWDON, CAPTAIN: Retired military officer, who does law-writing under the name of Nemo. He lodges in extreme poverty over the premises of Krook, a rag-and-bone dealer. Hawdon was the lover of Lady Dedlock, before her marriage to Sir Leicester, and the father of Esther Summerson. He dies from an overdose of opium, and is buried in a pauper's grave. His only friend at the end is Jo, the crossing-sweeper. *Bleak House*

HAWK, SIR MULBERRY: A man about town and client of Ralph Nickleby. Nicholas Nickleby overhears him speaking disrespectfully of his sister Kate, and gives him a thrashing. It is over Kate that Sir Mulberry has a dispute with Lord Verisopht, his patron, resulting in a duel. Sir Mulberry kills Lord Verisopht and has to fly the country. *Nicholas Nickleby*

HAWKINS: A middle-aged baker, successfully sued by Miss Rugg for breach of promise. *Little Dorrit*

HAWKINSES, THE: An aristocratic family of Taunton Vale, with whom Mrs. Nickleby stayed when a girl. *Nicholas Nickleby*

HAWKINSON, AUNT: Aunt of Georgiana Podsnap, who left her a necklace, which Georgiana offered to give to her friend Mrs. Lammle to help her pay her debts. *Our Mutual Friend*

HEADSTONE, BRADLEY: A schoolmaster of a boys' school on the borders of Kent and Surrey. He is in love with Lizzie Hexam, a riverside girl, although he considers her beneath him, being uneducated. He tries to murder his rival, Eugene Wrayburn, by striking him down into the river, having first disguised himself as Rogue Riderhood, lock-keeper at Plashwater Weir Mill lock, to throw the suspicion on him. Riderhood suspects the plot, however, and in a fight beside the lock, they both fall in the river and are drowned. Bradley Headstone holds his adversary round the waist as if he were girdled with an iron ring. *Our Mutual Friend*

HEART'S DELIGHT: Captain Cuttle's nickname for Florence Dombey. *See* Dombey, Florence

HEATHFIELD, ALFRED: Dr. Jeddler's ward, in love with Marion Jeddler, who, however, pretends to elope with Michael Warden. Alfred eventually marries Marion's sister, Grace. He becomes a village doctor. *The Battle of Life*

HEATHFIELD, MRS.: *see* Jeddler, Grace

HEEP, MR.: (deceased). Uriah Heep's father. He was brought up at a foundation school for boys, and taught his son the value of being ''umble'. *David Copperfield*

HEEP, MRS.: Uriah Heep's mother, a widow. She was brought up at a public sort of charitable establishment. *David Copperfield*

HEEP, URIAH: Mr. Wickfield's red-headed clerk, who by fraud and dishonesty becomes his partner. His plots are found out by Mr. Micawber, who works for him, and he is exposed. 'His hair was cropped as close as the closest stubble. He had hardly any eyebrows, and no eyelashes, and eyes of a red-brown.' He is very jealous of David Copperfield and looks upon him as a rival both in business and in respect of Agnes Wickfield, whom Uriah plans to marry. He is eventually imprisoned for fraud, forgery, and conspiracy on the Bank of England. *David Copperfield*

HENRY: Cousin of Maria Lobbs and brother of Kate; he was Nathaniel Pipkins' rival for the hand of Maria. Interpolated story written by Mr. Pickwick from Sam Weller's dictation: The Parish Clerk. *Pickwick Papers*

HERBERT, M.P., MR.: The member who called attention to the fact that Lord George Gordon was sitting in the House of Commons with a blue cockade in his hat (a signal for rebellion). *Barnaby Rudge*

HEXAM, CHARLEY: Son of Gaffer Hexam who is educated against his father's wishes with his sister Lizzie's help. He renounces his sister because she will not accept Bradley Headstone as her suitor. *Our Mutual Friend*

HEXAM, 'GAFFER' JESSE: A waterman and night bird on the river, collecting bodies and robbing them before handing them over to the police and claiming whatever reward was offered. He is against his son's being educated. He gets entangled with the towing rope in his boat and gets drowned himself. *Our Mutual Friend*

HEXAM, LIZZIE: Hexam's daughter. She is against her father's means of making a living, although she helps him with the boat. She is most anxious that her younger brother should be educated and she makes sacrifices to ensure his getting that education. In spite of that, her brother turns on her. She is loved by a ne'er-do-well lawyer, Eugene Wrayburn, and also by her brother's schoolmaster, Bradley Headstone. When Eugene is attacked by Bradley she saves him from the river and nurses him back to life, finally marrying him. *Our Mutual Friend*

HEYLING, GEORGE: Cast into prison for debt by his father-in-law, his wife and child dying during his imprisonment; on leaving the prison, he devotes his life to revenge. Interpolated story: The Old Man's Tale About a Queer Client. *Pickwick Papers*

HEYLING, MARY: Wife of the debtor who dies in the Marshalsea Prison. *Pickwick Papers*

HIGDEN, MRS. BETTY: A poor woman who keeps a minding school, and does mangling. Terrified of the thought of being buried by the parish, she keeps a sovereign sewn in her clothes to pay for her funeral. She dies in a riverside town and is cared for at the last by Lizzie Hexam. *Our Mutual Friend*

HOMINY, MAJOR: Husband of Mrs. Hominy—'one of our choicest spirits; and belongs to one of our most aristocratic families'. *Martin Chuzzlewit*

HOMINY, MRS.: A writer whom Martin Chuzzlewit meets at the levée at the National Hotel and whom he conducts to New Thermopylae, where she visits her married daughter. *Martin Chuzzlewit*

HONEYTHUNDER, LUKE: Chairman of the Covened Chief Composite Committee of Central and District Philanthropists. Guardian of Neville and Helena Landless from Ceylon. A modern philanthropist who never sees a joke. He arranges for Helena to attend Miss Twinkleton's Academy as a pupil, and Neville to stay in Minor Canon Row with the Rev. Crisparkle, who is to be his tutor. *The Mystery of Edward Drood*

HOPKINS, CAPTAIN: Debtor in the King's Bench Prison. He occupies a room above that of Mr. Micawber, with his wife, 'a very dirty lady', and two daughters, 'girls with shock heads of hair'. *David Copperfield*

HOPKINS, JACK: A medical student from Bartholomew's Hospital and a friend of Bob Sawyer. He appears in a black velvet waistcoat with thunder-and-lightning buttons. He tells a remarkable story at Bob Sawyer's party of the child who swallowed the necklace made of large black wooden beads. *Pickwick Papers*

HOPKINS, VULTURE: *see* Boffin, N.

HORSE GUARDS: *see* Merdle, Mr.

HORTENSE, MLLE: Lady Dedlock's French maid, who is discarded for a young and pretty girl, Rosa. Mlle Hortense tries to put pressure on Mr. Tulkinghorn to find her a job, but he threatens her with prison. She shoots him and tries to put suspicion on Lady Dedlock. She is arrested by Inspector Bucket. *Bleak House*

HOWLER, THE REV. MELCHISEDECK: Minister known to Mrs. MacStinger; he officiates at her wedding, when she is married to Jack Bunsby, Captain Cuttle's friend. *Dombey and Son*

HUBBLE, MR.: A wheelright and friend of Mr. and Mrs. Joe Gargery, who attends the Christmas dinner at the forge. 'Of a saw-dusty fragrance, with his legs extraordinarily wide apart.' *Great Expectations*

HUBBLE, MRS.: Wife of the wheelwright, who spends Christmas Day with the Gargerys. *Great Expectations*

HUDIBRAS, LUD: King of Britain, father of Price Bladud. Interpolated story, read by Mr. Pickwick at Bath: The True Legend of Prince Bladud. *Pickwick Papers*

HUGH: Hostler at the Maypole Inn at Chigwell, who is the illegitimate son of Sir John Chester. He becomes one of the leaders of the Gordon Rioters, and one of their boldest spirits. He is finally captured, imprisoned at Newgate, and hanged, as his mother was. *Barnaby Rudge*

HUMM, ANTHONY: President of the Brick Lane Branch of the United Grand Junction Ebenezer Temperance Association. A sleek, white-faced man in a perpetual perspiration. He was a converted fireman. *Pickwick Papers*

HUMPHREY, DUKE: With whom Diggory Chuzzlewit frequently dines. *Martin Chuzzlewit*

HUNT: Captain Boldwig's head gardener, who with his fellow gardener, finds Mr. Pickwick asleep in a wheelbarrow on the Captain's land. *Pickwick Papers*

HUNTER, THE MISSES: Daughters of Mrs. Leo Hunter, who, at the garden party were dressed in very juvenile costumes, although they were twenty or more, possibly to make their mother look younger. *Pickwick Papers*

HUNTER, MR. LEO: Husband of Mrs. Leo Hunter, who basks in the splendour of his wife's fame as a poetess, and collector of literary lions. *Pickwick Papers*

HUNTER, MRS. LEO: Poetess and hostess of the *Fête Champêtre* given at The Den, Eàtanswill, and attended by Mr. Pickwick and his friends. She was the authoress of 'An Ode to an Expiring Frog'. At the fête, she was dressed as Minerva with a fan. *Pickwick Papers*

HUTLEY, JEM: *see* Dismal Jemmy

I

IMPUDENCE, LITTLE MISS: A nickname that Edwin Drood gave to Rosa Bud's portrait. *See* Bud, Rosa

INEXHAUSTIBLE, THE: *see* Bella

INFANT PHENOMENON, THE: *see* Crummles, Miss Ninetta

INSPECTOR, MR. 'NIGHT': He was in charge of the Rover Police Station to which the supposed body of John Harmon is taken. Mr. Inspector later arrests John Harmon or Rokesmith as he is known for his own murder, but very soon identifies him as the real John Harmon. *Our Mutual Friend*

IRREPRESSIBLE, THE: *see* Wilfer, Miss Lavinia

ISAAC: The sheriff's officer who takes Mrs. Bardell from the Spaniards Inn, Hampstead, to the Fleet Prison, on the warrant of Dodson and Fogg, her solicitors. *Pickwick Papers*

IZZARD, MR.: A member of the deputation that waited on Mr. Elijah Pogram in the National Hotel, to which Martin Chuzzlewit came from Eden. *Martin Chuzzlewit*

J

JACK: A man at the Blue Dragon in Mr. Pecksniff's village, driving the chaise cart for Mrs. Lupin. *Martin Chuzzlewit*

One of the police constables who arrest Jonas Chuzzlewit for murdering Tigg Montague. *Martin Chuzzlewit*

Of the little causeway; he was in the riverside public house where Pip, Herbert Pocket, and Startop put up with Magwitch, the returned convict, in their attempt to smuggle him out of the country. He had a bloated pair of boots on . . . taken from the feet of a drowned seaman. *Great Expectations*

JACKSON, MR.: Dodson and Fogg's chief clerk who served writs on the Pickwickians as witnesses in the Bardell *v.* Pickwick breach of promise case and also arrested Mrs. Bardell for debt and took her to the Fleet Prison. She had promised to pay the costs of the case to Dodson and Fogg, if they were not paid by Mr. Pickwick. *Pickwick Papers*

JACKSON: A former turnkey at the gate of the Marshalsea Debtors' Prison. *Little Dorrit*

An acquaintance of Cousin Feenix, who kept the boxing-rooms in Bond Street. *Dombey and Son*

JACKSON, MICHAEL: He helps Bucket in his search for Lady Dedlock. *Bleak House*

JACQUES, ONE, TWO, THREE, AND FOUR: Revolutionaries who are gathered together by Defarge the wine-shop keeper. They use his shop as a headquarters. *A Tale of Two Cities*

JACQUES, FIVE: The road-mender, who later becomes a wood-sawyer, a spy for the revolutionaries. *A Tale of Two Cities*

JAGGERS, MR.: A criminal lawyer who acts for Magwitch, the convict, in paying out his allowance to Pip. Also lawyer to Miss Havisham, with whom he places Estella. *Great Expectations*

JAMES, HENRY: Commander of the barque *Defiance*, who reports the loss of the *Son and Heir*, which had Walter Gay aboard. *Dombey and Son*

JAMES: Mr. and Mrs. Bayham Badger's butler. *Bleak House*

JANE: Servant of Mr. Pecksniff. *Martin Chuzzlewit*

Servant at Manor Farm, Dingley Dell. *Pickwick Papers*

Servant of Mr. and Mrs. Pott, at Eatanswill. *Pickwick Papers*

Servant in obscure public house where young Martin Chuzzlewit stays in London. *Martin Chuzzlewit*

Sister of the old lord's fiancée, who patronizes Madame Mantalini's salon. *Nicholas Nickleby*

JANE, AUNT: One of Silas Wegg's imaginary inhabitants of the corner house outside which his stall stands. *Our Mutual Friend*

JANET: Miss Betsey Trotwood's maid at Dover, she helps her mistress to drive away the donkeys that trespass on the green in front of the cottage. *David Copperfield*

JARDINE: *see* Boffin, N.

JARLEY, MRS.: The owner of the travelling waxworks, who employs Little Nell and her grandfather. She marries her handyman, George. 'A Christian lady, stout and comfortable to look upon, who wore a large bonnet trembling with bows.' *The Old Curiosity Shop*

JARNDYCE, JOHN: He owns and lives in Bleak House at St. Albans. He is guardian of Ada Clare and Richard Carstone. Esther Summerson becomes his housekeeper and he is known as 'Guardian' or Cousin John. He proposes marriage to Esther but relinquishes her to Dr. Woodcourt, a much younger man. *Bleak House*

JARNDYCE, OLD TOM: Involved in the Jarndyce and Jarndyce case in Chancery. At last, in despair he blows his brains out in a coffee-house in Chancery Lane. *Bleak House*

JARREL, DICK: *see* Boffin, N.

JASPER, JOHN: Known also as 'Mr. Jack'. Uncle of Edwin Drood and lay precentor in Cloisterham Cathedral. An opium-taker and possibly concerned with the disappearance of Edwin Drood. *The Mystery of Edwin Drood*

JEDDLER, DR.: A philosopher who looks upon the world as a great practical joke. Father of two daughters, Grace and Marion. *The Battle of Life*

JEDDLER, GRACE: Elder daughter of Dr. Jeddler. She marries Alfred Heathfield who was at one time engaged to her sister. Grace was so gentle and retiring, and loved Alfred in secret. They have a little daughter who is called Marion. *The Battle of Life*

JEDDLER, MARION: Younger daughter of Dr. Jeddler. Knowing that her sister secretly loves Alfred Heathfield, Marion pretends to run away with Michael Warden, leaving her sister free to marry Alfred. She really goes to stay with an aunt. Years later she returns home and marries Michael Warden. *The Battle of Life*

JEDDLER, MARTHA: Spinster aunt of Grace and Marion and sister of Dr. Jeddler. When Marion runs away from home, she stays with this aunt. *The Battle of Life*

JELLYBY, CADDY (CAROLINE): Eldest daughter of Mrs. Jellyby, who acts as amanuensis for her mother. She marries Prince Turveydrop, dancing master. 'From her tumbled hair to her pretty feet, which were disfigured with frayed and broken satin slippers, trodden down at heel, she really seemed to have no article of dress upon her, from a pin upwards, that was in its proper condition, or in its right place.' *Bleak House*

JELLYBY, MR.: Husband of Mrs. Jellyby. He becomes bankrupt. A mild, bald gentleman, merged in the more shining qualities of his wife. *Bleak House*

JELLYBY, MRS.: A woman who neglects her home and family for the sake of a mission—the general cultivation of the coffee-berry and the colonization of the natives of Borrioboola-Gha, on the banks of the Niger. Her mission fails and she turns to other causes. 'A pretty, plump, diminutive woman of from forty to fifty, with handsome eyes, though they had a curious habit of seeming to look a very long way off—good hair—but much too occupied to brush it.' *Bleak House*

JELLYBY, PEEPY: One of the many Jellyby children, with an unnaturally large head, hence he gets it stuck in the iron railings in front of their house. *Bleak House*

JEM: One of the men at Manor Farm, Dingley Dell. *Pickwick Papers*

JEMIMA: Mrs. Toodle's sister, who looks after the Toodle family whilst the mother, Polly Toodle, is acting as wet nurse to Paul Dombey. *Dombey and Son*

JEMMY: *see* Dismal Jemmy

JENKINS: Sir Mulberry Hawk's manservant. *Nicholas Nickleby*

JENKINSON: One of the Circumlocution Office messengers who was eating mashed potatoes and gravy behind a partition and resented being interrupted. *Little Dorrit*

JENNINGS: A pupil at Dotheboys Hall in Yorkshire who slept with four others in Brooks's bed. *Nicholas Nickleby*

JENNINGS, MISS: A pupil at the Nun's House, Miss Twinkleton's Academy at Cloisterham, who was told to stand upright. *The Mystery of Edward Drood*

JENNY: The brickmaker's wife who helps Lady Dedlock to elude her pursuers, by changing clothes with her. *Bleak House*

JERRY: A travelling showman, with performing dogs. Little Nell and the grandfather meet him in the wayside public house. Nell takes pity on the dog in disgrace, but Jerry will not let anyone feed the dogs but himself. *The Old Curiosity Shop*

JEWBY: One of Mr. Snagsby's clients for whom he gets copying of legal documents done. *Bleak House*

JINGLE, ALFRED: Alias Captain Charles Fitz-Marshall. A strolling player who becomes friendly with the Pickwickians by rescuing them from a pugilistic cabby. Jingle turns out to be an unprincipled rascal, and he plays several confidence tricks on Mr. Pickwick and his friends. Later he ends in the Fleet Prison, for debt, and Mr. Pickwick sets him free by paying the debt for him and also paying for him to go abroad and have another start in life. *Pickwick Papers*

JINIWIN, MRS.: Mrs. Betsey Quilp's mother, who is in dread of her fiendish son-in-law. She was known to be laudably shrewish in her disposition; but Quilp was impervious to this. *The Old Curiosity Shop*

JINKINS, MR.: The oldest boarder at Mrs. Todgers's—a fish salesman's book-keeper aged fifty. Of a fashionable turn. *Martin Chuzzlewit*

'JINKINS': Resident at an inn on the Marlborough Downs, who is stopped by Tom Smart from marrying the landlady of the inn. Tom is able to disclose to her that Jinkins is married already which leaves him free to propose himself, and he is accepted. Interpolated story: 'The Bagman's Story'. *Pickwick Papers*

JINKS, MR.: Clerk of Mr. Nupkins, magistrate and Mayor of Ipswich. *Pickwick Papers*

JO: A crossing-sweeper who is befriended by Captain Hawdon, a law writer, and Mr. Snagsby, a law stationer. He lives in a wretched slum called 'Tom-all-Alone's' and becomes mixed up in Lady Dedlock's secret. Nicknames suggested for him by the inhabitants of Tom-all-Alone's were: The Brick, Carrots, the Colonel, Young Chisel, Gallows, Lanky, Terriers Tip, and Toughy. He dies in George's Shooting Gallery. *Bleak House*

JOBLING, DR. JOHN: Medical officer to the Anglo-Bengalee Disinterested Loan and Life Assurance Company, who also attended old Anthony Chuzzlewit. *Martin Chuzzlewit*

JOBLING, TONY: Mr. Guppy's friend and a law writer who lodges above Mr. Krook's rag-and-bone shop, in the room where Captain Hawdon died. He has a midnight appointment with his landlord Krook to see some letters, but Krook dies of spontaneous combustion. *Bleak House*

JODD, MR.: A member of the committee welcoming Mr. Elijah Pogram at the National Hotel in America, to which Martin Chuzzlewit comes from Eden. *Martin Chuzzlewit*

JODDLEBY, MR.: Related to the Barnacle family by marriage. *Little Dorrit*

JOE: Driver of the bus bound for Cloisterham. *The Mystery of Edwin Drood*

The fat boy. Mr. Wardle's page at Manor Farm, who is always falling asleep, and only wakes at the appearance of food. Described as 'A fat and red-faced boy, in a state of somnolency'. *Pickwick Papers*

Guard of the Dover mail on which Mr. Jarvis Lorry is travelling. The coach is overtaken by Jerry Cruncher with a message for Mr. Lorry. *A Tale of Two Cities*

Dan'l Peggotty's brother and Ham's father. *David Copperfield*

A labourer working at the riverside wharf where Florence Dombey finds Walter Gay when she is lost. *Dombey and Son*

Cook in a family hotel near to Hyde Park where Rose Maylie is visited by Nancy to give her news of Oliver Twist. *Oliver Twist*

JOE, MRS.: *see* Gargery, Mrs. Joe

JOE, OLD: A dealer in rags and bones, who buys Scrooge's belongings from the undertaker, the laundress, and the charwoman. *A Christmas Carol*

JOEY, CAPTAIN: A bottle-nosed regular customer of the Six Jolly Fellowship Porters, in a glazed hat. *Our Mutual Friend*

JOGG, MISS: The model whose three-quarter-face portrait was in the Dedlock's town house. *Bleak House*

JOHN: Miss La Creevy's married brother, who has a house in the country with liveried servants and a farm. *Nicholas Nickleby*

A clown who sends for Jem Hutley when he is taken seriously ill. Interpolated story: 'The Stroller's Tale'. *Pickwick Papers*

A poor labourer working by the riverside and looking after his invalid daughter, Martha, who interests Florence Dombey, when she is staying with Sir Barnet and Lady Skettles at Fulham. Florence envies the girl with the love of a father. *Dombey and Son*

Waiter at the Saracen's Head, Towcester. *Pickwick Papers*

JOHN EDWARD: Old Nandy's youngest grandson and son of Mr. and Mrs. Plornish. *See* Plornish, John Edward

JOHNNY: Betty Higden's great-grandson, whom Mr. and Mrs. Boffin decide to adopt. He dies, however, in the Children's Hospital before they can do so. *Our Mutual Friend*

JOHNSON: The scholar at Dr. Blimber's school at Brighton, who choked at dinner and earned himself an imposition from the Greek Testament. *Dombey and Son*

JOHNSON, DR.: Nicholas refers to him as being a bookworm and odd looking. *Nicholas Nickleby*

JOHNSON, MR.: The name by which Nicholas Nickleby is known whilst he is in the Vincent Crummles Theatrical Company at Portsmouth. *See* Nickleby, Nicholas

JOHNSON, TOM: A wooden-legged acquaintance of Cousin Feenix, whom he sees from the coach at Mrs. Skewton's funeral at Brighton. *Dombey and Son*

JOLLSON, MRS.: Previous occupier of No. 9, Brig Place, before Mrs. MacStinger lived there. *Dombey and Son*

JONATHAN: One of the regular customers at the Six Jolly Fellowship Porters. *Our Mutual Friend*

JONES, GEORGE: One of the regulars at the Six Jolly Fellowship Porters in Limehouse, who wore a faded scarlet jacket. *Our Mutual Friend*

JONES, MARY: Hanged by Dennis at Tyburn. She had taken a piece of cloth off the counter of a shop and put it down again on being seen by the shopman. For that she is hanged. *Barnaby Rudge*

JONES, MASTER: A boy of no merit whom Miss Shepherd preferred to David Copperfield. *David Copperfield*

JONES, MR.: Employed by Messrs. Blaze and Sparkle, the jewellers. *Bleak House*

JONES, MRS. GEORGE: Wife of George Jones to whom Miss Abbey Potterson, owner of the Six Jolly Fellowship Porters, gave a promise that her husband would be home punctual. *Our Mutual Friend*

JONES OF BLEWBERRY: *see* Boffin, N.

JOPER, BILLY: One of Cousin Feenix's club friends. *Dombey and Son*

JORAM: Assistant to Mr. Omer, the undertaker in Great Yarmouth. He marries Omer's daughter Minnie, and becomes a partner in the business. *David Copperfield*

JORAM, MRS.: *see* Omer, Minnie

JORKINS, MR.: Mr. Spenlow's partner, who remains in the background but was made out to be quite ruthless and was blamed for all the favours refused by Mr. Spenlow. *David Copperfield*

JOWL, JOE: One of the gamblers at the Valiant Soldier, who tempts Nell's grandfather to gamble again, and to steal money from Mrs. Jarley with which to stake at cards. Referred to on one occasion as Mat. *The Old Curiosity Shop*

JUPE, CECILIA or **CISSY:** Daughter of Signor Jupe, a clown in Sleary's Circus. When her father deserts her she is taken by Gradgrind into his house. She brings kindness and humanity into his family. She marries happily and has a family, after the end of the story. *Hard Times*

JUPE, SIGNOR: A clown in Sleary's Circus, who finding that he is getting too old to carry out his circus routine, runs away, and leaves his daughter Cissy, so that he shall not be a drag on her. *Hard Times*

K

KAGS: A returned convict who was hiding in the house on Jacob's Island, where Bill Sikes finally took refuge after the murder of Nancy. *Oliver Twist*

KATE: An orphan who visits Sir Barnet and Lady Skettles when Florence is staying with them. Her aunt is with her. *Dombey and Son*

A cousin of Maria Lobbs, who makes fun of Nathaniel Pipkin, the teacher, when he tries to court Maria. Interpolated story, written by Mr. Pickwick, from Sam Weller's dictation: 'The Parish Clerk'. *Pickwick Papers*

KEDGICK, CAPTAIN: Landlord of the National Hotel in America, where a levée is arranged in honour of Martin Chuzzlewit before he and Mark Tapley leave for Eden. *Martin Chuzzlewit*

KENGE, MR.: Known as 'Conversation Kenge'. Solicitor of Kenge and Carboys in Old Square, Lincoln's Inn, who acts for Mr. John Jarndyce. *Bleak House*

KENWIGS, LILLYVICK: Baby son of Mr. and Mrs. Kenwigs, named after his Uncle Lillyvick, from whom the family have great expectations. *Nicholas Nickleby*

KENWIGS, MORLEENA: Eldest daughter of the Kenwigs family, who with her sister went twice a week to a dancing school. They had flaxen hair, tied with blue ribands, hanging in luxuriant pigtails down their backs; and wore little white trousers with frills round the ankles. *Nicholas Nickleby*

KENWIGS, MR.: A turner in ivory, lodging in the same house as Newman Noggs, Ralph Nickleby's clerk. Nicholas also stays in this house for a short time. *Nicholas Nickleby*

KENWIGS, MRS. SUSAN: Wife of Mr. Kenwigs and mother of five children. She gives a party especially to impress her friends with her Uncle Lillyvick, the water-rate collector. *Nicholas Nickleby*.

KETTLE, MR. LA FAYETTE: Secretary of the Watertoast Association of United Sympathizers, whom Martin Chuzzlewit meets in America. 'Languid and listless in his looks, his cheeks were so hollow, and he seemed to be always sucking them in. The sun had burnt him a dirty yellow . . . a cake of tobacco and a penknife in his hand.' *Martin Chuzzlewit*

KIBBLE, MR. JACOB: A fellow passenger with John Harmon on the way home from abroad, who later identifies Harmon as Rokesmith, and proves, of course, that Rokesmith could not have murdered himself. *Our Mutual Friend*

KIDDERMINSTER: A member of Sleary's Circus, who takes part in the equestrian displays and is sometimes referred to as 'Cupid', a part he sometimes plays. *Hard Times*

KIDGERBURY, MRS.: A charwoman engaged at recurring periods by David and Dora Copperfield, when their regular servants leave. 'The oldest inhabitant of Kentish Town . . . who went out charring, but was too feeble to execute her conception of that art.' *David Copperfield*

KITT, MISS: At a picnic near Guildford attended by David Copperfield, David flirted with her to make Dora Spenlow jealous, because she seemed to be occupied with his rival 'Red Whiskers'. 'She was dressed in pink, with little eyes.' *David Copperfield*

KITT, MRS.: Mother of the girl in pink, who was also at the picnic and who separated David and her daughter 'from motives of policy'. The mother was in green. *David Copperfield*

KNAG, MISS: Madame Mantalini's forewoman in the dressmaking establishment. She pretends to make friends with Kate Nickleby, but is later very jealous of her. *Nicholas Nickleby*

KNAG, MORTIMER: Miss Knag's brother, who keeps an ornamental stationers and small circulating library in a by-street off Tottenham Court Road. He was once very attached to Madame Mantalini, and thought that she would marry him. *Nicholas Nickleby*

KNAG, UNCLE OF MISS: He had a most excellent business as a tobacconist . . . and had such small feet, that they were no bigger than those which are usually joined to wooden legs. *Nicholas Nickleby*

KNIFE SWALLOWER: *see* African Knife Swallower

KÖLDWETHOUT, THE BARON: Of Grogzwig, in Germany, who decides to commit suicide, but decides otherwise after talking to a phantom. Interpolated story: The Baron of Grogzwig. *Nicholas Nickleby*

KÖLDWETHOUT, BARONESS: Wife of the Baron and daughter of Baron von Swillenhausen. She had thirteen children, and the Baroness parted the Baron from the hunting companions he had been used to before they were married, hence his despondence. Interpolated story: The Baron of Grogzwig. *Nicholas Nickleby*

KROOK, MR.: Drunken dealer in rags and bones, brother of Mrs. Smallweed and landlord of Miss Flite. Captain Hawdon and Tony Jobling also lodge above his shop. He is also known as 'Old Boguey' and drinks so much gin that he dies of spontaneous combustion. *Bleak House*

L

LA CREEVY, MISS: A miniature painter in the Strand, who becomes friendly with Mrs. Nickleby and Kate, who occupy rooms in her premises. She later gets to know Nicholas. She marries Tim Linkinwater, senior clerk of the Cheeryble Brothers. *Nicholas Nickleby*

LADY, OLD: With a hand-basket, who won David Copperfield's caul, and kept it against drowning. She lives to be 92 and never went over the water, except on a bridge. Her inevitable saying was, 'Let us have no meandering.' *David Copperfield*

LAGNIER: *see* Rigaud, Monsieur

LAMBERT, DANIEL: Mrs. Nickleby refers to him as a fat man who was proud of his legs. *Nicholas Nickleby*

LAMMLE, ALFRED: An acquaintance of the Veneerings and an adventurer, who is taken in by a penniless adventuress, Sophronia Akershem, to whom he gets married. Finding they have both deceived each other, they make a pact, on their honeymoon, to join forces in preying on other suitable victims in society. They fail, however, in one notable example with the Boffins, who see through them. Lammle is finally ruined by Fledgeby, upon whom he takes a violent but humorous revenge. *Our Mutual Friend*

LAMMLE, MRS.: *see* Akershem, Sophronia

LANCASTER, LORD: *see* Stiltstalking

LANDLESS, HELENA: A ward of Mr. Honeythunder, from Ceylon, who becomes a boarder at Miss Twinkleton's Academy for Young Ladies, in the Nun's House, at Cloisterham. Twin sister of Neville. She defends her brother when he is accused of murder and is obviously ready to defy John Jasper, who accuses him. *The Mystery of Edwin Drood*

LANDLESS, NEVILLE: Twin brother of Helena, who becomes a pupil of Canon Crisparkle and lodges with him. After being accused of the murder of Edwin Drood who has disappeared, Neville is released for want of evidence and he takes a room in Staple Inn, London. He comes from Ceylon with his sister and is also a ward of Mr. Honeythunder. *The Mystery of Edwin Drood*

LANE, MISS: Governess to the children in the Borum family, in Portsmouth. Nicholas Nickleby, Miss Snevellicci, and the Infant Phenomenon call on the Borums and solicit their support for Miss Snevellicci's benefit performance at the theatre. Miss Lane is reprimanded for allowing the children to torment the Infant Phenomenon—flattening her pink gauze bonnet, etc. *Nicholas Nickleby*

LANGDALE, MR.: A distiller in Holborn, a portly old man, with a very red, or rather, purple face. His premises are sacked and burned by the Gordon Rioters, but he escapes with the help of Joe Willet. *Barnaby Rudge*

LANKY: *see* Jo

LARKEY BOY, THE: Who beat the Game Chicken, Mr. Toots' boxing trainer. *Dombey and Son*

LARKINS, THE ELDEST MISS: One of David Copperfield's earliest loves, when he was seventeen; she was not a chicken, but might be about thirty. She is dressed in blue at the ball, with blue flowers in her hair—forget-me-nots! But she marries Mr. Chestle, a hop-grower. *David Copperfield*

LARKINS, MR.: Father of Miss Larkins, a gruff old gentleman with a double chin, and one of his eyes immovable. He is an unconscious object of veneration for David, the boy of seventeen, who has fallen in love with his daughter. *David Copperfield*

LAZARUS, ABRAHAM: 'Habraham Latharuth' who was suspected of stealing plate. Mr. Jaggers had been briefed to prosecute him. *Great Expectations*

LEDBROOK, MISS: A member of Mr. Vincent Crummles Theatrical Company, and a friend of Miss Snevellicci, who calls her 'Led'. She jokes with Miss Snevellicci about being smitten by the appearance of Nicholas Nickleby. She was one of the bridesmaids to Miss Henrietta Petowker of the Theatre Royal, Drury Lane. *Nicholas Nickleby*

LEEFORD, EDWARD: *see* Monks

LEEFORD, EDWIN: The betrayer of Agnes Fleming and natural father of Oliver Twist. Father also of Monks. He died before Oliver's birth, but left him part of his estate provided he did not become a criminal—hence the plot hatched by Monks to get his half-brother brought up by Fagin as one of his gang. *Oliver Twist*

LENVILLE, THOMAS: A tragedian and member of the Vincent Crummles Theatrical Company. He issues a challenge to Nicholas threatening to pull his nose and is made to look very silly before the whole company. *Nicholas Nickleby*

LENVILLE, MRS.: Wife of the tragedian and a member of the Crummles company. In a limp bonnet and veil. She tries to intervene when her husband insults Nicholas Nickleby and gets knocked down for his trouble. *Nicholas Nickleby*

LEWSOME, MR.: A doctor's assistant, in London. He provides Jonas Chuzzlewit with drugs, with which Jonas intends to poison his father. Lewsome is later overcome with remorse, rambles on about his secret whilst in a fever and finally confesses to John Westlock, an old schoolfellow. He is nursed in his fever by Sarah Gamp and Betsey Prig. *Martin Chuzzlewit*

LIGHTWOOD, MORTIMER: A solicitor, employed by Mr. Boffin, and a friend of Eugene Wrayburn, also in the law. He attends the Veneering's dinners and is goaded on by Lady Tippins, a friend of his boyhood, to tell the story of John Harmon, rich owner of dust-heaps. *Our Mutual Friend*

LIGNUM VITAE: *see* Bagnet, Matthew.

LILIAN: *see* Fern, Lilian

LILLYVICK, MR.: Uncle of Mrs. Kenwigs, and a collector of water rates. He is looked upon as very important in the family and the baby is named after him. The expectations of the Kenwig family are shaken when Mr. Lillyvick marries an actress, Miss Henrietta Petowker of Drury Lane. She leaves him, however, and Uncle Lillyvick returns to the bosom of his family. *Nicholas Nickleby*

LILLYVICK, MRS.: *see* Petowker, Miss Henrietta

LIMBKINS, MR.: Chairman of the Board of the Workhouse in which Oliver Twist was born, who tries to get Oliver apprenticed to a sweep, but the application is turned down by the magistrate who refuses to grant the indentures. *Oliver Twist*

LINKINWATER, MISS: Tim Linkinwater's sister, who is one of the guests at the dinner given by the Cheeryble Brothers. *Nicholas Nickleby*

LINKINWATER, TIM: Chief clerk to the Cheeryble Brothers, for whom he has worked forty-four years. In spite of appearing to be a confirmed bachelor, he marries Miss La Creevy, the miniature-portrait painter. He keeps a blind blackbird named Dick. When Nicholas Nickleby becomes clerk to the Cheerybles, Tim is very doubtful about his keeping the books, but he accepts him happily on seeing his careful writing. *Nicholas Nickleby*

LINKINWATER, MRS.: *see* La Creevy, Miss

LIST, ISAAC: A gambler with Mat Jowl at the Valiant Soldier, who encourages Little Nell's grandfather to gamble and even to thieve money to stake on the cards. *The Old Curiosity Shop*

LITTIMER: Servant of Steerforth who makes the arrangements for Little Em'ly to run away with his master. His great claim to consideration was his respectability. He finally arrives in a model prison, having been sentenced to transportation for robbing his master of £250. *David Copperfield*

LITTLE DORRIT: *see* Dorrit, Amy

LITTLE, JOHN: *see* Boffin, N.

LITTLE NELL: *see* Trent, Nelly

LITTLE SWILLS: *see* Swills, Little

LIVELY, MR.: Salesman and receiver of stolen property in Field Lane. He is sitting in a child's chair at his warehouse door, smoking a pipe, when Fagin passes by and asks him if there is anyone up at the Cripples. *Oliver Twist*

LIVERER, MR.: The name the Marchioness gives to Dick Swiveller. *See* Swiveller, Dick

LIZ: Wife of a brickmaker, who consoles her friend Jenny on the loss of her baby. She had no kind of grace about her but the grace of sympathy; but when she condoled with the woman, and her own tears fell, she wanted no beauty. *Bleak House*

LLANDAFF, THE RIGHT REV. THE BISHOP OF: Mrs. Nickleby imagines him marrying her daughter Kate to Sir Mulberry Hawk, at St. George's, Hanover Square. *Nicholas Nickleby*

LOBBS, MARIA: Daughter of Old Lobbs, with whom Nathaniel Pipkin, the humble teacher in the village school opposite to the saddler's premises, is in love. Nathaniel goes to tea with Maria, but her father returns unexpectedly. Interpolated story: 'The Parish Clerk', written from Sam Weller's dictation by Mr. Pickwick. *Pickwick Papers*

LOBBS, OLD: The saddler, who could have bought up the whole village at one stroke of his pen. Nathaniel Pipkin is terrified when Old Lobbs finds him hiding in a cupboard but a young cousin of Maria who is also present at the tea party takes the blame. The old man becomes friendly with Nathaniel and they smoke their pipes together of an evening. Interpolated story: 'The Parish Clerk'. *Pickwick Papers*

LOBLEY, MR.: Mr. Tartar's man, in charge of his yacht somewhere down by Greenhithe. *The Mystery of Edwin Drood.*

LONGFORD, MR. EDMUND: A student who lodges with the Tetterbys under the name of Edmund Denham. Under the influence of Redlaw, the haunted man, he becomes dissatisfied with his kind nurse Millie, but when the curse is removed he appreciates all she does once more. *The Haunted Man*

LORRY, JARVIS: Senior confidential clerk at Tellson & Co., bankers. He takes Lucie Manette to France to see her father who has been released after eighteen years in the Bastille. Lorry again goes to France to see to the affairs of the bank during the Revolution. He returns finally to England with Lucie, her daughter, father, and husband, the latter having been saved from the guillotine by Sydney Carton. *A Tale of Two Cities*

LOSBERNE, MR.: A surgeon and friend of the Maylies. He attends Oliver Twist when he is shot during the attempted burglary. Known for ten miles round as 'The Doctor', he had grown fat, more from good humour than from good living; kind and hearty and an eccentric old bachelor. He later took a cottage outside the village where Harry and Rose live, after their marriage and devotes himself to gardening, fishing, and carpentry. *Oliver Twist*

LOWTEN, MR.: Mr. Perker's confidential clerk who took the chair at the convivial evening at the Magpie and Stump, which Mr. Pickwick joined. *Pickwick Papers*

LUCAS, SOLOMON: A dealer in fancy dresses. He supplied the fancy costumes for Mrs. Leo Hunter's *fête champêtre*. His wardrobe was very extensive—not strictly classical perhaps, not quite new, nor did it contain any one garment made precisely after the fashion of any age or time, but everything was more or less spangled. *Pickwick Papers*

LUCIFER, SIR: The name by which Lawrence Boythorn refers to Sir Leicester Dedlock. *See* Dedlock, Sir Leicester

LUFFEY, MR.: The 'highest ornament of Dingley Dell' and star bowler for that team, selected to bowl against Dumkins (All Muggleton). He officiated as vice-chairman at the dinner following the cricket match. *Pickwick Papers*

LUKIN, YOUNG: He is recalled by Mrs. Nickleby as one of her dozen or so suitors before she got married. *Nicholas Nickleby*

LUMBEY, DR.: Medical adviser to the Kenwigs family, who was called in at the births of all the Kenwigs' children. *Nicholas Nickleby*

LUMMY NED: A musical guard on a coach, who went to America and made his fortune but lost it all when twenty-six banks failed. *Martin Chuzzlewit*

LUPIN, MRS.: A widow and landlady of the Blue Dragon in the Wiltshire village where Mr. Pecksniff lives. She marries Mark Tapley after his return from America. He had previously been handyman at the Blue Dragon. *Martin Chuzzlewit*

M

MACSTINGER, ALEXANDER, CHARLES, AND JULIANA: Children of Mrs. MacStinger. Alexander was always being slapped, after being inverted, then sat down on the ground to cool. Charles was popularly known as Chowley. *Dombey and Son*

MACSTINGER, MRS.: A widow and Captain Cuttle's landlady at Brig Place. He is very afraid of her and when he moves, has to do so secretly at night. She marries his friend Jack Bunsby. *Dombey and Son*

'MAGGY': Grand-daughter of Mrs. Bangham, Little Dorrit's protégé. She later became assistant to Mrs. Plornish. She called Little Dorrit, 'Little Mother'. *Little Dorrit*

MAGNUS, MR. PETER: He travelled on Mr. Pickwick's coach from London and consulted him as to the best way to propose to a lady whom he is on his way to meet at Ipswich. They stay at The Great White Horse and that night, Mr. Pickwick loses his way in the hotel and gets into a lady's bedroom by mistake. Next morning he discovers to his horror that the lady is Miss Witherfield, the would-be fiancée of Mr. Magnus. Misunderstandings follow and Miss Witherfield informs the Mayor that Mr. Pickwick has threatened to fight a duel, which results in the arrest of that unfortunate gentleman. *Pickwick Papers*

MAGWITCH, ABEL: Alias Provis. Alias Campbell. Escaped convict and father of Estella. He is grateful to Pip for bringing him food and drink and a file on to the marshes. After being transported, he becomes well off and makes a generous allowance to Pip, secretly through Mr. Jaggers, the criminal lawyer, with the idea of making Pip into a gentleman. He cannot resist returning to England and thereby becomes liable to hanging. Pip tries to get him out of the country. He is informed upon by his partner in crime, Compeyson, who is killed in trying to capture him. Magwitch is arrested and sentenced to death, but he dies before the sentence can be carried out. *Great Expectations*

MALDON, JACK: Mrs. Annie Strong's cousin, thought to be in love with her. Rather a shallow sort of gentleman. *David Copperfield*

MALLARD, MR.: Clerk to Serjeant Snubbin. Snubbin was Counsel for the defendant, Mr. Pickwick, in the Bardell *v.* Pickwick case. An elderly clerk, whose sleek appearance and heavy watch-chain presented imposing indications of the extensive and lucrative practice of Serjeant Snubbin. *Pickwick Papers*

MALLOWFORD, LORD: He was burnt to death in his bed the first day Arthur Gride, moneylender, put on his bottle-green suit. *Nicholas Nickleby*

MAN FROM SHROPSHIRE: *see* Gridley, Mr.

MANETTE, DR. ALEXANDRE: French doctor and prisoner in the Bastille for eighteen years. He is eventually rescued and cared for by his old servant Defarge. Dr. Manette's daughter, Lucie takes him to England where he again practises as a doctor in Soho. He eventually returns to France to rescue his son-in-law, Charles Darnay, from the revolutionaries. During his long and unjust imprisonment he makes shoes to pass away the time. *A Tale of Two Cities*

MANETTE, LUCIE: Daughter of Dr. Manette, born after he was shut up in the Bastille. She goes to Paris with Mr. Lorry to bring her father back to London. She falls in love with and marries Charles Darnay, whose real name is Charles St. Evrémonde, nephew of the Marquis who wrongfully imprisoned her father. She has a daughter, Little Lucie. She is also loved by a dissolute lawyer, Sydney Carton, who sacrifices himself to save her husband's life. *A Tale of Two Cities*

MANN, MRS.: The matron of the branch workhouse to which Oliver Twist was farmed until he was old enough to work. She was allowed sevenpence halfpenny a week for each child farmed on her, most of which she appropriated for herself. *Oliver Twist*

MANNING, SIR GEOFFREY: Owner of the land on which Mr. Wardle and his friends, including Mr. Pickwick meet for a shooting-party and picnic. *Pickwick Papers*

MANTALINI, ALFRED: Husband of Madame Mantalini, who lives on his wife's earnings from her dressmaking salon, and eventually causes the bankruptcy of the business. His real name was Muntle, but altered for the purposes of the business. 'Dressed in a gorgeous morning gown, with a waistcoat and Turkish trousers of the same pattern, a pink silk handkerchief, and bright green slippers, and had a very copious watch-chain round his body.' Imprisoned for debt, he is released by a laundress, who pays the money owing, and he is last seen in a basement doing mangling. *Nicholas Nickleby*

MANTALINI, MADAME: Dressmaker and milliner—a buxom person, handsomely dressed, who had her business near Cavendish Square. Kate Nickleby worked for her, her husband being a client of Ralph Nickleby, moneylender. She becomes bankrupt owing to her husband's extravagance. *Nicholas Nickleby*

'MARCHIONESS, THE': Servant of Sampson and Sally Brass. It is possible that she was the child of Sally Brass and Quilp. She nurses Dick Swiveller through a fever, and is able to clear Kit Nubbles of the accusation of theft. Dick Swiveller has her educated and later marries her. He gives her the name of Sophronia Sphynx. After marriage they live in a cottage at Hampstead. *The Old Curiosity Shop*

MARGARET: Mr. Winkle senior's maid at Birmingham. Bob Sawyer openly shows his admiration of her and she calls him an 'odous creetur' and slaps his face. *Pickwick Papers*

MARKER, MRS.: She offers eighteen guineas for a cook. *Nicholas Nickleby*

MARKHAM: A friend of Steerforth, who attends David Copperfield's bachelor dinner party. He always refers to himself indefinitely as 'a man'. *David Copperfield*

MARKLEHAM, MRS.: Annie Strong's mother who was called 'The Old Soldier' by the boys in Dr. Strong's school, on account of her generalship, and the skill with which she marshalled great forces of relations against the doctor. *David Copperfield*

MARLEY, JACOB: Ebenezer Scrooge's deceased partner in the business of bill discounting. He had been dead seven years when the story starts. His ghost returns to give Scrooge a chance of repenting his ways. 'Marley in his pigtail, usual waistcoat, tights and boots . . . The chain he drew was clasped about his middle . . . and it was made of cash-boxes, keys, padlocks, ledgers, deeds and heavy purses wrought in steel. His body was transparent.' *See also* Ghost of Jacob Marley. *A Christmas Carol*

MAROON, CAPTAIN: Concerned with Tip Dorrit and his debts, which Arthur Clennam discharged. *Little Dorrit*

MARSHALSEA, FATHER OF THE: *See* Dorrit, William

MARTHA: Daughter of a poor man who has no regular employment, but who went looking for scraps in the mud of the river. Florence Dombey sees her at Fulham, when staying with Sir Barnet and Lady Skettles, and envies her her father's love in spite of their poverty. *Dombey and Son*

See Cratchit, Martha

A withered old female pauper, hideously ugly, who attends at the death of old Sally. Old Sally had previously attended at the death of Oliver Twist's mother when he was born. *Oliver Twist.*

MARTHA, AUNT: *see* Jeddler, Martha

MARTIN: Sir Geoffrey Manning's gamekeeper—a tall, raw-boned man who protests against the inclusion of Mr. Pickwick at the shooting party being pushed by Sam Weller in a wheelbarrow. *Pickwick Papers*

MARTIN, BETSY: A convert to temperance in the Annual Report of the Brick Lane Branch of the United Grand Junction Ebenezer Temperance Association. Went out charring and washing by the day, and never had more than one eye. Knew her mother drank stout and shouldn't wonder if that caused it. *Pickwick Papers*

MARTIN, CAPTAIN: A rather distinguished Collegian (debtor and inmate of the Marshalsea Prison), who seeks Mr. Dorrit's advice regarding his daughter's marriage. *Little Dorrit*

MARTIN, JACK: The bagman's uncle who had the adventure in the old disused coach and saved the beautiful young lady from her abductors by fighting and killing them. Or perhaps it was all a dream following a very heavy dinner in Edinburgh. Interpolated story told by the one-eyed bagman in the Bush at Bristol: The Story of the Bagman's Uncle. *Pickwick Papers*

MARTIN, MR.: Servant of Benjamin Allen's aunt. A surly-looking man with his legs dressed like the legs of a groom, and his body attired in the coat of a coachman. He drives the aunt in a private fly, painted a sad green colour, and drawn by a chubby sort of brown horse. Martin is encountered by Sam Weller in the lane behind the houses at Clifton, when Sam is looking for Benjamin Allen's sister, Arabella. Sam suggests his name might be Brown, Vilson, or Walker. *Pickwick Papers*

MARTIN, TOM: A butcher and debtor, who is a prisoner in the Fleet Prison, and upon whose room Mr. Pickwick is 'chummed'. He 'whopped' the coal-heaver down Fox-under-the-Hill, by the wharf, when drunk and was arrested by two street-keepers. *Pickwick Papers*

MARTON, MR.: A kindly old schoolmaster who befriends Little Nell and her grandfather. He eventually catches up on the road with the two wanderers and arranges for them to stay at the village in which he has been appointed schoolmaster. *The Old Curiosity Shop*

MARWOOD, ALICE: *see* Brown, Alice

MARY: Handmaiden at the Peacock, Eatanswill. *Pickwick Papers*

The pretty housemaid, first at Mr. Nupkins' at Ipswich, and then employed by Arabella Allen, and continues to be her maid when she becomes Mrs. Winkle. Sam Weller is very struck by her, and writes his famous Valentine to her. Finally she marries Sam and becomes Mr. Pickwick's housekeeper. *Pickwick Papers*

Servant at Manor Farm, Dingley Dell, who, when the Pickwickians arrive rather dishevelled and clothes torn from their accident in the chaise, is told by Mr. Wardle to bring towels and water. *Pickwick Papers*

A young lady in a hypothetical case put by Mr. Toots to the Game Chicken as to what name he would give to a boat of his own. *Dombey and Son*

MARY ANNE: David and Dora's servant. She had a written character as large as a proclamation. A woman in the prime of life, subject to a sort of perpetual measles or fiery rash. Her cousin in the Life Guards deserted into the coal hole and was taken away handcuffed. Her name was Paragon. *David Copperfield*

Cousin to the females in Bleeding Heart Yard who said that Mrs. Merdle's dresses would fill three waggons. *Little Dorrit*

Favourite pupil and domestic help of Miss Peecher, who teaches at a girls' school near to the boys' school run by Bradley Headstone. Mary Anne reports to Miss Peecher on the comings and goings of Bradley Headstone, Miss Peecher being secretly in love with him. *Our Mutual Friend*

Wemmick's small servant at the Castle at Walworth, who was relieved of her duties by Pip, toasting a sausage for the Aged. *Great Expectations*

MAT: *see* Jowl, Joe

MATINTERS, THE TWO MISS: At the ball in the Assembly Rooms at Bath they paid great court to the Master of the Ceremonies—Angelo Cyrus Bantam, Esquire—in the hope of getting a stray partner now and then. *Pickwick Papers*

MATTHEWS: Servant of Mr. Gregsbury, M.P. A very pale, shabby boy, who looked as if he had slept underground from his infancy—as very likely he had. *Nicholas Nickleby*

MAYLIE, HARRY: Son of Mrs. Maylie, who is in love with Mrs. Maylie's adopted daughter, Rose Maylie. He marries her and becomes a clergyman. *Oliver Twist*

MAYLIE, MRS.: Owner of the house at Chertsey, which Bill Sikes attempts to burgle. She adopted Rose, Oliver's aunt, and looks after Oliver when he is shot during the burglary. *Oliver Twist*

MAYLIE, ROSE: Adopted daughter of Mrs. Maylie and sister of Agnes Fleming, Oliver's mother, and therefore his aunt. Her real name is Rose Fleming. She has a serious illness, but recovers and marries Harry Maylie. *Oliver Twist*

MAYPOLE HUGH: *see* Hugh

M'CHOAKUMCHILD, MR.: A schoolmaster at Mr. Gradgrind's model school. If he had only learnt a little less, how infinitely better he might have taught much more. *Hard Times*

MEAGLES, MINNIE (PET): Only daughter of Mr. and Mrs. Meagles, her twin sister Lillie having died when very young. She is loved secretly by Arthur Clennam, a man in his forties, but she marries a ne'er-do-well artist, Henry Gowan. *Little Dorrit*

MEAGLES, MR.: A retired banker and father of Minnie (Pet) Meagles. They lived at Twickenham. Although he travelled, he never by any accident acquired any knowledge whatever of the language of any country he visited. *Little Dorrit*

MEAGLES, MRS.: Wife of Mr. Meagles and mother of Pet. Like Mr. Meagles, comely and healthy, with a pleasant English face, which had been looking at homely things for five and fifty years or more, and shone with a bright reflection of them. *Little Dorrit*

MEALY POTATOES: He worked in the warehouse of Murdstone and Grinby with David Copperfield. This name had been bestowed upon him in the warehouse, on account of his complexion, which was pale or mealy. His father was a waterman, and also a fireman at one of the large theatres. His little sister did imps in the Pantomimes. *David Copperfield*

MELCHISEDECH: A solicitor in Clifford's Inn. Mr. Tulking-horn recommends Mr. George to see him about his debts. *Bleak House*

'MELIA (short name for Amelia): Housemaid at Dr. Blimber's school at Brighton, Paul Dombey being so young can hardly dress himself. He goes downstairs in search of help and a pretty young woman in leather gloves, cleaning a stove, ties some strings for him, rubs his hands to warm them and, gives him a kiss. She tells him to ask for 'Melia. *Dombey and Son*

MELL, CHARLES: One of the masters at Salem House School. He meets David Copperfield when he arrives in London from Blunderstone and takes him to the school, first breaking the journey to visit his old mother in an almshouse, to whom he plays a flute. Later, after a dispute with Steerforth, a favourite pupil, Mr. Mell leaves the school, his humble circumstances having been made known to Mr. Creakle, the principal. He finally emigrates to Australia, where he is very successful. *David Copperfield*

MELL, HELENA: Fourth daughter of Dr. Mell in Australia, who, at the public dinner given in honour of Mr. Micawber, distinguishes herself at dancing with Wilkins Micawber, junior. *David Copperfield*

MELL, MRS.: Mother of Charles Mell, and inmate of an almshouse, who cooked David Copperfield's breakfast for him when he arrived in London from Blunderstone. *David Copperfield*

MELVILLESON, MISS M.: One of the entertainers in the Harmonic Meetings held in the Sol's Arms. Her real name is Melvinson. She had been married a year and a half, and her baby is carried to the Sol's Arms each night to receive its 'natural refreshment'. *Bleak House*

MERCURY: Sir Leicester Dedlock's footman. 'Six foot two, I suppose?' says Mr. Bucket. 'Three,' says Mercury. Mr. Bucket mixes up this everyday conversation with enquiries about Lady Dedlock's movements. *Bleak House*

MERDLE, MR.: A London banker and financier who turns out to be a common swindler. When he commits suicide, he ruins many thousands of people who have trusted him with their investments. 'Mr. Merdle was immensely rich; and a somewhat uneasy expression about his coat cuffs as if they were in his confidence, and had reasons for being anxious to hide his hands.' To his dinners came representatives of various professions and callings—Bar, Brother Bellows, Bench, Bishop, Mrs. Bishop, Horse Guards, Physician, Treasury, etc. Among others he ruins Mr. Dorrit. *Little Dorrit*

MERDLE, MRS.: Wife of Mr. Merdle, who is her second husband. Mother of Edmund Sparkler, by her first husband. The lady was not young and fresh from the hand of Nature, but was young and fresh from the hand of her maid. She had a broad, unfeeling, handsome bosom . . . It was not a bosom to repose upon, but it was a capital bosom to hang jewels upon. Mr. Merdle wanted something to hang jewels upon, and he bought it for the purpose. *Little Dorrit*

MICAWBER, EMMA: Daughter of Mr. Micawber, aged about three. *David Copperfield*

MICAWBER, MASTER: Son of Mr. Micawber, aged about four. *David Copperfield*

MICAWBER, MR. WILKINS: An agent for Murdstone and Grinby's with whom David Copperfield lodges when he is working at the firm's warehouse. Always living beyond his income and always waiting for something to turn up. 'A stoutish middle-aged person in a brown surtout and black tights and shoes, with no more hair upon his head (which was a large one and very shiny) than there is upon an egg.' Mr. Micawber is always getting into debt, and lands in the King's Bench Debtors' Prison. Later he obtains a post in Mr. Wickfield's office in Canterbury and discovers that Uriah Heep is swindling his partner, and exposes him. Mr. Micawber and his family are helped by Miss Trotwood to emigrate to Australia, where he makes good and becomes a magistrate. *David Copperfield*

MICAWBER, MRS. EMMA: Wife of Mr. Micawber—a thin and faded lady, not at all young. David remarks that, in all his experience of the family, he hardly ever saw both the twins detached from Mrs. Micawber at the same time. One of them was always taking refreshment. She had great faith in her husband, in spite of his shortcomings and her invariable statement was: 'I will never desert Mr. Micawber.' The name of the boy twin was Wilkins. *David Copperfield*

MICAWBER'S MAMA, MRS.: Mrs. Micawber says that she departed this life before Mr. Micawber's difficulties commenced, or at least before they became pressing. Her papa lived to bail Mr. Micawber several times, and then expired, regretted by a numerous circle. *David Copperfield*

MIDDLESEX DUMPLING, THE: A pugilist; a bout between him and the Suffolk Bantam was prohibited by Mr. Nupkins, the Mayor of Ipswich. *Pickwick Papers*

MIFF, MR.: Deceased husband of Mrs. Miff. *Dombey and Son*

MIFF, MRS.: Pew opener at the church where Mr. Dombey marries his second wife and where Paul Dombey was christened. A vinegary face has Mrs. Miff, and a mortified bonnet, and a thirsty soul for sixpences and shillings. *Dombey and Son*

MIGGS, MISS: Domestic servant to the Vardens. She supports her mistress in all her varying moods against Gabriel Varden. She is in love with Sim Tappertit, the locksmith's apprentice, but is despised by him. She is captured by the Gordon Rioters and after some roughish treatment is rescued with Dolly Varden and Emma Haredale. Gabriel Varden finally decides to dispense with her services. Her nephew and married sister live at 'number twenty-sivin, second bell-handle on the right hand door post'. *Barnaby Rudge*

MIKE: A client of Mr. Jaggers, criminal lawyer. 'A gentleman with one eye, in a velveteen suit and knee-breeches', who, when Pip is shown into the office, is pushed out and his fur cap tossed out after him. His eldest daughter is taken up on suspicion of shoplifting. *Great Expectations*

MILLER, MR.: One of the guests at Manor Farm, Dingley Dell, at Christmas—described as 'the hard-headed old gentleman'. *Pickwick Papers*

MILLERS: The second nurse, with Flopson looking after the children of Mr. and Mrs. Matthew Pocket. She retired hurriedly into the house to stop the baby wailing. *Great Expectations*

MILLS, MISS JULIA: Close friend of Dora Spenlow, who acts as a go-between when David is courting Dora. 'Comparatively stricken in years . . . almost twenty.' She eventually goes to India and marries a Scotch Croesus. *David Copperfield.*

MILLS, MR.: The father of Miss Julia Mills, who is out when David Copperfield calls on her, really to see Dora Spenlow. His absence was naturally rather welcome. *David Copperfield*

MILVEY, MRS. MARGARETTA: Wife of the Rev. Frank Milvey—quite a young wife—a pretty, bright little woman, something worn by anxiety. They have six children. *Our Mutual Friend*

MILVEY, THE REV. FRANK: He and his wife are consulted by the Boffins who want to adopt an orphan. A number are suggested and considered and they finally decide upon old

Betty Higden's great grandson, Johnny, but he dies before they can adopt him. Mr. Milvey officiates at Betty Higden's funeral. *Our Mutual Friend*

MITHERS: A client of Miss Mowcher, the little dwarf chiropodist and hairdresser. *David Copperfield*

MITHERS, LADY: A client of Miss Mowcher. Steerforth is interested to know what she does for Lady Mithers. *David Copperfield*

MIVINS, MR.: Known also as 'The Zephyr'. A prisoner in the Fleet Prison—one of those with whom Mr. Pickwick shares a cell on his first night in prison. Mivins is sent to the coffee-room to obtain a jug of burnt sherry and cigars at Mr. Pickwick's expense. *Pickwick Papers*

MIZZLE, MR.: A solicitor who had been given imaginary appointments by his office boy to keep suitors at bay. *Bleak House*

MIZZLER, MARQUIS OF: One of the aristocratic friends, of whom Mr. Chuckster boasts. *The Old Curiosity Shop*

MOBBS: One of the pupils at Dotheboys Hall. His step-mother wrote that she took to her bed on hearing that he wouldn't eat fat. The London newspapers told her that he turned up his nose at the cow's liver broth, after his good master had asked a blessing on it. She stops his halfpenny-a-week pocket money and gives the double-bladed knife with a corkscrew in it to the Missionaries. He is accordingly flogged by Squeers. *Nicholas Nickleby*

MODDLE, AUGUSTUS: The youngest boarder at Mrs. Todgers'. He is in love with Mercy Pecksniff, but when she gets married is persuaded to transfer his affection to her sister Charity. He deserts her upon her wedding day. *Martin Chuzzlewit*

MOGLEY: One of Mrs. Nickleby's many suitors. *Nicholas Nickleby*

MOLLY: Mr. Jaggers' housekeeper; Pip finds out that she is Estella's mother. Mr. Jaggers had successfully defended her in court against a murder charge. One of her wrists is deeply scarred across and across. *Great Expectations*

MOLOCH, LITTLE: Tetterby's baby Sally, with whom little Johnny Tetterby staggered about, carrying it in his arms. *The Haunted Man*

MONFLATHERS, MISS: Principal of a boarding and day Establishment for young ladies. She admonishes Little Nell for wasting her time working for a waxworks, when she might have been working in a factory. *The Old Curiosity Shop*

MONKEY, MR.: The name that Mr. Justice Stareleigh inadvertently gives to Mr. Phunkey, junior counsel in the Bardell *v.* Pickwick case. *See* Phunky, Mr.

MONKS: Oliver Twist's half-brother, who is plotting with Fagin to bring Oliver up as a criminal. If he had succeeded he would have acceded to Oliver's part of his father's estate. This was the name adopted by Edward Leeford. He has to leave the country and dies abroad in prison. *Oliver Twist*

MONTAGUE, TIGG: *see* Tigg, Montague

MOONEY: Beadle of the district. He is concerned in the coroner's inquest on Captain Hawdon, the law writer, who died of an overdose of opium in Krook's house. *Bleak House*

MOPS: *see* Dorrit, W.

MORDLIN, BROTHER: A member of the Brick Lane Branch of the United Grand Junction Ebenezer Temperance Association, who adapted the beautiful words of 'Who hasn't heard of a Jolly Young Waterman?' to the tune of the Old Hundredth. This is sung at the Annual Meeting at Brother Mordlin's request. *Pickwick Papers*

MORFIN, MR.: Head clerk at the office of Dombey and Son. He is the 'unknown friend' of Harriet Carker and her brother John, and he eventually marries Harriet. He was an amateur musician and played the violincello. *Dombey and Son*

MORGAN AP KERRIG: An ancestor of Mrs. Woodcourt who boasts to Esther Summerson of her Welsh descent. She is trying to discourage any thoughts of Esther marrying her son. *Bleak House*

MORGAN, BECKY: David, deputy sexton, tells the sexton he saw seventy-nine on her coffin. *The Old Curiosity Shop*

MORTIMER: Assumed name of Mr. Micawber. *See* Micawber, Mr.

MOULD, MR.: The undertaker who officiates at the funeral of Anthony Chuzzlewit. He has a wife and two daughters. *Martin Chuzzlewit*

MOULD, MRS.: Wife of the undertaker, who was plumper than her two daughters together. Helpmate to Mr. Mould in his punch, as in all other things. *Martin Chuzzlewit*

MOULD, THE MISSES: Daughters of Mr. and Mrs. Mould. Plump as any partridge was each Miss Mould. So round and chubby were their round proportions, that they might have been the bodies once belonging to the angel's faces in the shop below, grown up, with other heads attached to them to make them mortal. Even their peachy cheeks were puffed out and distended, as though performing on celestial trumpets. *Martin Chuzzlewit*

MOWCHER, MISS: Dwarf chiropodist, hairdresser, and masseuse, of whom Steerforth is a client. She is partly concerned with the flight of Em'ly with Steerforth, having had prior knowledge of the event, but makes up for it later when she is instrumental in the arrest of Littimer, Steerforth's servant, who has turned criminal. *David Copperfield*

M. R. F. (My Respected Father): *see* Wrayburn, Senior

MUDBERRY, MRS.: Mrs. Sanders in giving evidence in the breach of promise case Bardell *v.* Pickwick, said that Mrs. Mudberry, who kept a mangle, was of the opinion that Mrs. Bardell was engaged to Mr. Pickwick. *Pickwick Papers*

MUDGE, JONAS: Secretary of the Brick Lane Branch of the United Grand Junction Ebenezer Temperance Association. He is a chandler's shopkeeper, an enthusiastic and disinterested vessel who sold tea to the members. *Pickwick Papers*

MULLINS, MR. JACK: A regular customer at the Six Jolly Fellowship Porters who was told by the proprietress, Miss Abbey Potterson, that, as his work began early the next day, it was time for him to be at home and asleep. *Our Mutual Friend*

MULLIT: A professor of education staying at the Pawkins Boarding Establishment in New York, who had written some powerful pamphlets under the signature of 'Suturb', or Brutus reversed. 'One of the most remarkable men in the country.' *Martin Chuzzlewit*

MUNTLE: Mr. Mantalini's real name. *See* Mantalini, Alfred

MURDSTONE, EDWARD: Mrs. Copperfield's second husband and David's step-father. He is jealous of David and treats him very severely to Mrs. Copperfield's great sorrow. When his wife dies, Murdstone neglects David and finally puts him to work in a warehouse. Mr. Murdstone marries again. *David Copperfield*

MURDSTONE, MISS JANE: Mr. Murdstone's sister. She helps her brother break his wife's spirit. Later she becomes companion to Dora Spenlow and meets David Copperfield again. *David Copperfield*

MURPHY: A lady in Dawlish, presumably a friend of Mrs. Nickleby. *Nicholas Nickleby*

'MURPHY': *see* Bonney, Mr.

MUTANHED, LORD: He is a member of the *élite* society in Bath, who was introduced to Mr. Pickwick by Angelo Cyrus Bantam, M.C. A splendidly-dressed young man with long hair and a particularly small forehead. *Pickwick Papers*

MUZZLE: The footman of Mr. Nupkins, Mayor of Ipswich. He had a long body and long legs. He conducts Sam Weller down to the kitchen where Sam meets Mary, the pretty housemaid, for the first time—Sam's future wife. Muzzle was keeping company with the cook. *Pickwick Papers*

N

NADGETT, MR.: A private detective working for Tigg Montague, of the Anglo-Bengalee Disinterested Loan and Life Assurance Company. In the course of his enquiries he discovers the secret movements of Jonas Chuzzlewit, which leads to Jonas being accused of the murder of Tigg Montague. He was Tom Pinch's landlord in Islington. *Martin Chuzzlewit*

NAMBY: Sheriff's officer who arrests Mr. Pickwick for non-payment of the damages awarded to Mrs. Bardell, for breach of promise of marriage. *Pickwick Papers*

NANCY: A member of Fagin's gang and mistress of Bill Sikes to whom she is devoted. She takes pity on Oliver Twist, and is against Fagin's making him a criminal. She contacts Oliver's people—Rose Maylie and Mr. Brownlow—with a view to rescuing the boy, but will not give up her confederates. Fagin has her watched, and gives her away to Bill Sikes, knowing full well what the consequences will be. Sikes murders her in a very brutal manner. *Oliver Twist*

NANDY, JOHN EDWARD (OLD NANDY): Mrs. Plornish's old father. He visits William Dorrit in the Marshalsea Prison and Dorrit makes much of his infirmities. 'A poor little reedy, piping old gentleman, like a worn-out bird . . .' He had been in the music-binding business, and had retired of his own accord to the workhouse. *Little Dorrit*

'NATIVE, THE': Major Bagstock's coloured servant. The Major treats him as a native servant, abusing him soundly and even resorting to physical violence at times by throwing objects at him. *Dombey and Son*

NECKETT, CHARLOTTE: Known as 'Charley', Neckett's eldest daughter, who is about thirteen and keeps her brother and sister by going out charring and washing. She is employed by the Smallweeds. She becomes maid to Esther Summerson, who nurses her while she is suffering from smallpox, caught from Jo the crossing-sweeper. She nurses Esther in turn when she catches the fever. She eventually marries a well-to-do miller. *Bleak House*

NECKETT, EMMA: Sister to Charley. Mr. Jarndyce has her taken care of when her father dies and she takes her sister's place as maid to Esther when Charley marries. *Bleak House*

NECKETT, MR.: Sheriff's officer in Bell Yard, referred to by Mr. Skimpole, a debtor, as Coavinses. He carries out his duties, unpleasant as they are, very conscientiously and when he dies his three children are looked after by Mr. Jarndyce. *Bleak House*

NECKETT, TOM: Neckett's son. When Tom's father dies, Mr. John Jarndyce puts Tom to school. He is afterwards apprenticed to a miller, whom his sister Charlotte marries. *Bleak House*

NED: A chimney-sweep, who has a very small boy working for him. Sikes wished he could have such a boy to help him in the burglary at Chertsey. *Oliver Twist*

Name by which Sikes calls Oliver. *See* Twist, Oliver

NEDDY: Assistant turnkey at the Fleet Prison, and friend of Tom Roker. *Pickwick Papers*

NELL, LITTLE: *see* Trent, Nelly

NEMO: *see* Hawdon, Captain

NEPHEW, SCROOGE'S: *see* Fred

NETTINGALL, THE MISSES: They keep the boarding-school for young ladies at Canterbury, which is attended by Miss Shepherd, with whom David Copperfield falls in love. *David Copperfield*

NEWCOME, CLEMENCY: Servant to Dr. Jeddler, whose reading was confined to mottoes on a thimble and a nutmeg-grater. The motto on the thimble was 'Forget and Forgive', and on the nutmeg-grater 'Do as you would be done by'. She marries one of Dr. Jeddler's servants—Benjamin Britain—and they run a public house called 'The Nutmeg Grater'. They have a little daughter, Clem. *The Battle of Life*

NICKITS: The former owner of Bounderby's country estate. Mr. Bounderby boasts about his own humble start compared with that of Nickits, who had got into financial difficulties. *Hard Times*

NICKLEBY, GODFREY: Father of Ralph and Nicholas Nickleby (senior) and grandfather of Nicholas Nickleby (junior). He got married rather late in life and not being young enough or rich enough to aspire to the hand of a lady of fortune, married an old flame. His income at the time of his marriage fluctuated between sixty and eighty pounds per annum. He was left five thousand pounds by his uncle Ralph, with which he bought a small farm near Dawlish. When he died he left the farm and one thousand pounds to his son Nicholas (senior) and three thousand pounds to his son Ralph. *Nicholas Nickleby*

NICKLEBY, KATE: Sister of Nicholas Nickleby (junior) and daughter of Mr. and Mrs. Nicholas Nickleby (senior). When her father dies she comes to London with her mother and brother Nicholas, and her uncle Ralph finds her a job with Madame Mantalini. Kate is subjected to the undesirable attentions of Sir Mulberry Hawk, a dissolute client of Ralph Nickleby. She is protected by her brother and later marries Frank Cheeryble, nephew of the well-to-do Cheeryble Brothers. *Nicholas Nickleby*

NICKLEBY, MRS.: Widowed mother of Kate and Nicholas. Daughter of a gentleman in Devon, well-meaning, but weak and exceedingly talkative. She comes to London with her children when her husband dies and applies to Ralph for help. After the marriages of Kate and Nicholas she lives with each alternately. *Nicholas Nickleby*

NICKLEBY, MRS. GODFREY: Wife of Godfrey Nickleby and, after five years, mother of two sons, Nicholas (senior) and Ralph. *Nicholas Nickleby*

NICKLEBY, NICHOLAS (JUNIOR): Son of Nicholas (senior) and hero of the story. His uncle Ralph found him a job with Squeers, as assistant at Dotheboys Hall in Yorkshire. He runs away to London after giving Squeers a thrashing and is joined by a poor drudge from the school named Smike. They find jobs with a theatrical company at Portsmouth, run by Vincent Crummles, and act under the pseudonyms of Johnson and Digby. Nicholas has to return to London to protect his sister, becomes clerk to the Cheeryble Brothers, and eventually marries Madeline Bray, one of their charges. *Nicholas Nickleby*

NICKLEBY, NICHOLAS (SENIOR): Father of Kate and Nicholas (junior), and brother of Ralph. Left with a small fortune he speculated on his wife's advice and lost what little he had. He commended his wife and children to the care of his brother Ralph. *Nicholas Nickleby*

NICKLEBY, RALPH: Uncle of Kate and Nicholas (junior). When his father dies and leaves him three thousand pounds, he becomes a successful moneylender in London, with a good and fashionable clientéle. He obtains work for Kate and Nicholas, but hates the latter and tries to harm him through Smike, upon whom Nicholas has taken pity. Ralph, however, later learns that he is the father of Smike, and that he has been persecuting his own son. He is eventually ruined and hangs himself. *Nicholas Nickleby*

NICKLEBY, RALPH (SENIOR): Uncle of Godfrey Nickleby, who left him the bulk of his property—five thousand pounds, having originally left it to the Royal Humane Society, but had revoked this bequest in a codicil, because the Society had saved a poor relative of his, to whom he allowed three shillings and sixpence a week. *Nicholas Nickleby*

NIPPER, SUSAN: Maid to Florence Dombey, who speaks her mind to Mr. Dombey, when he is laid up, and chides him with the neglect of his daughter, for which she is dismissed. She later marries Mr. Toots. *Dombey and Son*

NOBBY SHROPSHIRE ONE: One of the opponents of The Game Chicken. *Dombey and Son*

NOBLEY, LORD: A name bandied about by Mr. Pip and Mr. Wolf, two guests at the dinner party given by Tigg Montague, with the intention of impressing Jonas Chuzzlewit. *Martin Chuzzlewit*

NOCKEMORF, LATE: This was the name of the medical surgery taken over by Bob Sawyer and Ben Allen in Bristol, which became known as 'Sawyer, late Nockemorf'. It does not prove a very great success. *Pickwick Papers*

NODDY, MR.: He was the scorbutic youth in a long stock who attends the party given by Bob Sawyer to Mr. Pickwick and his friends. He quarrels with Mr. Gunter, who threatens to throw him out of the window. The quarrel was eventually made up and they became bosom friends. *Pickwick Papers*

NOGGS, NEWMAN: Ralph Nickleby's clerk. He was once a gentleman, but falls on bad days and loses his self-respect while working for Ralph. He becomes friendly with Nicholas Nickleby, and is able to disclose to him some of his uncle's plots. Nicholas helps him to gain his self-respect once more. *Nicholas Nickleby*

NOLLY: The nickname given by Nancy to Oliver Twist. *See* Twist, Oliver

NORRIS, MR.: An American gentleman, engaged in mercantile affairs, to whose house Martin Chuzzlewit is taken by Mr. Bevan, an acquaintance he has made. There was also a Mrs. Norris, his wife, who 'looked much older and more faded than she ought to have looked'; two daughters, one eighteen and the other twenty, both slender, but very pretty, who sang in all languages except their own; a son, who was a student at college; and a grandmother, 'a little, sharp-eyed, quick old woman'. They turn out to be terrible snobs when they find out that Martin travelled steerage from Liverpool. *Martin Chuzzlewit*

NO-ZOO, THE LORD: Toby Chuzzlewit's grandfather. *Martin Chuzzlewit*

NUBBLES, CHRISTOPHER (KIT): Errand boy to Grandfather Trent. Little Nell is teaching him to write and Kit is in love with her. He calls Quilp an ugly dwarf and gains the dwarf's enmity. Quilp turns the grandfather against Kit. Later Kit becomes servant to the Garlands, and looks after and drives their fractious pony, Whisker. Quilp plots with the help of Sampson Brass to get Kit accused of thieving, but the Marchioness overhears the plot and is instrumental in clearing him. He travels with the Single Gentleman to find Little Nell dead. He marries Barbara, another servant of the Garlands, and they have a number of Kits and Barbaras. *The Old Curiosity Shop*

NUBBLES, MRS.: Kit's mother and a widow. She works hard as a laundress to keep the children. Besides Kit there are two brothers, one named Little Jacob. When Kit marries Barbara, the two mothers live together very harmoniously. *The Old Curiosity Shop*

NO. 20 COFFEE-ROOM FLIGHT: A prisoner in the Fleet, who, after seventeen years, had a fancy to see the market outside the prison. The turnkey trusted him out, but after two minutes he came back protesting that he had nearly been run over. He stayed in another five years then had a fancy to taste the beer at the new public house over the way. He was let out again and on several more occasions, but he began to drink and get later and later returning. At last the turnkey threatened to lock him out altogether, and after that he never wanted to go out again. *Pickwick Papers*

NUMSKULL, SIR ARROGANT: The name Mr. Boythòrn gave to Sir Leicester Dedlock. *See* Dedlock, Sir Leicester

NUPKINS, MISS HENRIETTA: Daughter of the Mayor of Ipswich. She joins with her mother in laying on her father's shoulders all blame for anything that went wrong. *Pickwick Papers*

NUPKINS, MR. GEORGE: Magistrate and Mayor of Ipswich. Mr. Pickwick is brought before him as having threatened to fight a duel. Mr. Pickwick obtains his release by disclosing to Mr. Nupkins that his newly-found friend, Captain Fitz-Marshall, is a swindler named Jingle. *Pickwick Papers*

NUPKINS, MRS.: Wife of the Mayor of Ipswich. She and her daughter join forces against Mr. Nupkins when they learn that Captain Fitz-Marshall is an adventurer. *Pickwick Papers*

O

'OLD BRICKS AND MORTAR': A nickname given to Mr. Vincent Crummles because of his heavy acting. *See* Crummles, Vincent

OLD SOLDIER, THE: Name given by the pupils of Dr. Strong's school to Mrs. Markleham. *See* Markleham, Mrs.

OLD 'UN: Dan'l Peggotty's name for the late Mr. Gummidge, when his widow appears to be melancholy—'She's thinking of the old 'un.' *David Copperfield*

OMER, MINNIE: Daughter of Mr. Omer, draper, haberdasher, and undertaker, in Great Yarmouth. She does needlework for the business, making the mourning, etc., and attends the funeral of David's mother, as a sort of day out with her young man. She marries Joram, who later takes over the business from her father. *David Copperfield*

OMER, MR.: An asthmatical draper, tailor, haberdasher, and undertaker in Great Yarmouth, who officiates at the funeral of David Copperfield's father, his mother, and his baby brother. *David Copperfield*

ORFLING, THE: The Micawbers' maid. *See* Clickett

ORLICK, DOLGE: An assistant blacksmith employed by Joe Gargery. Orlick is jealous of Pip, brother of the blacksmith's wife. He attacks Mrs. Gargery and injures her so badly that she becomes paralysed and loses her power of speech. She finally dies as a result of the injury, but nothing is proved against Orlick. He obtains a post with Miss Havisham, as gate-keeper, but is dismissed on the recommendation of Pip. Orlick later entices Pip on to the marshes where he attempts to kill him, but Pip is rescued just in time, and Orlick escapes. *Great Expectations*

OVERS, JOHN: *see* Boffin, N.

OWEN, JOHN: One of the pupils taken over by Mr. Marton, the old schoolmaster. *The Old Curiosity Shop*

P

PACKER: One of Mr. Snagsby's clients, who is registered in his book as having had some law-copying done. *Bleak House*

PACKLEMERTON, JASPER: A murderer whose effigy was in Mrs. Jarley's Waxworks. He murdered fourteen wives by tickling the soles of their feet. *The Old Curiosity Shop*

PANCKS, MR.: Mr. Casby's agent and rent-collector. Casby appears to his tenants as benefactor and Pancks has to take all the blame for grinding the rent out of them. He found out that Mr. Dorrit in the Marshalsea was entitled to a large fortune. *Little Dorrit*

PANKEY, MISS: A boarder at Mrs. Pipchin's school at Brighton, to which Paul Dombey went. 'A mild, little blue-eyed morsel of a child, who was shampooed every morning and seemed in danger of being rubbed away altogether.' *Dombey and Son*

PARAGON: see Mary Anne

PARDIGGLE, EGBERT (12 years), OSWALD (10½), FRANCES (9), FELIX (7), ALFRED (5): Sons of Mrs. Pardiggle, all of whom had to contribute their pocket money to various causes sponsored by their mother, which they very much resented. *Bleak House*

PARDIGGLE, F.R.S., MR. O. A.: Husband of Mrs. Pardiggle who 'brings up the rear' as his wife puts it and contributes one pound to various causes. *Bleak House*

PARDIGGLE, MRS.: A charity worker who makes a great deal of fuss about what she does. Whenever she goes visiting she seems to knock furniture and ornaments down with her sweeping dresses. *Bleak House*

PARKER, UNCLE: One of the imaginary inhabitants of the corner house so called by Silas Wegg, who keeps the stall outside on the pavement. *Our Mutual Friend*

PARKES, PHIL: A tall taciturn man and a ranger. He is one of the accepted regulars who sit round the boiler in the Maypole Inn. *Barnaby Rudge*

PASSNIDGE, MR.: One of the gentlemen with whom Mr. Murdstone went on board a yacht at Lowestoft when he took little David with him. *David Copperfield*

PATRIARCH, THE: *see* Casby, Christopher

PAWKINS, MAJOR: Husband of Mrs. Pawkins who kept the Boarding House in New York, to which Martin Chuzzlewit is taken on his arrival in that city. In commercial affairs he was a bold speculator—in plainer words, he had a most distinguished genius for swindling. *Martin Chuzzlewit*

PAWKINS, MRS.: She kept the boarding house in New York where Martin Chuzzlewit and Mark Tapley stayed. *Martin Chuzzlewit*

PAYNE, DR.: Surgeon of the Forty-Third Regiment, and friend of Dr. Slammer (97th Regiment). He calls on Mr. Winkle at the Bull Inn, Rochester, on behalf of his friend Dr. Slammer and issues a challenge to a duel, failing a written apology for his conduct the previous evening. *Pickwick Papers*

PEAK: Sir John Chester's manservant, who was as cool and negligent in his way as his master. On Sir John's death, he takes all the cash and movables and sets up as a finished gentleman on his own account. He would have married an heiress, but got himself into jail and sank under jail fever. *Barnaby Rudge*

PECKSNIFF, CHARITY: Elder daughter of Mr. Pecksniff, nicknamed 'Cherry'. She leaves home when her father plans to marry Mary Graham, young companion of old Martin Chuzzlewit, and lodges with Mrs. Todgers in London. Betrothed to Augustus Moddle, boarder at Mrs. Todgers', but he deserts her on her wedding day. *Martin Chuzzlewit*

PECKSNIFF, MERCY: Younger daughter of Mr. Pecksniff, nicknamed 'Merry'. Jonas Chuzzlewit marries her out of spite, because she had always laughed at and mocked him. He leads her an unhappy life and after being caught for murder, commits suicide. Then she is cared for by old Martin Chuzzlewit, who had tried to warn her against marrying Jonas. *Martin Chuzzlewit*

PECKSNIFF, MR. SETH: A widower, architect, and land surveyor who took in pupils for a premium of three or four hundred pounds, and was not above 'borrowing' their designs for his own ends. He was a cousin of old Martin Chuzzlewit and did everything possible, while not appearing to do so, to alienate Martin from the rest of his family and obtain his fortune, besides aspiring to the hand of Martin's young companion, Mary Graham. He is one of the greatest hypocrites among all the characters in Dickens and inspired the adjective 'Pecksniffian'. His downfall was at last brought about by old Martin, who had seen through his schemes and led him on. *Martin Chuzzlewit*

PEDDLE AND POOL: Solicitors of Monument Yard. They were instructed by Edward (Tip) Dorrit to forward to Mr. Arthur Clennam, the sum of twenty-four pounds, nine shillings, and eightpence, being the amount of principal and interest for which he believed he was indebted to Mr. Clennam, and to point out that this had not been asked of him. This was Tip Dorrit's ungrateful way of repaying the amount of a debt which Arthur Clennam had voluntarily liquidated to get him out of jail. *Little Dorrit*

PEECHER, MISS EMMA: Schoolmistress of the girls' school near to that of Bradley Headstone. She secretly loves Bradley, but her affection is not returned. *Our Mutual Friend*

PEERYBINGLE, MR. JOHN: Carrier. Married to Dot Peerybingle, much younger than him. A sturdy figure of a man, he had to stoop a long way down to kiss her. He is made jealous by the appearance of a mysterious stranger, but the mystery is cleared up at last and he finds that he has no reason to suspect his little wife. *The Cricket on the Hearth*

PEERYBINGLE, MRS. MARY: Known as Dot because of her size. Wife of the carrier. They have a young baby almost referred to by her husband as 'Dot and carry one'. *The Cricket on the Hearth*

PEFFER: Deceased partner of Peffer and Snagsby, law stationers. *Bleak House*

PEGGOTTY, CLARA: David's nurse and servant to Mrs. Copperfield; sister of Dan'l Peggotty, the old fisherman. When Mrs. Copperfield dies, Clara Peggotty is dismissed by Mr. Murdstone. She marries Mr. Barkis, the old carrier, who plies his cart between Blunderstone and Great Yarmouth. *David Copperfield*

PEGGOTTY, DAN'L: An old Yarmouth fisherman, Clara Peggotty's brother. He lived in a boat converted into a house and standing on the beach at Great Yarmouth, and had with him his niece Em'ly, the widow of his partner, Mrs. Gummidge, and his nephew Ham. When Little Em'ly runs away with Steerforth, Dan'l goes in search of her and finally finds her, when she has been discarded by Steerforth. He emigrates with her to Australia. Mrs. Gummidge accompanies them. *David Copperfield*

PEGGOTTY, HAM: Dan'l's nephew, also a fisherman. He is engaged to Little Em'ly but she runs away with Steerforth. He is later drowned in trying to save Steerforth from a wreck off the Yarmouth coast. *David Copperfield*

PEGLER, MRS.: Mr. Bounderby's mother, who keeps in the background so that she will not disgrace him. She visits Coketown at intervals to look at him from a distance and admire him. She kept a little village shop and he allowed her thirty pounds a year. *Hard Times*

PELL, MRS.: A widow before she married Mr. Pell. According to him—'A very elegant and accomplished woman.' *Pickwick Papers*

PELL, SOLOMON: An attorney, who is employed by Tony Weller on his affairs. *Pickwick Papers*

PELTIROGUS, HORATIO: A son of an old neighbour of Mrs. Nickleby who was supposed to have entertained an attachment for her daughter, Kate. *Nicholas Nickleby*

PEPPER: Called 'The Avenger'. Pip's boy from his washerwoman's family. Pip had to find him a little to do and a great deal to eat. *Great Expectations*

PEPS, DR. PARKER: The doctor who attends Mrs. Dombey at the birth of Little Paul and pretends that he is confused with the names of his aristocratic patients. He later attended Little Paul during his last illness and Paul liked him because he had attended his mother. *Dombey and Son*

PERCH, MR.: The messenger at the office of the firm of Dombey and Son, in the City, who lived at Balls Pond. When he sees his master come in, he hurries into Mr. Dombey's room, stirs the fire, hangs the newspaper to air upon the fender, puts the chair ready, and is round upon his heel on the instant of Mr. Dombey's entrance, to take his greatcoat and hat, and hang them up. *Dombey and Son*

PERCH, MRS.: Wife of Mr. Perch. When Mr. Dombey is ruined she visits his house and in the kitchen discusses his affairs with the cook and servants. *Dombey and Son*

PERCY, LORD ALGERNON: During the Gordon Riots he was in command of the Northumberland Militia. *Barnaby Rudge*

PERKER, MR.: Of Gray's Inn. Mr. Pickwick's lawyer. He first meets Mr. Pickwick when he is acting for Mr. Wardle against Jingle who proposes to marry Rachael Wardle, Mr. Wardle's sister. Later he is agent for the Blue candidate at the Eatanswill Election, the Hon. Samuel Slumkey. *Pickwick Papers*

PERKINS, MRS.: When Mr. Pecksniff called on Mrs. Gamp to obtain her services in the laying-out of old Anthony Chuzzlewit, she asks if she is being called out to Mrs. Perkins, one of her lady clients, expecting a baby. *Martin Chuzzlewit*

PERKINS, MRS.: She lived in the court where Krook's rag-and-bone shop was situated, and in the excitement of the inquest on Captain Hawdon, who died in a room on Krook's premises, she is reconciled to her neighbour Mrs. Piper, with whom she had not been on speaking terms. *Bleak House*

PERKINS, YOUNG: The cause of his mother's quarrel with Mrs. Piper, a near neighbour, because young Perkins fetched young Piper 'a crack'. *Bleak House*

PERT, MISS SCORNFUL: Edwin Drood's nickname for Rosa Bud. *See* Bud, Rosa

PET: *see* Meagles, Minnie

PETOWKER, HENRIETTA: An actress of the Theatre Royal, Drury Lane, who is a friend of the Kenwigs family. At their parties she used to let down her back hair and recite 'The Blood Drinker's Burial'. She appeared at a special performance at Portsmouth for Mr. Vincent Crummles and married Mr. Lillyvick, the water-rate collector, and Mrs. Kenwigs' uncle. She soon left him for a half-pay captain. *Nicholas Nickleby*

PHENOMENON, THE INFANT: *see* Crummles, Ninetta

'PHIB': Fanny Squeers' handmaiden, who curled her hair and administered as much flattery as she could get up. Phib was a shortened name for Phoebe. *Nicholas Nickleby*

PHIL: *see* Squod, Phil

PHILIPS: A constable to whom the Lord Mayor refers Mr. Langdale, the vintner, for protection against the Gordon Rioters. *Barnaby Rudge*

PHUNKY, MR.: Junior barrister who appears with Serjeant Snubbin for Mr. Pickwick, in the Bardell *v.* Pickwick case. His name was taken down by the judge as Monkey. *Pickwick Papers*

PHYSICIAN: *see* Merdle, Mr.

PICKWICK, SAMUEL: General Chairman and founder of The Pickwick Club, and chief character in the book. The humour of the book lies partly in the indignities suffered by this gentleman, and his cheerful acceptance of his misfortunes. Besides tracing the mighty ponds of Hampstead to their source and agitating the Scientific World with his Theory of Tittlebats, he founded the Corresponding Society of the Pickwick Club, comprising himself, Mr. Tupman, Mr. Snodgrass, and Mr. Winkle. Wrongfully taken to court by his landlady, Mrs. Bardell, for breach of promise of marriage, he has damages awarded against him, which he refuses to pay, on principle, and he serves some months in the Fleet Debtors' Prison. To save his landlady from being also imprisoned, he pays the costs of the case, is released, and cleared by Mrs. Bardell. He finally retires to Dulwich with his servant, Sam Weller. *Pickwick Papers*

PIDGER, MR.: Once a suitor of Lavinia Spenlow, one of Dora Spenlow's aunts. He would doubtless have declared his passion if he had not been 'cut short in his youth' (at about sixty) by overdrinking his constitution, and overdoing an attempt to set it right by swallowing Bath water. *David Copperfield*

PILKINS, MR.: Family practitioner to the Dombey family. He made very much of the fact that he was working with the famous Dr. Parker Peps, when Mrs. Dombey was confined. *Dombey and Son*

PIMKIN AND THOMAS: Solicitors, whose outdoor man attends the gathering at the Magpie and Stump, and who could sing a comic song. *Pickwick Papers*

PINCH, RUTH: Tom Pinch's sister. She was governess in a wealthy brass- and copper-founder's family at Camberwell. Tom took her away from Camberwell and he and Ruth took rooms at Islington. Ruth eventually marries John Westlock, Tom's friend, and Tom goes to live with them. *Martin Chuzzlewit*

PINCH, TOM: Assistant to Mr. Pecksniff, in whom Tom has great faith. At last, however, he is disillusioned when Pecksniff dismisses him and Tom realizes his hypocrisy. He moves to London, where he lives with his sister and is secretly given work by old Martin Chuzzlewit. *Martin Chuzzlewit*

PIP: *see* Pirrip, Philip

PIP, MR.: A theatrical man, and friend of Tigg Montague. He is guest at the dinner attended by Jonas Chuzzlewit. He used an oath for the introduction of everything he said. *Martin Chuzzlewit*

PIPCHIN, MR.: Mrs. Pipchin's late husband, who broke his heart in pumping water out of the Peruvian mines, which in the view of Mr. Dombey conferred a sense of respectability to his widow. *Dombey and Son*

PIPCHIN, MRS.: A widow, whose husband broke his heart pumping water out of the Peruvian mines. She runs a boarding-school for young people at Brighton. Paul Dombey becomes one of her boarders. 'A marvellously ill-favoured old lady, of a stooping figure, with a mottled face, like bad marble, a hook nose, and a hard grey eye, that looked as if it might have been hammered at on an anvil without sustaining any injury.' She later becomes housekeeper to Mr. Dombey. *Dombey and Son*

PIPER, ALEXANDER JAMES: Son of Mrs. Piper, half-baptized, aged eighteen months and four days, not being expected to live, suffering in his gums. Young Perkins 'fetched him a crack' and his mother stopped talking to Mrs. Perkins. *Bleak House*

PIPER, MR.: Husband of Mrs. Piper living in the court where Krook's rag-and-bone shop is situated. He is a cabinet-maker. *Bleak House*

PIPER, MRS. ANASTASIA: She gives evidence at the inquest on Captain Hawdon, the law writer (lover of Lady Dedlock), who died through an overdose of opium. *Bleak House*

PIPER, PROFESSOR: A member of the Committee who waited on the Hon. Elijah Pogram and arranged a levée for him at the National Hotel, which Martin Chuzzlewit attends on his way back from Eden. *Martin Chuzzlewit*

PIPKIN, NATHANIEL: Parish clerk of a little town, and schoolmaster, who falls in love with Maria Lobbs, daughter of the fierce and rich old saddler. He was led on by Maria who was really in love with her cousin. He later becomes friendly with old Lobbs. Interpolated story: 'The Parish Clerk', written by Mr. Pickwick from Sam Weller's dictation and read aloud by Mr. Pickwick when he is laid up with rheumatism in The Angel, Bury St. Edmunds. *Pickwick Papers*

PIRRIP FAMILY, THE: Mr. Pirrip, deceased father of Philip Pirrip, or Pip. Mrs. Georgiana: Pip's mother. Also his sister and brothers—Abraham, Alexander, Bartholomew, Roger, and Tobias, all deceased. *Great Expectations*

PIRRIP, PHILIP: Known as Pip—hero of the story. He and his sister who brings him up by hand, are the only survivors of the family. He is apprenticed to the blacksmith, Jo Gargery, who is his sister's husband. He comes into a lot of money and is brought up on his unknown benefactor's instructions as a gentleman. He goes to London where he stays with Herbert Pocket. He later finds to his dismay that his benefactor is an escaped convict, Magwitch, who was helped by him as a boy with food and a file. The convict comes to England, thereby making himself liable to hanging. Pip tries to get him out of the country, but Magwitch is betrayed by his partner in crime, is injured in the escape attempt, and dies before the sentence of hanging can be carried out. Pip loses all his money, which is forfeit to the Crown, and he joins the firm of Clarriker and Pocket as a clerk. Pip is in love with Estella, who he later finds out is the daughter of the convict, Magwitch. Herbert Pocket, Pip's friend, called him Handel, because he had been a blacksmith. *Great Expectations*

PITCHER: A young pupil at Dotheboys Hall, who, while Squeers was away in London, had a fever, which Mrs. Squeers considers due to his obstinacy, and should be beaten out of him. *Nicholas Nickleby*

PLORNISH, JOHN EDWARD: The Plornish's youngest son and Nandy's grandson. *Little Dorrit*

PLORNISH, MRS. SALLY: Wife of Plornish, the out-of-work plasterer. They lived in rooms in a large house in Bleeding Heart Yard. *Little Dorrit*

PLORNISH, THOMAS: A plasterer, living in Bleeding Heart Yard, tenant of Christopher Casby, and finding it difficult to obtain work and make a living. Arthur Clennam makes friends with the Plornishes and they visit him when he is in the Debtors' Prison. *Little Dorrit*

PLUCK, MR.: A toady of Sir Mulberry Hawk and business acquaintance of Ralph Nickleby. He is usually accompanied by his fellow toady, Mr. Pyke. They play an important part in trying to bring Kate Nickleby and Sir Mulberry Hawk together. *Nicholas Nickleby*

PLUMMER, BERTHA: Blind daughter of Caleb Plummer. She helps with the toy business by making and dressing dolls. She is in love with her employer, Tackleton, a stern, ill-natured toymaker, who treats her with contempt. *The Cricket on the Hearth*

PLUMMER, CALEB: A poor toymaker employed by Tackleton (trading as Gruff and Tackleton), toy-merchant. He tries to deceive his blind daughter into believing that he is dressed comfortably and that their home is a handsome one. She finally finds out the truth. *The Cricket on the Hearth*

PLUMMER, EDWARD: Son of Caleb; he becomes a sailor and goes away, but returns in time to save his sweetheart, May Fielding, who believed him to be dead, from marrying Tackleton. Edward marries her himself. *The Cricket on the Hearth*

POCKET FAMILY, THE: ALICK: Who with his sister Jane was warned by their nurses that if they bounced up and down against the bushes, they would fall into the river; BABY: Who was nursed by his mother Mrs. Pocket and given the nutcrackers to play with; JOE: He had a hole in his frill, and Flopson, his nurse, was going to mend it when she had time; FANNY: Daughter of Mr. and Mrs. Matthew Pocket, who had a whitlow. Millers, the nurse, was going to poultice it, when she didn't forget. *Great Expectations*

POCKET, HERBERT: Eldest son of Matthew Pocket. The 'pale young gentleman with red eyelids and light hair' whom Pip first meets at Miss Havisham's in the garden and fights with him. Pip later shares chambers with him at Barnard's Inn, and becomes very friendly with him, and buys for him a partnership in Clarriker & Co. Herbert marries Clara Barley, daughter of a retired purser, and they go abroad for the business. *Great Expectations*

POCKET, MATTHEW: A cousin of Miss Havisham who helps Pip in his studies when he comes to London to be made into a gentleman. As a result of Pip's intervention on his behalf, Miss Havisham leaves him £4,000. *Great Expectations*

POCKET, MRS. MATTHEW (BELINDA): Wife of Matthew Pocket, a highly ornamental, but perfectly helpless and useless woman. Only daughter of a certain deceased knight. She has a number of young children being brought up by nurses. *Great Expectations*

POCKET, SARAH: One of Miss Havisham's fawning relatives. Miss Havisham leaves her £25 to buy pills, because she is always bilious. *Great Expectations*

PODDER, MR.: Hitherto unconquered batsman of the All-Muggleton cricket team, against whom Mr. Struggles, a Dingley-Deller, was selected to bowl. Podder and Dumkins made a great stand and the Dingley Dell team were never able to make up lost ground. At the dinner following the cricket match, Podder is toasted with Dumkins, by Mr. Staple. *Pickwick Papers*

PODDLES: A little girl left to be minded by Mrs. Betty Higden, who is therefore called a 'minder'. For this, Betty Higden was paid fourpence a week. *Our Mutual Friend*

PODSNAP, MISS GEORGIANA: She was scared of being taken notice of and is taken in hand by the Lammles, two adventurers, who scheme to get her married to Fledgeby. Their schemes are upset by Mr. and Mrs. Boffin, who, simple though they appear to be, see through the Lammles and 'pay them off'. Miss Podsnap wants to help the Lammles when they are ruined. *Our Mutual Friend*

PODSNAP, MR. JOHN: In the Marine Insurance business. Mr. Podsnap had acquired a peculiar flourish of his right arm in often clearing the world of its most difficult problems, by sweeping them behind him with a flushed face and the words: 'I don't want to know about it. I don't choose to discuss it; I don't admit it!' A friend of the Veneerings. The Podsnaps lived in a shady angle adjoining Portman Square. *Our Mutual Friend*

PODSNAP, MRS.: His wife. Fine woman, quantity of bone, neck and nostrils like a rocking-horse, hard features, majestic head-dress in which Podsnap has hung golden offerings. *Our Mutual Friend*

POGRAM, ELIJAH: A member of Congress who meets Martin Chuzzlewit on the river-boat returning from Eden. He was given a reception at the National Hotel. *Martin Chuzzlewit*

POLLY: Waitress at the 'Slap Bang', the restaurant to which Young Smallweed, Tony Jobling, and Mr. Guppy go for lunch. *Bleak House*

PORKENHAM FAMILY, THE: MISS P.: daughter of the Porkenhams; MRS. P.: wife of old Porkenham; MR. P.: 'Old Porkenham'. A rival in magisterial circles of Mr. Nupkins; SIDNEY: son of the Porkenhams, whose addresses to Miss Nupkins were discarded for those of Captain Fitz-Marshall, who was really the strolling player, Jingle. The Porkenhams were 'bosom' friends and rivals of the Nupkins family in Ipswich. *Pickwick Papers*

PORKIN AND SNOB: The bass voice called out that firm's name when Mr. Pickwick was waiting at the office of Namby. *Pickwick Papers*

PORSON: Nicholas refers to him as being odd-looking. *Nicholas Nickleby*

PORTERS, 'FOOLISH MR.': A certain gentleman who declares his regard for Miss Twinkleton at Tunbridge Wells. *The Mystery of Edwin Drood*

POTATOES, MEALY: *see* Mealy Potatoes

POTKINS, WILLIAM: Waiter at the Blue Boar in Rochester. He waits on Uncle Pumblechook and Pip. *Great Expectations*

POTT, MR.: Editor of the *Eatanswill Gazette* and rival of Mr. Slurk, editor of the *Eatanswill Independent*. Mr. Pott attends Mrs. Leo Hunter's *fête champêtre* as a Russian officer, with a knout. *Pickwick Papers*

POTT, MRS.: Wife of the editor, Mr. Pott. She was tired of her husband's quarrels with his rival newspaper. She goes to Mrs. Leo Hunter's party as Apollo—with a gown on. Mr. Pott is very jealous of Mr. Winkle and the attentions he pays to his wife, but Mrs. Pott gets out of the affair by having hysterics, and becoming the aggrieved party, aided and abetted by her maid. *Pickwick Papers*

POTTERSON, ABBEY: Her name was said to be short for Abigail. She is proprietress of the riverside public house, The Six Jolly Fellowship Porters. She befriends Lizzie Hexam when her father is accused of murder and when Gaffer Hexam is eventually drowned. *Our Mutual Friend*

POTTERSON, JOB: A ship's steward and brother of Abbey Potterson. He returns to this country on a ship on which an attempt is made on the life of John Harmon. Later Job is able to identify John Rokesmith as the missing John Harmon. *Our Mutual Friend*

POUCH, MRS. JOE: Mrs. Bagnet, a great friend of George Rouncewell, is always advocating that he should have married Joe Pouch's widow, and that if he had done so, he would never have got himself into financial difficulties. *Bleak House*

POWLERS: They were said to be relations of Mrs. Sparsit, Mr. Bounderby's housekeeper, which added so much to her respectability. *Hard Times*

'PRENTICE KNIGHTS: *see* Bulldogs, United

PRICE: A coarse, vulgar young man who was under arrest for debt, in the Sheriff Officer's sponging-house, when Mr. Pickwick was taken there. *Pickwick Papers*

PRICE, 'TILDA (MATILDA): Friend of Miss Fanny Squeers, a miller's daughter, who marries the corn-factor, John Browdie. Fanny Squeers is her bridesmaid. *Nicholas Nickleby*

PRIG, BETSEY: A nurse from Bartholomew's Hospital who nurses patients with Mrs. Gamp, 'turn and turn about'. She finally quarrels with Mrs. Gamp, by declaring that Mrs. Harris, Mrs. Gamp's fictitious friend, does not exist. *Martin Chuzzlewit*

PRISCILLA: Mrs. Jellyby's maid who drinks too much. She wore a flannel bandage, and dropped everything on the table at dinner, wherever it happened to go, and never moved it again until she put it on the stairs. *Bleak House*

PROSEE, MR.: The eminent counsel who was at a dinner party with Mr. Perker. *Pickwick Papers*

PROSS, MISS: Lucie Manette's nurse and companion, and sister of Barsad, the spy. She accompanies Lucie to Paris and stays behind when Lucie leaves with her husband, to cover the escape. She is challenged by Madame Defarge, the revolutionary, and kills her in a struggle with a gun. *A Tale of Two Cities*

PROSS, SOLOMON: Brother of Miss Pross, whom he defrauds of her money. He becomes a spy, known as John Barsad and going to Paris acts as a sort of turnkey at the prison. Knowledge of Barsad's identity enables Sydney Carton to gain access to Darnay's cell. *A Tale of Two Cities*

PROVIS: Assumed name. *See* Magwitch, Abel

PRUFFLE: The scientific gentleman's servant at Clifton. Mr. Pickwick's dark lantern arouses many theories in the scientist's mind, but his servant, when appealed to for his opinion, gives a down-to-earth explanation of the phenomenon, for which he is called a fool. *Pickwick Papers*

PUBSEY & CO.: *see* Fledgeby

PUFFER, PRINCESS: An old woman who runs an opium den in the East End of London, which is patronized by John Jasper. She follows him back to Cloisterham to try to find out who he is and what is his secret. *The Mystery of Edwin Drood*

PUGSTYLES, MR.: A plump old gentleman and the leader of the deputation waiting on Mr. Gregsbury, M.P., to tell him that his constituency was dissatisfied with his conduct. *Nicholas Nickleby*

PUMBLECHOOK, UNCLE: Joe Gargery's uncle, a corn-chandler and seedsman. He had his business in Rochester and was very well off. He gets Pip a job at Miss Havisham's. Later his shop is broken into by Orlick, Joe Gargery's journeyman, and Pumblechook is roughly handled. *Great Expectations*

PUPKER, SIR MATTHEW: Chairman of the United Metropolitan Improved Hot Muffin and Crumpet Baking and
Punctual Delivery Company, the annual meeting of which
was attended by Ralph Nickleby. *Nicholas Nickleby*

PYEGRAVE, CHARLEY: The duke's son and a client of
Miss Mowcher. He tried to do without her and got into
great difficulties trying to obtain a bottle of Madagascar
Liquid for his moustachios. *David Copperfield*

PYKE, MR.: A sharp-faced gentleman who with Mr. Pluck
was a toady to Sir Mulberry Hawk and business acquaintance of Ralph Nickleby. *Nicholas Nickleby*

Q

QUALE, MR.: A friend of Mrs. Jellyby and a philanthropic
worker. He was intended as a husband for Caddy Jellyby,
but she refuses him. *Bleak House*

QUANKO SAMBO: A bowler in Mr. Jingle's famous cricket
match in the West Indies. He was the last bowler left and
finally bowled Jingle out, but died as a result of his exer-
tions in the scorching sun. *Pickwick Papers*

QUILP, DANIEL: A dwarf moneylender and dealer in
second-hand ship's fittings, whose business was on a wharf
opposite the Tower of London; he himself lived on Tower
Hill. He has a young and pretty wife whom he terrorizes,
as he does her mother, Mrs. Jiniwin. He sells up Grandfather Trent, who owes him money, and pursues him and
Little Nell. His plotting is finally given away by his servile
confederate, Sampson Brass. Fleeing from the police in
thick fog, he falls into the river and, as he has locked them
out, they cannot get to him to save him, and he is drowned.
His discoloured fangs gave him the appearance of a panting
dog. *The Old Curiosity Shop*

QUILP, MRS. BETSY: The dwarf's wife who lives in constant fear of her husband and what he might do. When Quilp is drowned she inherits his wealth and marries a smart younger fellow. *The Old Curiosity Shop*

QUINION, MR.: Manager of Murdstone and Grinby's wine warehouse, where David Copperfield is put to work by Mr. Murdstone. Mr. Quinion first sees David at Lowestoft, when Mr. Murdstone takes him there before marrying his mother, Mrs. Copperfield. *David Copperfield*

R

RACHAEL: A mill-hand and friend of Stephen Blackpool, whom he wants to marry. He cannot afford to get a divorce from his drunken wife. *Hard Times*

RACHAEL, MRS.: *see* Chadband, Mrs.

RADDLE, MR.: A gentleman of heavy and subdued nature. His wife calls him a base, faint-hearted, timorous wretch, because he will not support her against their lodgers, Bob Sawyer and Ben Allen, and the guests. *Pickwick Papers*

RADDLE, MRS. MARY ANN: Bob Sawyer's landlady at his lodgings in Lant Street, in the Borough. A little fierce woman, sister to Mrs. Cluppins. She demands her outstanding rent the night Bob Sawyer gives a party for Mr. Pickwick and his friends and makes herself generally awkward, by taking away the kettle so they cannot get any hot water. She attends the picnic at The Spaniards at Hampstead when Mrs. Bardell is arrested. *Pickwick Papers*

RADFOOT, GEORGE: Third mate on the ship on which John Harmon returned to England. He drugged and robbed John Harmon, but was himself set upon and murdered. Being in John Harmon's clothes his body is mistaken for Harmon's. *Our Mutual Friend*

RAMSEY, MR.: A client of Dodson and Fogg—who came to the office too late to pay off his debt, but had further costs added on. *Pickwick Papers*

RAYMOND, COUSIN: *see* Camilla, Mr. Raymond

REDLAW, MR.: The haunted man—learned in chemistry, and a teacher. He relinquishes his memory of the past, but with it loses, not only his sad and unpleasant memories, but the pleasant and happy ones as well. He also gains the gift of passing this on to everyone with whom he comes into contact with very unhappy results. Eventually he begs for his memory to be restored, and it is. *The Haunted Man*

REYNOLDS, MISS: A pupil at Nun's House, Miss Twinkleton's Academy at Cloisterham. When rumours are being passed round concerning the quarrel between Edwin Drood and Neville Landless, Miss Reynolds pretends to stab herself in the hand with a pin, and is reproved by Miss Twinkleton. *The Mystery of Edwin Drood*

RIAH, MR.: A benevolent Jew who is used by Fledgeby and made to appear to be the hard, grinding principal of Pubsey & Co., moneylenders. In reality the business is owned by Fledgeby. He makes a friend of Lizzie Hexam and little Jenny Wren, and, when Lizzie wants to hide, he finds work for her with his friends up river. Derisively nicknamed 'Aaron' by Eugene Wrayburn. *Our Mutual Friend*

RICHARD: Meg's sweetheart. He and Meg are discouraged by the advice of Alderman Cute against poor people marrying, but they decide to ignore his warnings and Trotty Veck, Meg's father, awakes from a disturbing dream about them to find that they are happily getting married. *The Chimes*

One of the waiters at the Saracen's Head, Snow Hill, London, where Mr. Squeers waits to collect the new boys for his school in Yorkshire. *Nicholas Nickleby*

'RICHARDS': The name given to Paul's nurse. *See* Toodle, Polly

RICKITTS, LITTLE: A pupil at Nun's House, Cloisterham. During the Christmas celebration, various club suppers were held among the girls and cowslip wine had been drunk from the small squat measuring-glass in which little Rickitts, a junior of weakly constitution, took her steel drops, daily. *The Mystery of Edwin Drood*

RIDERHOOD, MRS.: Pleasant's deceased mother, who had established the business of unlicensed pawnbroker, popularly known as a Leaving Shop. *Our Mutual Friend*

RIDERHOOD, PLEASANT: Daughter of Rogue Riderhood, who acted as an unlicensed pawnbroker to seamen wishing to raise money on their belongings. She eventually marries a Mr. Venus, taxidermist. *Our Mutual Friend*

RIDERHOOD, ROGUE (ROGER): A waterside character living on what he finds in the pockets of drowned people and not averse to helping them into the river. He becomes lock-keeper at Plashwater Weir Mill Lock up the river and is drowned in a fight with Bradley Headstone, a schoolmaster who tries to throw suspicion of murder on to Riderhood. *Our Mutual Friend*

RIGAUD, MADAME: *see* Barroneau, Madame

RIGAUD, MONSIEUR: Alias Lagnier—alias Blandois. Although in prison in Marseilles on suspicion of having murdered his wife, he is released for want of evidence. He comes to England and becomes involved with Flintwinch, learning certain secrets concerning Mrs. Clennam. He attempts to blackmail her, but is killed in the collapse of her old house. *Little Dorrit*

ROB THE GRINDER: *see* Toodle, Robin

ROBINSON: An aspiring rival to the acknowledged wit in the City counting house of the firm of Dombey and Son. The rival wits make it up in view of the disaster to the firm. *Dombey and Son*

ROCKINGHAM, LORD: His house in Grosvenor Square was occupied by the military and guns pointed from the windows ready to sustain a siege against the Gordon Rioters. *Barnaby Rudge*

ROGERS: A friend of Mrs. Nickleby living at Dawlish. *Nicholas Nickleby*

ROGERS, MRS.: When Mr. Pickwick leaves his lodgings with Mrs. Bardell, Mrs. Rogers takes his rooms. She attends the picnic at the Spaniards Inn, at Hampstead, when Mrs. Bardell is arrested. *Pickwick Papers*

ROKER, TOM: Turnkey at the Fleet Prison, who receives Mr. Pickwick on his arrival. *Pickwick Papers*

ROKESMITH, JOHN: *see* Harmon, John

ROKESMITH, MRS. JOHN: *see* Wilfer, Bella

ROSA: Mrs. Rouncewell, housekeeper to the Dedlocks at Chesney Wold, takes her from the village to train as maid. Lady Dedlock takes a fancy to her and makes her her personal maid in place of Mlle Hortense, the French woman, who becomes violently jealous. Mrs. Rouncewell's grandson, Watt, falls in love with Rosa. His father asks permission to take Rosa away from domestic service at Chesney Wold, to have her educated, and made suitable to marry his son. *Bleak House*

ROSE: Oliver Twist's aunt. *See* Maylie, Rose

ROSEBUD: *see* Bud, Rosa

ROUNCEWELL, MR.: An ironmaster. Son of Sir Leicester Dedlock's housekeeper. *Bleak House*

ROUNCEWELL, MR. GEORGE: Trooper George, or 'Bluffy' as his friend Bagnet calls him. An ex-trooper and owner of a shooting-gallery in London. Son of Mrs. Rouncewell. He is wrongfully accused and arrested under suspicion of the murder of Mr. Tulkinghorn, but released when the real murderer is found and arrested. He becomes a servant-companion to Sir Leicester Dedlock, during his illness. *Bleak House*

ROUNCEWELL, MRS.: A widow whose husband died some time before the decease of the pretty fashion of pigtails. Housekeeper to Sir Leicester and Lady Dedlock at Chesney Wold. Mother of George and his brother, the ironmaster. Devoted to the Dedlock family. *Bleak House*

ROUNCEWELL, WATT: Son of the ironmaster; in love with Rosa, Lady Dedlock's maid. Rosa is eventually sent to Germany to finish her education and Watt's father agrees to their marrying after a twelve-month. *Bleak House*

ROVINGHAMS: Commission merchants to whom all consignments dealt with by Mrs. Clennam are made. Arthur Clennam does not therefore see any necessity for him to take part in the business, in which he has little interest. *Little Dorrit*

RUDDLE: Client of Ralph Nickleby to whom a mortgage has been granted. *Nicholas Nickleby*

RUDGE, BARNABY: Son of Rudge, the murderer—half-witted and terrified at the sight of blood. He wanders the countryside in company with a tame raven, Grip. Barnaby gets involved in the Gordon Riots and led away by the rough and unscrupulous leaders, Hugh and Dennis. He is imprisoned in Newgate and condemned to be hanged, but a pardon is obtained for him at the last minute, at the instigation of Gabriel Varden, the locksmith. *Barnaby Rudge*

RUDGE, MR.: Steward of Reuben Haredale, and Barnaby's father. He murders Reuben Haredale and his gardener, who surprises him, and with whom he changes clothes. The body found in the lake is assumed to be that of Rudge. Mr. Geoffrey Haredale, Reuben's brother later discovers the truth and captures Rudge who has joined the Gordon Rioters. Rudge is thrown into prison with his son and later hanged. *Barnaby Rudge*

RUDGE, MRS. MARY: Wife of Rudge, the murderer, and mother of Barnaby. She later learns the truth of her husband's crime, when he returns and demands money from her to stay away from their son. *Barnaby Rudge*

RUGG, MISS ANASTASIA: Daughter of Rugg; she was successful in a breach of promise case against a baker. *Little Dorrit*

RUGG, MR.: General agent, accountant and collector of debts, and landlord of Mr. Pancks. He helps Pancks to establish Mr. Dorrit's claim to a fortune. *Little Dorrit*

RUMTY: Nickname. *See* Wilfer, R.

S

ST. EVRÉMONDE, MARQUIS DE: The younger of twin brothers and uncle of Charles Darnay. He runs over and kills a child in the streets of Paris. The child's father, Gaspard, follows him back to his château and stabs him to death. *A Tale of Two Cities*

Deceased elder twin brother of the above and father of Charles Darnay. He seduced the sister of Madame Defarge, killed her brother and locked up Dr. Manette, who had tended them, in the Bastille. On his death his younger brother succeeds to the estate. *A Tale of Two Cities*

See Darnay, Charles

ST. EVRÉMONDE, MARQUISE DE: Mother of Charles Darnay, who wished her son to seek out the wronged girl's sister and make amends for his father's crime. *A Tale of Two Cities*

SALLY: *see* Compeyson, Mrs.

SALLY, OLD: She nursed Agnes Fleming at the birth of Oliver Twist in the workhouse. She robs Oliver's mother of a locket establishing Agnes Fleming's identity. When Sally dies the locket passes to Mrs. Corney, matron of the workhouse, who sells it to Monks, Oliver's half-brother, to destroy. *Oliver Twist*

SAM: The cab driver, No. 924, who drives Mr. Pickwick from St. Martins-le-Grand to the Golden Cross and fights Mr. Pickwick and his friends, whom he accuses of being informers. This was because Mr. Pickwick made notes about his very old horse. *Pickwick Papers*

Mr. Pecksniff's hostler who looks after the raw-boned haggard horse. *Martin Chuzzlewit*

SAMKIN AND GREEN: Solicitors, whose managing clerk attended the gathering at the Magpie and Stump, to which Mr. Pickwick was invited by Mr. Lowten. *Pickwick Papers*

SAMPSON, GEORGE: He first of all courted Bella Wilfer, but later, when Bella was adopted by the Boffins, transfers his attentions to her sister Lavinia. *Our Mutual Friend*

SAMSON: The executioner who operated the guillotine in Paris. Referred to by the little wood-sawyer as 'The Barber', whom he watched doing his shaving. *A Tale of Two Cities*

SANDERS, MRS. SUSANNAH: A big, fat, heavy-faced woman, who is a friend of Mrs. Bardell. She gave evidence in the Bardell *v.* Pickwick case. She stated that during her courtship, Mr. Sanders had often called her a 'duck', but never 'chops' or 'tomato sauce'. *Pickwick Papers*

SAPSEA, MR. THOMAS: Auctioneer and Mayor of Cloisterham. He composes an epitaph for his late wife's tombstone, the installing of which is presumably going to be instrumental in clearing up the mystery surrounding the disappearance of Edwin Drood. Sapsea dressed like the Dean of the Cathedral, and had been mistaken for the Dean. *The Mystery of Edwin Drood*

SAPSEA, MRS. ETHELINDA: The late Mrs. Sapsea, who before her marriage had been a Miss Brobity, schoolteacher, keeping a rival establishment to the Nun's House. She is so overcome when proposed to by Mr. Sapsea that she is only able to articulate the two words 'O Thou!'. She died owing to a feeble action of the liver. *The Mystery of Edwin Drood*

SARAH: One of the domestic staff at Westgate House, the Seminary for Young Ladies at Bury St. Edmunds, over the wall of which Mr. Pickwick has himself put at night. *Pickwick Papers*

SAUTEUSE, MADAME: She runs the dancing-school where Georgiana Podsnap suffers, being taught dancing. *Our Mutual Friend*

SAVILLE, SIR GEORGE: He brought in the Catholic Bill and his house in Leicester Fields was to be burnt by the Gordon Rioters. *Barnaby Rudge*

SAWYER, BOB: A medical student from Guy's Hospital, who lives in lodgings in Lant Street, in the Borough, let to him by Mrs. Raddle. Bob's great friend was another student from Guy's, Benjamin Allen. Bob sets up in practice unsuccessfully in Bristol and goes finally to Bengal with his friend in the service of the East India Company. *Pickwick Papers*

SCADDER, ZEPHANIAH: Agent of the Eden Land Corporation in America, and real estate swindler. Although appearing to discourage him, he persuades young Martin Chuzzlewit to purchase worthless swamp land in Eden. *Martin Chuzzlewit*

SCADGERS, LADY: Great aunt of Mrs. Sparsit. Mr. Bounderby, banker and millowner, proud of his so-called humble beginning, gained some satisfaction from the knowledge of his housekeeper, Mrs. Sparsit's aristocratic connections. 'An immensely fat old woman, with an inordinate appetite for butcher's meat, and a mysterious leg which had now refused to get out of bed for fourteen years.' *Hard Times*

SCALEY, MR.: A bailiff or sheriff's officer who takes possession of Madame Mantalini's millinery and dressmaking business, on account of a writ of execution for fifteen hundred and twenty-seven pounds, four and ninepence ha'penny—debts incurred by her husband. *Nicholas Nickleby*

SCIENTIFIC GENTLEMAN, THE: An elderly gentleman of scientific attainments, writing a philosophical treatise, who lives at Clifton. He is gazing out of the window one evening when he sees a strange phenomenon—a travelling light, which he attributes to the effect of electricity, especially as, when he looks out of his back gate, he receives a shock which stuns him for a quarter of an hour. The truth is that Mr. Pickwick is operating a dark lantern in his endeavour to meet Miss Arabella Allen in the next garden, and, when the scientific gentleman looks out, Sam Weller gives his head a gentle tap with his clenched fist which knocks it against the gate. *Pickwick Papers*

SCOTT, TOM: Quilp's boy at his wharf. He defies Quilp by walking on his hands with his feet in the air, a habit which particularly annoys the dwarf. Quilp maltreats him and yet he is quite devoted to his master in his defiant way. When Quilp is drowned, Tom Scott becomes an Italian tumbler and assumes the name of an Italian image lad. *The Old Curiosity Shop*

SCREWZER, TOMMY: A bilious acquaintaince of Cousin Feenix. *Dombey and Son*

SCROOGE, EBENEZER: A squeezing, wrenching, grasping, scraping, clutching, covetous old sinner. Hard and sharp as flint—secret and solitary as an oyster. The surviving partner of Scrooge and Marley—moneylenders and bill-discounters. A vivid dream on Christmas Eve transforms him into a better man. *A Christmas Carol*

SCROOGE'S NEPHEW AND NIECE: *see* Fred and Mrs. Fred

SCROOGE'S NIECE'S SISTER: The plump one with the lace tucker, who was being courted by Topper and who played blind man's buff at the Christmas party given by Scrooge's nephew. *A Christmas Carol*

SEAMSTRESS, THE LITTLE: She is in the La Force Prison with Charles Darnay and later goes to the guillotine with Sydney Carton, realizing that he is taking Darnay's place and finding comfort in his brave sacrifice. *A Tale of Two Cities*

SERAPHINA, LADY: She was the second daughter by the third marriage of Lord Decimus Barnacle, according to Mr. Meagles, who was trying to trace the position of Clarence Barnacle in the great family. *Little Dorrit*

SEXTON, THE OLD: An old man in the village where Little Nell dies. He shows her about the church and churchyard. *The Old Curiosity Shop*

SHARP, MR.: First master at Salem House, the school attended by David Copperfield, who dined and supped at the headmaster's table. *David Copperfield*

SHEEN AND GLOSS: Mercers who dealt only with the fashionable people in Society. *Bleak House*

SHEPHERD, MISS: A boarder at the Misses Nettingall's Establishment, with whom David, as a boy, falls in love. She eventually expresses preference for Master Jones, and the romance is over. *David Copperfield*

SHEPHERD, THE: *see* Stiggins, Mr.

SHINY WILLIAM: *see* William, Shiny

SHORT TROTTERS: *see* Harris (Punch and Judy man)

SHROPSHIRE, THE MAN FROM: *see* Gridley, Mr.

SIKES, BILL: A burglar and ferocious member of Fagin's gang. He plans the burglary of a house at Chertsey. Sikes, goaded on by Fagin, brutally murders his mistress, Nancy, is pursued by an infuriated mob, and is hanged by accident in trying to escape. *Oliver Twist*

SIMMERY, FRANK: In the office of Wilkins Flasher Esq., of the Stock Exchange, who makes various bets on all sorts of contingencies with Flasher. Tony Weller applies to the office regarding the sale of the shares left to him by Mrs. Weller. *Pickwick Papers*

SIMMONDS, MISS: One of the young ladies in the dressmaking and millinery workroom of Madame Mantalini's. She acts as a sort of chorus to Miss Knag, the forewoman. *Nicholas Nickleby*

SIMMONS, MRS. HENRIETTA: One of the guests at Mrs. Quilp's tea-party at Tower Hill, when Quilp suddenly appears to the great discomfiture of the ladies as they have all been discussing and criticizing him. *The Old Curiosity Shop*

SIMMONS, WILLIAM: Better known as Bill. Driver of a light van drawn by four horses who picks up young Martin Chuzzlewit at a small wayside public house and conveys him to Hounslow, on his way to London. He first gives the idea to Martin of going to America to make his fortune. *Martin Chuzzlewit*

SIMON: Servant of a drunken J.P., whose master wants to buy Barnaby's pet raven, Grip. *Barnaby Rudge*

SIMPSON, MR.: Prisoner in the Fleet, who was once a horse-chaunter. Mr. Pickwick was 'Chummed' on him and two others in cell No. 27. The three occupants of the cell decide to pay off Mr. Pickwick, who finds himself private lodgings elsewhere. *Pickwick Papers*

SINGLE GENTLEMAN, THE: The brother of Little Nell's grandfather, who took lodgings with Sampson Brass from whence he pursues his enquiries as to the whereabouts of the two wanderers. *The Old Curiosity Shop*

SKETTLES, LADY: Wife of Sir Barnet Skettles, with whom Florence Dombey stays at Fulham. She makes quite a fuss of Paul Dombey when he is taken ill at Dr. Blimber's, when she meets him at the school party. *Dombey and Son*

SKETTLES, MASTER: Son of Sir Barnet and Lady Skettles. He attends Dr. Blimber's school, at Brighton, and revenges himself for the studies to come, on the plum cake. When at home, on holiday, he was much stiffened as to his cravat, and sobered down as to his spirits. *Dombey and Son*

SKETTLES, SIR BARNET: An M.P., living at Fulham in a house on the banks of the Thames. A friend of Mr. Dombey, Sir Barnet's object in life was constantly to extend the range of his acquaintances. *Dombey and Son*

SKEWTON, THE HON. MRS.: Referred to also as Cleopatra. Mrs. Granger's mother, whose wish seemed to be to retreat to a Swiss Farm and live entirely surrounded by cows and china. Although the lady was not young, she was very blooming in the face—quite rosy—and her dress and attitude were perfectly juvenile. Her age was about seventy—her dress would have been youthful for twenty-seven . . . slightly setting her false curls and false eyebrows with her fan, and showing her false teeth, set off her false complexion. *Dombey and Son*

SKIFFINS: An accountant and agent, and brother of Miss Skiffins. Wemmick consults him on behalf of Pip to find a suitable business partnership for Pip to purchase for his friend Herbert Pocket. *Great Expectations*

SKIFFINS, MISS: She attended at the Castle at Walworth every Sunday afternoon, when the young servant was off duty, prepared tea, and washed up. She is courted by Wemmick and they eventually get married at Camberwell. *Great Expectations*

SKIMPIN, MR.: Junior barrister for Mrs. Bardell, under Sergeant Buzfuz. He examines Mr. Winkle and completely confuses him. *Pickwick Papers*

SKIMPOLE, ARETHUSA: Mr. Skimpole's beauty daughter, who plays and sings odds and ends like her father. *Bleak House*

SKIMPOLE, HAROLD: A friend of John Jarndyce, upon whom he depends for loans of money and getting him out of financial scrapes. He accepts no responsibility, is without principle and pretends to be a child, completely indifferent to the meaning or significance of money. Originally a medical man, but too lazy to turn his hand to anything. *Bleak House*

SKIMPOLE, KITTY: Harold Skimpole's comedy daughter, who, according to her father 'sings a little, but don't play'. *Bleak House*

SKIMPOLE, LAURA: Harold Skimpole's sentiment daughter, who, he says, 'plays a little but don't sing'. *Bleak House*

SKIMPOLE, MRS.: Wife of Harold Skimpole, who had once been a beauty, but was now a delicate, high-nosed invalid, suffering under a complication of disorders. *Bleak House*

'SKYLARK', MR.: A boatman whom David Copperfield meets when he is taken by Mr. Murdstone to Lowestoft. He had 'Skylark' printed across his barred shirt or vest, and David took this to be his name, which he put there because he lived aboard a ship and had no front door upon which to put it. *David Copperfield*

SLACKBRIDGE: A trade union agitator, who declaimed himself into a violent heat, and was as hoarse as he was hot. As a result of his agitation, Stephen Blackpool, who will not join the Union because of a promise he has given to Rachael, is sent to Coventry by his fellow workers and finally leaves his job. *Hard Times*

SLADDERY, MR.: A librarian who is concerned only with aristocratic circles. *Bleak House*

SLAMMER, DR.: Surgeon to the 97th Regiment at Chatham, who is insulted at the Charity Ball by Jingle. Jingle is wearing Mr. Winkle's special blue dress coat with Pickwick

Club buttons. This results in Mr. Winkle being challenged by Dr. Slammer to a duel. *Pickwick Papers*

SLASHER, MR.: Surgeon at St. Bartholomew's Hospital, London. According to Jack Hopkins, a medical student, Slasher took a boy's leg out of its socket and the boy ate five apples and a gingerbread cake exactly two minutes after it was all over. *Pickwick Papers*

SLEARY, JOSEPHINE: Daughter of Mr. Sleary, the circus proprietor. She marries E. W. B. Childers and they have a boy who takes to circus riding. *Hard Times*

SLEARY, MR.: Owner of the circus, who is instrumental in getting Tom Gradgrind out of the country when he is in danger of being captured and accused of robbing Bounderby's bank. *Hard Times*

SLIDERSKEW, PEG: Housekeeper to Arthur Gride, the ancient old moneylender. She is very put out when Arthur Gride proposes marrying a very young girl, Madeline Bray. She is concerned with Squeers in the destruction of documents, and, being found guilty, was sent overseas at the same time as Squeers and never returned. *Nicholas Nickleby*

SLINGO: A dealer in horses, who is in the debtors' prison. When he comes out he promises to give Tip Dorrit a berth. This results in Tip himself coming back to the prison as one of the debtors. *Little Dorrit*

SLOPPY: A love-child who is cared for by old Betty Higden, and helps her with her mangling. He is taken by the Boffins and looked after when Betty Higden goes away and eventually dies, and is taught woodwork, at which he becomes very useful. He gets to know Jenny Wren, the doll's dressmaker, and he makes several useful gadgets in wood for her. *Our Mutual Friend*

SLOUT, MR.: Master of the workhouse, whose place Mr. Bumble plans to take if Mrs. Corney consents to marry him. *Oliver Twist*

SLOWBOY, TILLY: Servant to Mr. and Mrs. Peerybingle, and nurse to the baby. She is always getting the baby into difficulties and endangering its head. *The Cricket on the Hearth*

SLUM, MR.: He is a poet who sells rhymes advertising various commodities and businesses. He offered Mrs. Jarley an acrostic which he would adapt from Warren's. *The Old Curiosity Shop*

SLUMKEY, THE HON. SAMUEL: Of Slumkey Hall. The successful Blue candidate for Parliament in the Eatanswill election. He shook hands with twenty washed workmen, patted the babies on the head and kissed them all. *Pickwick Papers*

SLUMMINTOWKENS, THE: Social acquaintances of the Nupkins family at Ipswich, about whose opinion Mrs. Nupkins is particularly worried, should it come out that the particular 'catch' the Nupkins had flourished—Captain Fitz-Marshall—is in reality the strolling player, Jingle. *Pickwick Papers*

SLURK, MR.: Editor of the *Eatanswill Independent*, the Buff newspaper and great rival of Mr. Pott, who runs the *Eatanswill Gazette*. *Pickwick Papers*

SLYME, CHEVY: A relative of old Martin Chuzzlewit, who makes his way through life with the assistance of his friend Montague Tigg. He was said to be perpetually round the corner. *Martin Chuzzlewit*

SMALDER GIRLS, THE: Acquaintances of Cousin Feenix who sees them when he is attending Mrs. Skewton's funeral at Brighton. *Dombey and Son*

SMALLCHEEK: Sam Weller's name for the half-booted leather-legginned boy, who at the shooting party mentions that there is a barrow the other side of the hedge, in which Mr. Pickwick can be wheeled. *Pickwick Papers*

SMALLWEED, JOSHUA: Grandfather of the family. A moneylender and discounter of bills. He tries to blackmail Sir Leicester Dedlock by the production of a will found in Krook's papers, but is frustrated by Inspector Bucket. 'A leech in his disposition, a screw and a vice in his actions, a snake in his twistings, and a lobster in his claws.' *Bleak House*

SMALLWEED, JUDITH: Known as Judy, she is the sister of Bartholomew Smallweed. She never owned a doll and never played at any game. Whenever her grandfather falls back in his chair, after throwing a cushion at his wife, she shakes him up like a great bottle and sits him up again. *Bleak House*

SMALLWEED, MRS.: Grandmother of the family. Sister of Krook, the rag-dealer. She is stone deaf and whenever she sees her husband speaking, counts up large sums of money. He calls her various names—brimstone chatterer, jade of a magpie, jack-daw, poll-parrot, brimstone pig, etc. She has an eternal disposition to fall asleep over the fire and into it. *Bleak House*

SMALLWEED, YOUNG BARTHOLOMEW (BART): Twin with Judith. He works as clerk at Kenge and Carboys, solicitors, and is a friend of Mr. Guppy and Jobling. He has various nicknames and is known as 'Chick'. *Bleak House*

SMANGLE, MR.: Prisoner in the Fleet Prison, in whose cell Mr. Pickwick is accommodated for his first night. He suggests that Mr. Pickwick should pay for burnt sherry for all the occupants of the cell. *Pickwick Papers*

SMART, TOM: A friend of the bagman's uncle and traveller for the firm of Bilson and Slum. He prevents the marriage of Jinkins to the landlady of the inn on the Marlborough Downs, by disclosing to her that Jinkins is already married. Tom eventually marries her himself. Interpolated story: 'The Bagman's Story'. Told by the one-eyed bagman in the Peacock at Eatanswill. *Pickwick Papers*

SMAUKER, JOHN: Angelo Bantam's footman, who invites Sam Weller to the 'swarry' at Bath. *Pickwick Papers*

SMIF, PUTNAM: A clerk in Hancock and Floby, a dry-goods store in America. *Martin Chuzzlewit*

SMIFSER: One of Mrs. Nickleby's suitors. *Nicholas Nickleby*

SMIGGERS, JOSEPH: Perpetual Vice-president of the Pickwick Club, who presides over the meeting of the club, at which the Corresponding Society is formed. *Pickwick Papers*

SMIKE: Son of Ralph Nickleby. A clerk in Ralph's employ, Brookes, conceals the survival of the boy, and Smike, by which name he is known, is put with Mr. Squeers at Dotheboys Hall, where he remains as a lame half-witted drudge. He escapes from the school and joins Nicholas Nickleby, who has also run away, after giving the schoolmaster a thrashing. Nicholas and Smike journey to London and then to Portsmouth, where they obtain work under the names of Johnson and Digby, with the Vincent Crummles Theatrical Company. On returning to London to rescue his sister, Nicholas brings Smike with him and he is accommodated with Mrs. Nickleby and Kate. Smike falls in love with Kate, but becomes ill and dies in Devonshire. *Nicholas Nickleby*

SMITHERS, MISS: A boarder at Westgate House, Bury St. Edmunds, a young ladies' boarding establishment. When Mr. Pickwick gets into the garden at night to prevent an elopement, Miss Smithers sees him hiding behind the door leading into the garden and gives the alarm. *Pickwick Papers*

SMITHERS AND PRICE: A legal firm whose chancery clerk attended the social gathering at the Magpie and Stump. *Pickwick Papers*

SMITHIE FAMILY, THE: Husband, wife and two daughters attending the charity ball at the Bull Inn, Rochester. They were said to be something in the Yard and were acknowledged and bowed to by Sir Thomas Clubber, who was Commissioner and Head of the Yard, and Lady Clubber and her daughters. *Pickwick Papers*

SMIVEY, CHICKEN: Of Holborn—26½b, lodger. The name and address given by Montague Tigg to the pawnbroker, when young Martin Chuzzlewit pawned his watch. *Martin Chuzzlewit*

SMORLTORK, COUNT: A foreign visitor, interested in literature, who attends Mrs. Leo Hunter's *fête champêtre*. He was gathering materials for his 'great work on England'. *Pickwick Papers*

SMOUCH: The sheriff's assistant who helps in taking Mr. Pickwick from the George and Vulture to the Fleet. *Pickwick Papers*

SNAGSBY, MR.: Law stationer in Cook's Court, near Lincoln's Inn. He becomes slightly involved with Lady Dedlock's secret, rather against his will, and incurs the suspicion of his wife. He is kind to Jo, the crossing-sweeper, which increases his wife's suspicion. *Bleak House*

SNAGSBY, MRS.: Wife of the law stationer and niece of Mr. Peffer, his late business partner. Her unjustified suspicion of her husband is eventually dissipated by Inspector Bucket. *Bleak House*

SNAWLEY, MR.: Stepfather of two boys—Snawley junior and his brother, left with Squeers as pupils. He is later paid by Ralph Nickleby to declare himself the father of Smike in an endeavour to take the boy away from Nicholas. Ralph does not realize that he is persecuting his own son. Squeers lodges with Snawley's wife. *Nicholas Nickleby*

SNEVELLICCI, MISS: A member of the Vincent Crummles Theatrical Company, who takes a fancy to Nicholas, but he does not return her feelings. She could do anything from a medley dance to Lady Macbeth, and always played some part in blue silk knee-smalls, at her benefit—glancing from the depths of her coal-scuttle bonnet. She was one of Henrietta Petwoker's bridesmaids. She was later married to an affluent young wax-chandler, who had supplied candles to the theatre. *Nicholas Nickleby*

SNEVELLICCI, MR.: Father of Miss Snevellicci and rather given to drinking. He had been in the theatrical profession since he first played ten-year-old imps in Christmas pantomimes. He occasionally beats his wife, Mrs. Snevellicci, who is still a dancer with a neat little figure. *Nicholas Nickleby*

SNEWKES, MR.: He was supposed to entertain honourable designs on a sister of Mrs. Kenwigs, who is asked to the party to meet Uncle Lillyvick. *Nicholas Nickleby*

SNICKS, MR.: Life Office Secretary, who attends the dinner party given by Mr. Perker. *Pickwick Papers*

SNIGGLE AND BLINK: One of the firms called out in the office of Namby, the sheriff, while Mr. Pickwick was waiting to be committed to the Fleet Prison. *Pickwick Papers*

SNIGSWORTH, LORD: Of Snigsworthy Park. Cousin of Mr. Twenlow, for which connection Twenlow was much in demand in Society. *Our Mutual Friend*

SNIPE, THE HONOURABLE WILMOT: According to Mr. Tupman's impression he was a 'little boy with the light hair and pink eyes'. He was an Ensign in the 97th Regiment and came from a great family. *Pickwick Papers*

SNITCHEY, JONATHAN: Attorney-at-law and partner of the firm of Snitchey and Craggs. He is like a magpie or raven, only not so sleek. *The Battle of Life*

SNITCHEY, MRS.: His wife, who is highly suspicious of his partner Craggs, as Mrs. Craggs is of Snitchey. In general they are all very friendly. *The Battle of Life*

SNOBB, THE HONOURABLE MR.: A guest of Ralph Nickleby at his dinner party, given to get business from Lord Verisopht. *Nicholas Nickleby*

SNOBBY: *see* Nubbles, Kit. (Mr. Chuckster's nickname for him)

SNODGRASS, AUGUSTUS: A close friend of Mr. Pickwick, member of the Pickwick Club and also of the Corresponding Society. Reputed to be a great poet. He marries Emily Wardle in Dulwich Church and settles down on a small farm near to Dingley Dell. *Pickwick Papers*

'SNOOKS': *see* Bonney, Mr.

SNOOKS: *see* Dorrit, W.

SNUBBIN, SERJEANT: Senior counsel for Mr. Pickwick, in the Bardell *v.* Pickwick case. He was 'a lantern-faced, sallow-complexioned man, of about five and forty . . . or fifty'. *Pickwick Papers*

SNUFFIM, SIR TUMLEY: The doctor who attends Mrs. Wittitterly, Kate Nickleby's employer. He told Mr. Wittitterly that her complaint was soul. *Nicholas Nickleby*

SNUPHANUPH, THE DOWAGER LADY: One of the old harridans with whom Mr. Pickwick plays whist in the Assembly Rooms at Bath. 'Of an ancient and whist-like appearance.' Lady Snuphanuph and Mrs. Colonel Wugsby won. *Pickwick Papers*

SOLS, MR.: Toots' name for old Sol Gills. *See* Gills, Sol

SOPHIA: Daughter in the brass- and copper-founder's family at Camberwell, and pupil of Ruth Pinch who is encouraged by her parents to look upon Miss Pinch as a beggar. *Martin Chuzzlewit*

Housemaid to Mr. and Mrs. Matthew Pocket. *Great Expectations*

SOWERBERRY, MR.: Undertaker who carries out the parochial funerals for paupers. Oliver Twist is apprenticed to him and trained as a mute for children's funerals. He is kindly disposed towards Oliver, but when the boy fights the other apprentice, Noah Claypole, for saying insulting things about Oliver's mother, Sowerberry is obliged to thrash Oliver, who runs away. *Oliver Twist*

SOWERBERRY, MRS.: The undertaker's wife—a short, thin, squeezed-up woman, with a vixenish countenance. She feeds Oliver on scraps intended for the dog. *Oliver Twist*

SOWNDS, MR.: The beadle at the church where Paul Dombey is christened and where Mr. Dombey marries his second wife, Edith Granger. *Dombey and Son*

SPARKLER (DECEASED), COLONEL: First husband of Mrs. Merdle. They had one son, Edmund. *Little Dorrit*

SPARKLER, EDMUND: Son of Colonel Sparkler—'of a chuckle-headed, high-shouldered make, with a general appearance of being, not so much a young man as a swelled boy'. He marries Fanny Dorrit, who, prior to her coming into money, he had known as a dancer at the theatre. *Little Dorrit*

SPARSIT (DECEASED), MR.: The late husband of Mr. Bounderby's housekeeper, Mrs. Sparsit. He had been on his mother's side, what Mrs. Sparsit called a 'powler'. *Hard Times*

SPARSIT, MRS.: Mr. Bounderby's housekeeper. In her elderly days, with the Coriolanian style of nose, and the dense black eyebrows, she had captivated Sparsit. She unwisely discovers Mr. Bounderby's old mother, for which she is discharged. *Hard Times*

SPENLOW, CLARISSA AND LAVINIA: Two maiden sisters of Mr. Spenlow, living at Putney. When her father dies, Dora goes to live with them. David courts Dora at Putney, having obtained the permission of her aunts. *David Copperfield*

SPENLOW, DORA: Only daughter of Mr. Spenlow, a proctor in Doctors' Commons, and David Copperfield's employer. David and Dora fall in love and after Mr. Spenlow's sudden death, they marry. She proves quite hopeless in domestic affairs and dies after losing her baby. *David Copperfield*

SPENLOW, FRANCIS: Father of Dora Spenlow and partner in the firm of Spenlow and Jorkins, Proctors of Doctors' Commons. David is articled to the firm, but Mr. Spenlow dies, leaving his affairs in a chaotic state, and his daughter to live with her two maiden aunts. *David Copperfield*

SPHYNX, SOPHRONIA: *see* Marchioness, The

SPIDER, THE: *see* Drummle, Bentley. (Mr. Jaggers' nickname for Bentley Drummle)

SPIKER, HENRY: A solicitor to someone connected with the Treasury. He is a guest at Mr. Waterbrook's where Agnes Wickfield stays when in London. David visits her at this house. *David Copperfield*

SPIKER, MRS. HENRY: Wife of Henry Spiker, was also a visitor at Mr. Waterbrook's, and great deference was shown to both of them. 'A very awful lady in a black velvet dress, and a great black velvet hat . . . looking like a near relative of Hamlet's—say his aunt.' *David Copperfield*

SPILLER AND SPOKER: Who executed the portrait and bust of Mr. Pecksniff. *Martin Chuzzlewit*

SPOFFINS: Name given by Lavinia Wilfer to the Boffins. *See* Boffin, Mr. and Mrs.

SPOTTLETOE, MR: Husband of old Martin Chuzzlewit's niece. He and his wife join a number of other members of the Chuzzlewit family at a meeting at Mr. Pecksniff's house. He withdrew from the meeting after holding his clenched fist close to Mr. Pecksniff's eye. *Martin Chuzzlewit*

SPOTTLETOE, MRS.: Old Martin Chuzzlewit's niece—at one time his favourite. She also withdraws from the meeting at Mr. Pecksniff's house—following her husband. *Martin Chuzzlewit*

SPRODGKIN, MRS. SALLY: A parishioner of the Rev. Frank Milvey, and one of the plagues of his life. *Our Mutual Friend*

SPYERS, JEM: A police officer who arrests the criminal, Conkey Chickweed. *Oliver Twist*

SQUEERS, FANNY: Daughter of Squeers, the schoolmaster, who took a fancy to Nicholas Nickleby, when he came to Dotheboys Hall, as teacher. She turns against Nicholas when she finds that he does not return her 'love'. *Nicholas Nickleby*

SQUEERS, MASTER WACKFORD: Only son of Mr. Squeers. A striking likeness of his father. The strange thing was that the new clothes of every boy who came to the school seemed to fit him. When his father was sentenced to transportation and Dotheboys Hall broke up, the boys dipped his head into the bowl of brimstone and treacle. *Nicholas Nickleby*

SQUEERS, MRS.: Wife of the schoolmaster, who dosed the boys with brimstone and treacle to take away their appetites for breakfast. She called Nicholas 'Knuckleboy', and hated him. She was eventually made to take her own brimstone and treacle by the boys. *Nicholas Nickleby*

SQUEERS, WACKFORD: The Yorkshire schoolmaster of Dotheboys Hall, brutal and ignorant. 'He had but one eye, and the popular prejudice runs in favour of two. The eye he had was unquestionably useful, but decidedly not ornamental, being of a greenish grey, and in shape resembling the fan-light of a street door.' He was eventually caught trying to suppress some documents and was transported for seven years. *Nicholas Nickleby*

SQUOD, PHIL: Lame man-of-all-work in George Rouncewell's shooting-gallery. He was picked out of the gutter by George Rouncewell and cared for. *Bleak House*

STABLES, THE HONOURABLE BOB: Cousin to Sir Leicester Dedlock, admirer of Lady Dedlock. *Bleak House*

STAGG: A blind man who keeps an underground cellar where Sim Tappertit, the locksmith's apprentice, holds the meetings of the United Bull Dogs. He becomes acquainted with Rudge the elder, and on his behalf traces Mrs. Rudge and Barnaby to the country, where they are hiding. He blackmails Mrs. Rudge into giving him money. *Barnaby Rudge*

STANLEY, SIR HUBERT: The Dombey family doctor refers to Doctor Parker Peps by this name to flatter him. *Dombey and Son*

STAPLE, MR.: A member of the Dingley Dell cricket team. He was called upon by the Vice-chairman at the cricket dinner following the match with All Muggleton, to propose a toast to the Chairman, Mr. Dumkins. *Pickwick Papers*

STARELEIGH, MR. JUSTICE: The judge who presides over the case Bardell *v.* Pickwick; he sat in the absence of the Chief Justice, who was indisposed. He was so fat that he seemed all face and waistcoat. *Pickwick Papers*

STARTOP: One of Mr. Matthew Pocket's living-in pupils. A friend of Pip. He and Herbert Pocket eventually help Pip in an endeavour to smuggle Magwitch, the escaped convict, out of the country. *Great Expectations*

STEERFORTH, JAMES: Head boy at Salem House when David Copperfield joins the school. Later he becomes a close friend of David, who introduces him into the Peggotty household at Great Yarmouth. He seduces Little Em'ly who goes abroad with him, but he abandons her. He is later drowned in his yacht in a storm off Yarmouth, and Ham Peggotty, the man he wronged, is also drowned in trying to save him. *David Copperfield*

STEERFORTH, MRS.: Steerforth's mother who idolizes her son, but is estranged from him when he deserts her to go abroad with a common fisherman's niece, Little Em'ly. She later becomes mentally unbalanced and is left with Rosa Dartle, a cruel companion, to look after her. *David Copperfield*

STETTA, VIOLETTA: Of the Italian Opera, who had a certain income guaranteed by the Duke of Thigsberry. *The Old Curiosity Shop*

STIGGINS, MR.: A 'shepherd' who frequented the Marquis of Granby, at Dorking, and was addicted to pineapple rum, with which he frequently replenished his bottle. When

Mrs. Weller dies he tries to resume his place in the Marquis of Granby, but is kicked out by Tony Weller and his head ducked in the horse-trough outside. *Pickwick Papers*

STILTSTALKING, AUGUSTUS, TOM, DICK, HARRY, and TUDOR: All members of the great and noble family who married into the Barnacle family. *Little Dorrit*

STILTSTALKING, LORD LANCASTER: He had been maintained by the Circumlocution Office for many years as a representative of the Britannic Majesty abroad. He attends a dinner in Mrs. Gowan's Grace and Favour apartments in Hampton Court Palace. *Little Dorrit*

STORR AND MORTIMER: Fashionable jewellers to whom Mr. Merdle was likened as he married Mrs. Merdle 'to hang jewels on'. *Little Dorrit*

STRONG, DR.: Schoolmaster at the school in Canterbury to which David Copperfield is sent by his aunt, Betsey Trotwood. He was married to a very young wife, Annie, and was engaged on the compilation of a new dictionary, which the boys in the school calculated, at the doctor's rate of going, would be completed in one thousand six hundred and forty-nine years. *David Copperfield*

STRONG, MRS. ANNIE: Dr. Strong's young and beautiful wife, who before her marriage had been inclined towards her cousin Jack Maldon. An attempt by Uriah Heep to cause a rift between the doctor and Annie fails. *David Copperfield*

STRUGGLES, MR.: A bowler in the Dingley Dell Club who was put on to bowl against the hitherto unconquered Podder, of All Muggleton. *Pickwick Papers*

STRYVER, MR.: Counsel for Charles Darnay when he was tried as a spy at the Old Bailey. Stryver decided to offer himself to Lucie Manette as a desirable suitor, but was dissuaded from doing so by Mr. Lorry, the banker, who gave the opinion that he would be unsuccessful. He was stout, loud, red, bluff and free from any drawback of delicacy. *A Tale of Two Cities*

STRYVER, MRS.: Wife of Mr. Stryver—a florid widow with property and three boys, who had nothing particularly shining about them but the straight hair of their dumpling heads. *A Tale of Two Cities*

STUMPS, BILL: A labourer in the village of Cobham said to have been responsible for the inscription on the stone discovered by Mr. Pickwick and thought to be of very ancient origin. The inscription was said by Mr. Blotton, Mr. Pickwick's rival in the Pickwick Club, to stand for 'Bill Stumps His Mark'. *Pickwick Papers*

STUMPY AND DEACON: One of the firms called out in Namby's sponging-house. *Pickwick Papers*

SUFFOLK BANTAM, THE: A pugilist, whose contest with the Middlesex Dumpling was prohibited by Mr. Nupkins, Mayor of Ipswich. *Pickwick Papers*

SUMMERSON, ESTHER: Illegitimate daughter of Lady Dedlock and Captain Hawdon; niece of Miss Barbary and narrator of part of the story. She becomes housekeeper to John Jarndyce and companion of Ada Clare, one of his Wards in Chancery. Esther is proposed to by Mr. Guppy, clerk of Kenge and Carboy, but accepts the proposal of John Jarndyce to become the mistress of Bleak House. Jarndyce, however, relinquishes her to a younger man, with whom she is secretly in love—Alan Woodcourt, a doctor. She eventually marries him. She was given various nicknames—Dame Durden, Cobweb, etc. *Bleak House*

SUSAN: Servant of Mrs. Mann, matron of the branch workhouse for younger children, where Oliver is sent. *Oliver Twist*

SWALLOW: The owner of a chaise, which Mrs. Squeers takes in her search for Smike. *Nicholas Nickleby*

SWALLOW, MR.: A correspondent to whom Mrs. Jellyby is dictating a letter when Esther Summerson, Ada Clare, and Richard Carstone are made known to her. *Bleak House*

SWEEDLEPIPE, PAUL (POLL): Barber and bird fancier, who has his business in Kingsgate Street, and is Mrs. Gamp's landlord. *Martin Chuzzlewit*

SWEET WILLIAM: *see* William, Sweet

SWIDGER, PHILIP: An old man—former custodian of the institution in which Mr. Redlaw is lecturer, and head of the family of Swidgers. CHARLEY, JUNIOR: Nephew of Mrs. Swidger, aged twelve, who rowed her into the piers at Battersea. GEORGE: Eldest son of old Philip, a bold man who died under unhappy circumstances. WILLIAM: Youngest son of old Philip, servant to Mr. Redlaw, and husband of Milly. MRS. MILLY: Wife of William Swidger, the embodiment of good who has an improving influence on all the family. *The Haunted Man*

SWILLENHAUSEN, BARON VON: His daughter was demanded in marriage by the Baron von Koëldwethout of Germany. Interpolated story, told at the inn where the coach passengers rest, including Nicholas Nickleby and Squeers, following the accident to the coach on the way to Yorkshire. *Nicholas Nickleby*

SWILLS, LITTLE: A comic singer and entertainer, who appears at the harmonic meetings held at the Sol's Arms, in the court near Lincoln's Inn. *Bleak House*

SWIVELLER, REBECCA: Dick Swiveller's aunt in Chiselbourne, Dorset, who instead of a sum of five and twenty thousand pounds, left him an annuity of one hundred and fifty pounds a year. *The Old Curiosity Shop*

SWIVELLER, RICHARD (DICK): Dissipated friend of Fred Trent, Little Nell's brother. Dick was founder of the drinking club, the 'Glorious Apollers'. Quilp plans that he should marry Little Nell and come into her supposed fortune and Dick breaks off his engagement to Sophy Wackles. The scheme comes to nothing. Dick Swiveller is nursed through a serious illness by the Marchioness, servant of

Sampson and Sally Brass. After having her educated, Dick marries her. *The Old Curiosity Shop*

SWOSHLE, MRS. HENRY GEORGE ALFRED: Née Tapkins, who with many other members of her family—Mrs. Tapkins, Miss Tapkins, Antonia, Euphemia, Frederica, and Malvina Tapkins, finds that she has omitted to leave a card on Mr. and Mrs. Boffin and Miss Bella Wilfer—most important as the Boffins have come into money. *Our Mutual Friend*

SWOSSER, CAPTAIN: Of the Royal Navy and the 'dear old *Crippler*'. He is the first husband of Mrs. Bayham Badger. She was barely twenty when she married him. It was at a ball on board the *Crippler*, in Plymouth Harbour, when, Captain Swosser used to say, he fell—raked fore and aft by the fire from her tops (a naval way of mentioning her eyes). *Bleak House*

T

TACKER: The chief mourner of Mr. Mould, the undertaker, who arranges the funeral of Anthony Chuzzlewit. An obese person, with his waistcoat in closer connection with his legs than is quite reconcilable with the established ideas of grace. *Martin Chuzzlewit*

TACKLETON: Owner of Gruff and Tackleton, toy merchants. He employs an old man, Caleb Plummer and his blind daughter, Bertha. Bertha idolizes him, thinking in her blindness that he is kind and benevolent, and hides it under his brusque manner, but he openly despises her. He plans to marry a young girl, May Fielding, whose sailor lover has disappeared. Her lover returns, however, in time to prevent the marriage. *The Cricket on the Hearth*

TADGER, BROTHER: Member of the Brick Lane Branch of the United Grand Junction Ebenezer Temperance Association. He introduces Mr. Stiggins to the meeting, who, being the worse for drink himself, accuses Brother Tadger of being drunk. *Pickwick Papers*

TAMAROO: Supposed to be the name of the successor to Bailey junior at Mrs. Todgers' Boarding Establishment. Mrs. Todgers vowed that she would have no more boys working for her as servants. She was an ancient female 'chiefly remarkable for a total absence of all comprehension upon every subject whatever. She was a perfect tomb for messages and small parcels'. She waited at table in a bonnet. *Martin Chuzzlewit*

TANGLE, MR.: He knew more about the case of Jarndyce and Jarndyce than anybody. *Bleak House*

TAPKINS, MISS: *see* Swoshle, Mrs. Henry George Alfred

TAPLEY, MARK: Odd-job man and hostler at the Blue Dragon, he later attaches himself to young Martin Chuzzlewit and goes to America to look after him. Having contributed part of the money to purchase a plot of land at Eden, he becomes the 'Co' of Chuzzlewit & Co. He returns to England with Martin and eventually marries Mrs. Lupin, owner of the Blue Dragon, which is re-named the Jolly Tapley. *Martin Chuzzlewit*

TAPPERTIT, SIMON (SIM): Apprentice to Gabriel Varden, locksmith. He makes himself head of the 'United Bull Dogs', a band of dissatisfied apprentices. He fancies himself in love with Gabriel Varden's daughter, Dolly, and is loved himself in turn by Miggs, the maidservant and companion in the Varden household. Sim defies his master and joins the Gordon Rioters. Both his little spindly legs, of which he is very proud, are crushed in the Riots and he sets up with two wooden legs as a shoe-black, under an archway, by the Horse Guards. He later marries the widow of a rag-and-bone merchant. *Barnaby Rudge*

TAPPERTIT, MRS.: Widow of a rag-and-bone merchant, who keeps control of Simon by taking away his wooden legs and rendering him immobile. *Barnaby Rudge*

TAPPLETON, LIEUTENANT: Friend of Dr. Slammer, who calls on Mr. Winkle, on the morning after the charity ball at the Bull Inn, Rochester, and arranges details of the duel between Slammer and Winkle. He finds Mr. Winkle by the description of his special Pickwick Club coat, which, unknown to them, Mr. Jingle borrowed and wore at the ball. *Pickwick Papers*

TARTAR, MR.: A retired naval lieutenant living in chambers in Staple Inn. He makes the acquaintance of Rosa Bud and appears to be much attracted by her. *The Mystery of Edwin Drood*

TARTARY, EMPEROR OF: Referred to by the old lunatic next door, who courted Mrs. Nickleby by throwing vegetables into the garden. *Nicholas Nickleby*

TATTYCORAM: Pet Meagles' maid, who came from the Foundling Hospital. Her real name is Harriet Beadle. She is jealous of Pet and rather passionate. She runs away with Miss Wade, a bitter and sullen woman, full of fancied wrongs. Tattycoram is later glad to return to Mr. and Mrs. Meagles. *Little Dorrit*

TAYLOR, JEMMY: *see* Boffin, N.

TELLSON & CO.: A French/English bank by Temple Bar, for which Mr. Jarvis Lorry is confidential clerk. *A Tale of Two Cities*

TERRIERS TIP: *see* Jo

TETTERBY, ADOLPHUS: A newsvendor who had seven boys and one girl, and had a small corner shop under the name of A. Tetterby & Co. He also dealt in walking-sticks, marbles, bull's eyes and wax dolls, but most of these items were failures and remained in the window in great confusion. *The Haunted Man*

TETTERBY, 'DOLPHUS: Elder son of the Tetterbys. He was in the newspaper line, being employed to sell newspapers at a railway station, where his shrill little voice became as well known as the panting of the locomotives. *The Haunted Man*

TETTERBY, JOHNNY: Second son of the Tetterbys, whose knees were considerably affected by the weight of a large baby, Sally, the Moloch (the youngest in the family), whom he was usually carrying about, trying to hush to sleep. *The Haunted Man*

TETTERBY, MRS. SOPHIA: Although referred to by her husband as his little woman, she would have made two editions of himself quite easily. *The Haunted Man*

TETTERBY, SALLY: *see* Moloch, Little

THIGSBERRY, DUKE OF: Who guarantees an income to Violetta Stetta, of the Italian Opera. *The Old Curiosity Shop*

THOMAS: Groom to Sir Leicester Dedlock, who tells Mrs. Rouncewell, the housekeeper, that Lady Dedlock has not been well in town. *Bleak House*

Mr. Mortimer Knag's boy who works in the ornamental stationery and circulating library shop, in a by-street off Tottenham Court Road. He was told to close the warehouse at ten. *Nicholas Nickleby*

Waiter at the restaurant where the gentleman dined—a cut off the joint for one and nine, every night on principle. *Pickwick Papers*

TICKIT, MRS.: Cook and housekeeper to the Meagles family at Twickenham. When the family were away she established herself in the breakfast-room and sat looking over the blind all day. She had a grandchild who came to see her occasionally. *Little Dorrit*

TIFFEY, MR.: An old clerk at Spenlow and Jorkins, Doctors' Commons. He had a stiff brown wig that looked as if it was made of gingerbread. He had been to Mr. Spenlow's house on business several times and had partaken of brown East India Sherry in the breakfast parlour, of a quality so precious that it made him wink. *David Copperfield*

TIGG, MONTAGUE: A disreputable friend of Chevy Slyme (one of the Chuzzlewit family). He is paid money for services by old Martin Chuzzlewit, with which he forms a bogus insurance company called the Anglo-Bengalee Disinterested Loan and Life Insurance Company, and changes his name to Tigg Montague, and lives on credit. By obtaining a hold on Jonas Chuzzlewit, he forces him to join the company and to introduce Mr. Pecksniff. Jonas eventually murders him in a thicket in Wiltshire, whilst on a business trip. As Montague Tigg he was shabby genteel, but as Tigg Montague he was exceedingly smart. *Martin Chuzzlewit*

TIGGIN AND WELPS: Employers of the bagman's uncle, in the calico and waistcoat piece line. Interpolated story told by the one-eyed bagman in The Bush at Bristol. *Pickwick Papers*

TIM, TINY: Youngest son of Bob Cratchit, and a cripple. In Scrooge's dream he dies, but, after reforming, Scrooge looks after him with the rest of the family. *A Christmas Carol*

TIMBERRY, SNITTLE: An actor in the Crummles company, who played a faithful black in the last piece, and it took him longer than the others to wash himself. He was vice-chairman at the farewell dinner given to Mr. Crummles in a tavern, prior to the departure of the Crummles family for America. *Nicholas Nickleby*

TINKLER, MR.: Valet to Mr. Dorrit, after the latter's acquisition of riches. Mr. Dorrit watches him closely to see if he has anything on his mind prejudicial to the family dignity. *Little Dorrit*

TIPKINS: A churchwarden in a case heard in Doctors' Commons, against Bullock, one of whom was alleged to have pushed the other against a pump. The handle of the pump projecting into a schoolhouse, which in turn was under a gable of the church roof, made it an ecclesiastical offence. The case was attended by David Copperfield. *David Copperfield*

TIPP: A carman in the warehouse of Murdstone and Grinby, Blackfriars, who wore a red jacket. He sometimes calls David Copperfield, David, although the others mostly speak of him as 'the little gent', or 'the young Suffolker'. *David Copperfield*

TIPPINS, LADY: Guest of Mr. and Mrs. Veneering, scandalmonger and generally the 'voice of Society'. 'With an immense, obtuse, drab, oblong face, like a face in a tablespoon.' She raps the knuckles of her left hand—which is particularly rich in knuckles and calls upon her so-called lovers ('a grizzly little fiction') to do her bidding. Her late husband, Sir Thomas, was knighted in mistake for somebody else. *Our Mutual Friend*

TIPSLARK: One of the many suitors recalled by Mrs. Nickleby. *Nicholas Nickleby*

TISHER, MRS.: Miss Twinkleton's companion in the Nun's House, at Cloisterham. She is a deferential widow who looks after the young ladies' wardrobes, and leads them to infer that she has seen better days. The servants have decided among themselves that the departed Tisher was a hairdresser. *The Mystery of Edwin Drood*

TIX, TOM: A bailiff who accompanies Scaley when they take possession of Madame Mantalini's dressmaking establishment, on account of Mr. Mantalini's debts. He is left in possession overnight by Scaley. *Nicholas Nickleby*

TOCKAHOOPO INDIANS: To whom Egbert Pardiggle sent his pocket money of five and threepence. At the mention of the Tockahoopo Indians, Egbert gives a savage frown. *Bleak House*

TODDLES: The pet name of a boy who was a 'minder', and who had been left with Poddles, to be minded by Mrs. Betty Turner, for fourpence a week. *Our Mutual Friend*

TODGERS, MRS. M.: Proprietress of a communal boarding establishment near the Monument. She is an old friend of Mr. Pecksniff and his two daughters and had once had hopes of his marrying her. Pecksniff lodges with Mrs. Todgers, and when Charity Pecksniff leaves her father's house in the country, she lives with Mrs. Todgers and would have been married from that establishment if her fiancé had not deserted her on the day of her wedding. Mrs. Todgers also looks after the other sister, Mercy, when her husband, Jonas Chuzzlewit, commits suicide. Her great anxiety in life was to satisfy her gentleman boarders with enough gravy. *Martin Chuzzlewit*

TOLLIMGLOWER, LADY: A friend of old Mrs. Wardle, recalled by her on two occasions, once at the wedding of Trundle and Isabella and again at the wedding of Snodgrass and Emily Wardle. *Pickwick Papers*

TOM: One of the undertaker's men at Anthony Chuzzlewit's funeral. *Martin Chuzzlewit*

A stout country lad at the Leather Bottle who shows Mr. Pickwick and his friends into the parlour where they find Mr. Tupman enjoying his lunch, although he was supposed to have taken leave of the world. *Pickwick Papers*

Mr. Wardle's coachman who drove the barouche at the military tournament and the gig in pursuit of Jingle and Rachael Wardle. *Pickwick Papers*

See also Cripps, Tom

The boy in the General Agency Office to whom Nicholas Nickleby applies for a job. He is later knocked down by Frank Cheeryble for making disparaging remarks about a lady known to Frank. *Nicholas Nickleby*

The driver of the Dover Mail, in which Mr. Jarvis Lorry is travelling as a passenger on his way to France and which is stopped by Jerry Cruncher with a message for Mr. Lorry— 'Wait at Dover for Mam'selle', which he answered with the message, 'Recalled to life'. *A Tale of Two Cities*

Dan'l Peggotty's brother-in-law, who is Little Em'ly's father. According to Mr. Peggotty, he was 'drowndead'. *David Copperfield*

One of the officers arresting Jonas Chuzzlewit for the murder of Tigg Montague. *Martin Chuzzlewit*

TOM, CAPTAIN: A prisoner in Newgate seen by Mr. Wemmick. *Great Expectations*

TOM, HONEST: *see* Honest Tom

TOM, UNCLE: The pawnbroker with whom Jingle had pawned his coat and other belongings when he was in the Fleet Debtors' Prison. *Pickwick Papers*

TOMKINS, MISS: The proprietress of Westgate House, Bury St. Edmunds, a girls' school, over the wall of which Mr. Pickwick is put at night by Sam Weller, in his attempt to prevent an elopement—in reality a plot of Mr. Jingle to fool Mr. Pickwick. She questions Mr. Pickwick. *Pickwick Papers*

TOMPKINS: A pupil at Dotheboys Hall, who had the temerity to suggest that Smike had run away, for which he was soundly beaten until he rolled away out of Mr. Squeers' grasp. *Nicholas Nickleby*

TOMLINSON, MRS.: The post-office keeper who attends the charity ball at the Bull Inn, Rochester, and who seems to have been chosen, by mutual consent, to be the leader of the trade party. *Pickwick Papers*

TOMMY: The waterman who calls the first cab for Mr. Pickwick from the coach-stand at St. Martin's le Grand. This is when Mr. Pickwick begins his travels. *Pickwick Papers*

TOOBY: Poet of the local newspaper in Pip's village. *Great Expectations*

TOODLE, MR.: A stoker on the railway whose wife, Polly, is engaged by Mr. Dombey to be wet nurse to Paul Dombey, when his mother dies. He has four sons and a daughter. *Dombey and Son*

TOODLE, MRS. POLLY: Wife of Toodle the stoker and foster-mother to little Paul Dombey. Mother of five children —rosy in appearance and apple-faced. Mr. Dombey names her Richards. *Dombey and Son*

TOODLE, ROBIN: Otherwise known as Rob, the Grinder, or Biler. Mr. Dombey uses his influence to get him into an educational institution called the 'Charitable Grinders'. hence his nickname. He is made the butt of the neighbourhood because of the uniform he has to wear. *Dombey and Son*

TOOTLE, TOM: One of the regular customers at the Six Jolly Fellowship Porters. Because he was going to be married next month, Abbey Potterson, the proprietress of the public house, tells him it is time for him to be at home and asleep. *Our Mutual Friend*

TOOTS, MR.: Head boy at Dr. Blimber's School at Brighton, who gets very fond of Paul Dombey. He is also in love with Paul's sister, Florence, but she marries Walter Gay. Toots eventually marries Florence's maid Susan Nipper and they have several children. *Dombey and Son*

TOOTS, MRS. SUSAN: *see* Nipper, Susan

TOOZELLEM, THE HONOURABLE CLEMENTINA: Second wife of the fifteenth Earl of Stiltstalking, whose daughter was Lady Jemima. *Little Dorrit*

TOPE, MR.: Chief verger of Cloisterham Cathedral, whose vacant lodgings are taken by the mysterious character, Mr. Datchery. The rooms overlook the doorway in the cathedral gate and winding stairway leading to John Jasper's rooms. *The Mystery of Edwin Drood*

TOPE, MRS.: A comely dame, and wife of the chief verger. The breakfast she prepares for Mr. Datchery and his recording of the clues on his cupboard door with chalk lines are the very last incidents in the unfinished story. (Written the day before Dickens died.) *The Mystery of Edwin Drood*

TOPPER: A guest of Scrooge's nephew who clearly has his eye on one of Scrooge's niece's sisters—the plump one with the lace tucker. When playing blind man's buff, she was the only one he would catch. They finished up being very confidential behind the window-curtains. *A Christmas Carol*

TOPPIT, MISS: A literary lady in a brown wig of uncommon size. She and Miss Codger with Mrs. Hominey 'splashed up words in all directions' in conversation with Elijah Pogram at his levée at the National Hotel and all four got out of their depths and were unable to swim. *Martin Chuzzlewit*

TOPSAWYER, MR.: The gentleman who, according to the waiter's story to David Copperfield, ordered a glass of ale, drank it, and fell dead. To oblige David the waiter drinks the glass of ale ordered for him. *David Copperfield*

T'OTHER GOVERNOR: Rogue Riderhood's name for Eugene Wrayburn (*q.v.*).

T'OTHEREST GOVERNOR: Rogue Riderhood's name for Bradley Headstone (*q.v.*).

TOUGHY: *see* Jo

TOWLINSON, THOMAS: Footman in Mr. Dombey's domestic household. When Mr. Dombey becomes bankrupt and the household breaks up, Towlinson marries the housemaid, Anne, and they settle in Oxford Market in the general greengrocery and herb and leech line. *Dombey and Son*

TOX, LUCRETIA: A friend of Mr. Dombey's sister, Mrs. Chick. She greatly admires Mr. Dombey and even hopes that he might take her for his second wife. Mrs. Chick cuts her when she discovers her aspirations. 'A long, lean figure wearing such a faded air, that she seemed not to have been made in what linen-drapers call "fast colours" originally, and to have, little by little, washed out.' She introduces the Toodle family to Mr. Dombey when a nurse is needed for Paul. *Dombey and Son*

TOZER: A pupil at Dr. Blimber's school at Brighton and room mate of Paul Dombey, together with Briggs. *Dombey and Son*

TRABB, MR.: Tailor and undertaker. He provides Pip with his 'town' suit after Pip's fortune has been realized. He also officiates at the funeral of Pip's sister, Mrs. Joe Gargery. *Great Expectations*

TRABB'S BOY: He is errand boy to Trabb, the tailor. He mocks Pip on his first appearance in the little country town after becoming a 'gentleman', and pretends to be overcome by Pip's grandeur. Later, however, he is instrumental in saving Pip's life by guiding the rescuers to where Orlick has Pip in captivity and is preparing to murder him. *Great Expectations*

TRADDLES, THOMAS: David Copperfield's school friend who is with him at Salem House. Later, Traddles lodges with the Micawbers and gets involved in Mr. Micawber's affairs by standing guarantor for him. He is also instrumental in foiling the criminal plots of Uriah Heep and freeing Mr. Wickfield from suspicion. He marries Miss Sophy Crewler—'the dearest girl in the world'. *David Copperfield*

TREASURY: *see* Merdle, Mr.

TRENT, FREDERICK: Little Nell's dissolute brother. He has an idea of marrying her to his friend Dick Swiveller, thinking that his sister will get all his grandfather's money. After falling in with a gang of gamblers and card-sharpers he goes abroad where he lives by his wits. His drowned body, disfigured by bruises, said to have been caused in a scuffle, was finally recognized in a hospital in Paris. *The Old Curiosity Shop*

TRENT, GRANDFATHER: He is a little old man with long grey hair. He was obsessed with the idea that he could gain a fortune for his little granddaughter, Nell, by gambling. He borrowed sums of money from Quilp with this end in view and mortgages all his property. He loses all the money and is ruined. The business is taken over and sold up by Quilp. After a severe illness, Grandfather Trent is taken away by Nell to get him away from the temptation of gambling. After much hardship and wandering through the countryside they settle in a village where Little Nell dies. Her grandfather dies soon after, brokenhearted at her loss. *The Old Curiosity Shop*

TRENT, NELLY: 'Little Nell', the heroine of the story, who after leaving their home wanders through the countryside with her grandfather trying to keep him away from the temptation to gamble. They meet many strange people and for a time Nell works for Mrs. Jarley, as guide to her wax-works. Her grandfather's gambling habits break out again, and Nell takes him away as there is the possibility of his turning thief to obtain money to play cards. Finally, in a state of collapse she is rescued by an old schoolmaster she had met previously, who takes her to a village where he has obtained work, and gets her taken on as guide in the old village church. Her health has broken down, however, as a result of her many privations and she dies. Her grandfather's brother who has been searching for them, arrives too late to save her. *The Old Curiosity Shop*

TRIMMERS, MR.: He got up a subscription for the widow and family of six children of a man killed in the East India Docks—smashed by a cask of sugar. The Cheeryble Brothers donated forty pounds. *Nicholas Nickleby*

TROTTER, JOB: Jingle's servant and fellow conspirator. He finally ends up in the Fleet Prison with Jingle, from which both are rescued by Mr. Pickwick who pays their debts. Job Trotter goes to the West Indies with Jingle after being released from prison. *Pickwick Papers*

TROTTERS: *see* Harris, Mr.

TROTTY: *see* Veck, Trotty.

TROTWOOD, BETSEY: David Copperfield's great-aunt, who appears at his birth, but vanishes on finding that the baby is a boy, having set her heart on a girl. After being ill-treated by his stepfather, Mr. Murdstone, and being put to work in a wine-bottling factory, David runs away to his aunt in Dover. She decides to take care of him and have him educated. Miss Trotwood has a ne'er-do-well husband who turns up occasionally and demands money. He eventually dies. For a time Miss Trotwood is under the impression that she has been ruined by Mr. Wickfield who deals with her affairs. Mr. Micawber reveals that it was owing to the machinations of Uriah Heep, who attempted to throw the blame on his partner, Wickfield. Her money is restored to her and she uses some of it to help Mr. Micawber and his family. She looks after Mr. Dick, an old lunatic. She has a great antipathy to anyone riding a donkey over the green in front of her cottage. *David Copperfield*

TRUMAN, HANBURY & BUXTON: Brewers mentioned by Mrs. Micawber. *David Copperfield*

TRUNDLE, MR.: The suitor of Miss Isabella Wardle, to whom he is married. They later attend the wedding of Mr. Snodgrass and Emily Wardle, Isabella's sister. *Pickwick Papers*

TUCKLE, MR.: A footman who attends the 'swarry' in Bath. A stoutish gentleman in a bright crimson coat, with long tails, vivid red breeches and a cocked hat. Sam Weller calls him 'Blazes'. *Pickwick Papers*

TUGBY, MR.: The breathless porter of Sir Joseph Bowley, who opened the door to Trotty Veck. He later marries Mrs. Chickenstalker, and helps to look after the little general shop. *The Chimes*

TUGBY, MRS.: *see* Chickenstalker, Mrs. Anne

TULKINGHORN, MR.: Lawyer to Sir Leicester Dedlock, among many other great families, whose secrets he retains. Finding out that Lady Dedlock had a lover prior to her marriage to Sir Leicester and by whom she had a child, he threatens to reveal this secret to her husband. Mr. Tulkinghorn is shot and several people including Lady Dedlock are suspected. Later, Hortense, Lady Dedlock's late maid, is arrested for the murder, which she has tried to throw upon her mistress. Mr. Tulkinghorn had threatened her with prison if she did not cease to pester him to get her a job, and this was her revenge. *Bleak House*

TUNGAY: Wooden-legged gatekeeper at Salem House, the boys' school attended by David Copperfield. The schoolmaster, Mr. Creakle, could only speak in a whisper, so Tungay used to stump along beside him and repeat everything he said in a loud voice. *David Copperfield*

TUPMAN, TRACY: A member of the Pickwick Club who accompanies Mr. Pickwick on his travels. At Manor Farm, Dingley Dell, he fell for the charming Rachael Wardle, but she was enticed away from him by Mr. Jingle. Mr. Tupman, finally, when his friends Winkle and Snodgrass got married, took lodgings at Richmond. There he walks constantly on the terrace during the summer months, with a youthful and jaunty air, which has rendered him the admiration of the numerous elderly ladies of single condition, who reside in the vicinity. He never proposes again. *Pickwick Papers*

TURVEYDROP, PRINCE, (JUNIOR): The son of Mr. Turveydrop, senior, who runs the Dancing Academy and plays a little fiddle (or kit) to accompany the dances. He was called Prince in remembrance of the Prince Regent. He married Caddy Jellyby. They have a daughter, Esther —a tiny little old-faced mite, with a countenance that seemed to be scarcely anything but cap-border. *Bleak House*

TURVEYDROP, MR., (SENIOR): A widower and father of Prince Turveydrop. He had married a little dancing-mistress, who had worked herself to death for him, and he had continued to live on his son, and was celebrated for his deportment. After his son's marriage to Caddy, old Turveydrop continues to live with the young couple, taking the best rooms for himself. *Bleak House*

TURVEYDROP, MRS.: *see* Jellyby, Caddy

TWEMLOW, MELVIN: First cousin to Lord Snigsworth, who made him an allowance, and a friend of the Veneerings. He is in demand at society receptions and functions because of his high connexion. *Our Mutual Friend*

TWINKLETON, MISS: Headmistress of Nun's House, Cloisterham, school for young ladies. She comes to London as companion to Rosa Bud, one of her pupils, and carries on a war with the Billickin', landlady of a lodging house in Bloomsbury. *The Mystery of Edwin Drood*

TWIST, OLIVER: Hero of the story—born in a workhouse, where the children are starved. The illegitimate son of Agnes Fleming and Leeford (senior) and half-brother to Monks (Edward Leeford). Because he dares to ask for more he is apprenticed to an undertaker, Sowerberry. Oliver runs away to London, is met by the Artful Dodger, and is taken to Fagin's den. Monks pays Fagin to make Oliver a thief, because if that happens the boy forfeits his share of Leeford senior's estate. Oliver is saved from a life of crime by Mr. Brownlow and cared for. After being recaptured by the thieves and used by Bill Sikes in an attempted burglary, Oliver again falls into kind hands, in a house where his mother's sister, Rose Maylie, lives. Oliver lives happily with his newly-found friends and is eventually restored to Mr. Brownlow, who knew and loved his mother. He is known to the thieves as 'Nolly'. Sikes, on one occasion calls him Ned. *Oliver Twist*

U

UPWITCH, RICHARD: A greengrocer. One of the ordinary jurymen, who is pressed into the special jury to make up the number required for the Bardell *v.* Pickwick case. *Pickwick Papers*

V

VARDEN, DOLLY: Daughter of Gabriel Varden, the locksmith. A little coquette who is sorry when she finds that Joe Willet has gone away to be a soldier. She is captured by the Gordon Rioters with Emma Haredale, but rescued by Joe, who has returned from the war minus one arm. They get married and have a number of little Joes and Dollys. *Barnaby Rudge*

VARDEN, GABRIEL: Locksmith. He is forced by the mob to go to Newgate Prison where they demand that he picks the lock of the gate. This he refuses to do and the mob begins to get ugly. He is saved in time by Joe Willet and Edward Haredale. *Barnaby Rudge*

VARDEN, MRS. MARTHA: Wife of Gabriel. At first she appears as a shrew, but later reforms. A lady of what is commonly called uncertain temper—a phrase which being interpreted signifies a temper tolerably certain to make everybody more or less uncomfortable. *Barnaby Rudge*

VECK, MARGARET (MEG): Toby Veck's daughter. She brings him a meal of hot tripe and a potato to his windy corner by the church, where he waits for jobs. She marries a handsome young smith—Richard. *The Chimes*

VECK, TOBY, OR TROTTY: He was called Trotty because of his pace. He is a ticket-porter who waited on the corner beside a church in the City. Discouraged by the words of Alderman Cute, for whom he does an errand, and Sir Joseph Bowley, his faith in himself and the poor people begins to falter. He falls asleep on New Year's Eve and dreams that the chimes show him the importance of not doubting ourselves nor one another and he wakes to a happy New Year and his daughter's forthcoming wedding. *The Chimes*

VENEERING, HAMILTON: Of Chicksey, Veneering and Stobbles, a drug-house. Once their traveller and commission agent, Veneering had absorbed both his partners. He eventually becomes bankrupt, retires to Calais, where he lives on Mrs. Veneering's jewellery. *Our Mutual Friend*

VENEERING, MRS. ANASTASIA: Wife of Hamilton Veneering. 'Bran-new' people in a 'bran-new' house in a 'bran-new' quarter of London. They had a 'bran-new' baby. *Our Mutual Friend*

VENGEANCE, THE: A leading revolutionary among the women in Saint Antoine, Paris. The short, rather plump wife of a starved grocer and close friend of Madame Defarge. *A Tale of Two Cities*

VENUS, MR.: A taxidermist and preserver of animals and birds, who has a little shop in Clerkenwell. He plotted with Silas Wegg against Mr. Boffin, but eventually changes sides and marries Pleasant Riderhood. *Our Mutual Friend*

VERISOPHT, LORD FREDERICK: Client of Ralph Nickleby and one of Sir Mulberry Hawk's tools. He finally quarrels with Sir Mulberry over Kate Nickleby, which culminates in a duel at Ham, beside the river. Sir Mulberry kills him. *Nicholas Nickleby*

VHOLES, CAROLINE, EMMA, AND JANE: The three daughters of Mr. Vholes, whom he supports. *Bleak House*

VHOLES, MR.: A lawyer and widower who supports an aged father in the Vale of Taunton, besides three daughters. He had also supported his grandmother who died in her hundred and second year. He becomes Richard Carstone's solicitor and encourages Richard to put faith in the Jarndyce and Jarndyce suit. *Bleak House*

VUFFIN, MR.: A travelling showman, proprietor of a giant and a little lady without legs or arms. *The Old Curiosity Shop*

W

WACKLES, JANE: Youngest daughter of Mrs. Wackles. She teaches the art of needlework, marking, and samplery, in her mother's ladies seminary. *The Old Curiosity Shop*

WACKLES, MELISSA: Eldest daughter of Mrs. Wackles. She teaches English grammar, composition, geography, and the use of dumb-bells. *The Old Curiosity Shop*

WACKLES, MRS.: She runs a ladies' seminary at Chelsea. She saw to corporal punishment, fasting, torturing, and other terrors. *The Old Curiosity Shop*

WACKLES, SOPHIA: 'Sophy'. The middle daughter. She teaches writing, arithmetic, dancing, music, and general fascination. She was being courted by Dick Swiveller, but when Dick throws her over, she marries Mr. Cheggs, a market-gardener. *The Old Curiosity Shop*

WADE, MISS: A handsome young Englishwoman, travelling on her own. She had a sullen disposition and was worried by fancied wrongs. She entices Tattycoram away from the Meagles family, by making her dissatisfied with her lot, but Tattycoram later leaves her and returns to her old master and mistress. *Little Dorrit*

WALDENGARVER, MR.: The name taken by Mr. Wopsle, when he took up acting. *See* Wopsle, Mr.

WALKER, MICK: Boy at Murdstone and Grinby's warehouse, who works with David Copperfield. His father was a barge-man, and walked, in a black velvet head-dress, in the Lord Mayor's Show. *David Copperfield*

WALKER, MR. H.: A tailor, with a wife and two children, and a convert to temperance, whose case is cited in the annual report of the Brick Lane Branch of the United Grand Junction Ebenezer Temperance Association. When in better circumstances owned to have been in the constant habit of drinking ale and beer. Probably, twice a week for twenty years tasted 'dog's nose'. Had a rusty needle stuck into him. Is out of work and penniless; has nothing but cold water to drink and never feels thirsty. *Pickwick Papers*

WALTERS, LIEUTENANT: Name given by Mr. Toots to Walter Gay. *See* Gay, Walter

WARDEN, MICHAEL: A client of Snitchey and Craggs, solicitors, who was almost ruined because of his own improvident ways. He is in love with Dr. Jeddler's youngest daughter, Marion, who is already engaged to Alfred Heathfield. Michael Warden is persuaded to go away so that his affairs can be put in order. This he does and Marion makes it look as though she has run away with him, to leave Alfred for her sister, Grace, whom she knows loves him, and who finally marries Alfred. Eventually Marion returns, having been living with an aunt. Warden also returns and marries her. *The Battle of Life*

WARDEN, MRS. MICHAEL: *see* Jeddler, Marion

WARDLE, EMILY: Mr. Wardle's daughter, who marries Mr. Snodgrass in Dulwich Church and they settle down on a farm at Dingley Dell. *Pickwick Papers*

WARDLE, ISABELLA: Another of Mr. Wardle's daughters, who marries Mr. Trundle. *Pickwick Papers*

WARDLE, MR.: A gentleman farmer and widower who lives with his daughters, his sister and his mother at Manor Farm, Dingley Dell, where he entertains Mr. Pickwick and his friends. *Pickwick Papers*

WARDLE, MRS.: Mr. Wardle's mother. She is seventy-three and very deaf. *Pickwick Papers*

WARDLE, RACHAEL: Mr. Wardle's sister—a lady of doubtful age. Mr. Tupman falls in love with her, but by a trick, Mr. Jingle persuades her to transfer her affections to him. They elope and are pursued by Mr. Wardle and Mr. Pickwick, to the White Hart Inn, London. Mr. Jingle, for a monetary consideration, is persuaded to abandon Miss Rachael and she returns home with her brother. *Pickwick Papers*

WATERBROOK, MR.: Mr. Wickfield's agent in London, who lives in Ely Place and invites Mr. Wickfield and his daughter, Agnes, to stay with him in London, where David Copperfield calls on them. 'A middle-aged gentleman with a short throat and a good deal of shirt collar, who only wanted a black nose to be the portrait of a pug dog.' *David Copperfield*

WATERBROOK, MRS.: Wife of Mr. Waterbrook, a large lady in a large dress. David did not know which was dress and which was lady. *David Copperfield*

WATERS: A young lady recollected by Mrs. Nickleby, who went as a companion to a married lady. *Nicholas Nickleby*

WATERTOAST SYMPATHIZERS: Name of an American Association, a meeting of which Martin Chuzzlewit attended in the National Hotel, a spectacle 'calc'lated to make the British lion put his tail between his legs'. *Martin Chuzzlewit*

WATKINS, MR.: Mr. Nickleby, senior, went bail for him. He is Kate Nickleby's godfather. *Nicholas Nickleby*

He kept the Old Boar in a village in Devonshire. He borrowed twenty pounds from Mr. Nickleby senior. *Nicholas Nickleby*

WATTY, MR.: A bankrupt client of Mr. Perker, to whom Mr. Perker is not at home. *Pickwick Papers*

WEEVLE: *see* Jobling, Tony

WEGG, SILAS: A stallkeeper with a wooden leg who sells halfpenny ballads, nuts, apples, oranges, and gingerbread. He is engaged by Mr. Boffin to read to him and Mrs. Boffin, of an evening, at twopence halfpenny per hour. He plots to blackmail Mr. Boffin, but his scheme is frustrated and he is thrown into a refuse cart by Sloppy. *Our Mutual Friend*

WEGG, THOMAS: Father of Silas Wegg—a waterman, who was promoted to a situation under Government, and who said farewell to his old calling in rhyme. *Our Mutual Friend*

WELLER, MRS. TONY (SUSAN): Wife of Tony Weller and, prior to that, Susan Clarke, a widow. She kept the Marquis of Granby at Dorking, while Tony drove his coach. She becomes very friendly with Mr. Stiggins, a drunken cleric, who takes advantage of her generosity. *Pickwick Papers*

WELLER, SAMUEL: Son of Tony Weller and manservant to Mr. Pickwick. Mr. Pickwick found him cleaning boots at the White Hart Inn, Southwark. He accompanies Mr. Pickwick on his travels. He falls in love with Mary the pretty housemaid, who he first meets when she is employed in Ipswich by Mr. Nupkins, Mayor of the town. Later she gets married to Sam, and they have two sturdy little boys, Tony and Sam. *Pickwick Papers*

WELLER, TONY: Sam Weller's father, and a coach-driver. His wife keeps the Marquis of Granby, Dorking. She dies and leaves him a comfortable sum of money which Mr. Pickwick invests for him to great advantage. Later, when gout compels him to relinquish coach-driving, he retires to an excellent public house near Shooter's Hill. He had a great aversion to widows. *Pickwick Papers*

WEMMICK, JOHN: Clerk to Mr. Jaggers. In business he is hard like Mr. Jaggers, but at home in the Castle at Walworth, he is kind and good-hearted. His mouth was so straight and so much like a post office, he didn't eat his food—he posted it. He married Miss Skiffins. *Great Expectations*

WEMMICK, MRS.: *see* Skiffins, Miss

WEMMICK, SENIOR: The father of John Wemmick, known as the Aged P. A very old man in a flannel coat: clean, cheerful, comfortable, and well-cared-for, but intensely deaf. *Great Expectations*

WEST, DAME: Grandmother of Harry, the schoolmaster's best pupil. *The Old Curiosity Shop*

WESTLOCK, JOHN: Pupil of Mr. Pecksniff. He sees through the duplicity of Pecksniff and leaves him. Later he becomes very well off. He makes a friend of Tom Pinch and eventually marries Tom's sister, Ruth. They have Tom to live with them. *Martin Chuzzlewit*

WESTWOOD, MR.: A friend of Sir Mulberry Hawk who is a witness to the blow struck by Lord Verisopht on Sir Mulberry. He arranges the duel between them and acts as second for Sir Mulberry. *Nicholas Nickleby*

WHAT'S-HIS-NAME: Referred to by Mr. Squeers as one of the pupils at Dotheboys Hall, sleeping in Brooks's bed, which is full. *Nicholas Nickleby*

WHIFFERS, MR.: One of the footmen at the 'swarry' at Bath, attended by Sam Weller. He was dressed in orange-coloured plush. The uniform was extremely rich and expensive, the females in the family most agreeable, but—he had been required to eat cold meat—and so he had resigned. *Pickwick Papers*

WHIFFIN: The town crier at Eatanswill at the election. When required by the Mayor to proclaim silence, he performs a concerto on his bell, whereupon someone in the crowd shouts 'Muffins'. *Pickwick Papers*

WHILKS, MR.: When Mr. Pecksniff tries to engage Mrs. Gamp to lay out old Anthony Chuzzlewit and he raps on her bedroom window with the coachman's whip, she takes him for Mr. Whilks, whose wife is expecting another addition to the family. *Martin Chuzzlewit*

WHILKS, MRS.: One of Mrs. Gamp's clients. When Mrs. Gamp is woken up by Mr. Pecksniff to attend to Anthony Chuzzlewit, who has died, she thinks that it is Mrs. Whilks who needs her prematurely. *Martin Chuzzlewit*

WHIMPLE, MRS.: She kept the house at Chinks's Basin, Mill Pond Bank, down the river, where Magwitch, the convict, was hidden until Pip could get him out of the country. With her also Clara Barley lodges with her old bed-ridden father, Gruffandgrim, as Herbert Pocket called him. *Great Expectations*

WHISKER, RED: One of the picnic party near Guildford, who pretended that he could make a salad and voted himself in charge of the wine-cellar, in the hollow trunk of a tree. He becomes a rival of David Copperfield in giving attention to Dora Spenlow. *David Copperfield*

WHITROSE, LADY BELINDA: Who unknowingly did duty for Jenny Wren as model for her dolls. *Our Mutual Friend*

WICKAM, MRS.: Paul Dombey's nurse. She was a waiter's wife—always ready to pity herself, or to be pitied, or to pity anybody else. *Dombey and Son*

WICKFIELD, AGNES: Mr. Wickfield's only daughter. She acts as little housekeeper for her widowed father and is a companion to David, when they are girl and boy. Agnes becomes David Copperfield's second wife. They have a number of children, the eldest named Agnes. *David Copperfield*

WICKFIELD, MR.: A lawyer and widower. Legal adviser of Betsey Trotwood, David's aunt. David lives with the Wickfields when he is at school in Canterbury. Mr. Wickfield drinks rather heavily, and so gets into the power of Uriah Heep, his clerk, who becomes his partner. He is nearly ruined by Uriah Heep, but Mr. Micawber exposes Heep's villainies and Mr. Wickfield is cleared of suspicion of having lost his clients' money. *David Copperfield*

WICKFIELD, MRS. (DECEASED): Agnes's mother. She marries Mr. Wickfield against her father's wish and he renounces her and breaks her heart. *David Copperfield*

WICKS, MR.: One of Dodson and Fogg's clerks, who keeps Mr. Pickwick waiting when he calls at the office to see Mr. Fogg. *Pickwick Papers*

WIDEAWAKE: *see* Dorrit, W.

WIGGS AND CO.: Owners of the *Polyphemus*, a Private West Indian Trader of 350 tons. *Dombey and Son*

WILDSPARK, TOM: Tony Weller quotes him as having got off a charge of manslaughter because he had an 'alleybi' and he recommends the same procedure for Mr. Pickwick. *Pickwick Papers*

WILFER, BELLA: Elder daughter of Mr. and Mrs. Wilfer. She is 'left' in old John Harmon's will to his son. If he does not marry her, he forfeits his fortune. The Boffins, servants of old John Harmon, adopt her. John Harmon's son, thought to be murdered on his way back from abroad, reappears under the name of John Rokesmith and, as secretary to Boffin, watches Bella Wilfer, and finds her being spoilt by the thoughts of money. She reforms and marries John Rokesmith, thereby fulfilling the conditions of old John Harmon's will, and they both inherit the fortune. *Our Mutual Friend*

WILFER, LAVINIA: Younger daughter of the Wilfers and sister of Bella. After Bella is adopted by the Boffins, Lavinia (nicknamed Lavvy) takes on George Sampson, her sister's discarded suitor. Also called The Irrepressible. *Our Mutual Friend*

WILFER, MRS.: Wife of R. Wilfer, who makes her husband and the family generally uncomfortable. A tall angular woman, much given to tying up her head in a pocket handkerchief knotted under the chin. *Our Mutual Friend*

WILFER, REGINALD: A clerk working in the drug-house of Chicksey, Veneering and Stobbles. In view of his initial he was nicknamed 'Rumty'. He was also known as 'The Cherub'. Bella, his elder daughter, is very fond of him and gives him several treats when she has money given to her by the Boffins. He attends his daughter's secret wedding at Greenwich, to John Rokesmith. The Wilfers had numerous children, all but two out in the world—John, Susan, etc. *Our Mutual Friend*

WILKINS: Captain Boldwig's sub-gardener, who reveals to his master Mr. Pickwick asleep in a wheelbarrow, following the picnic on Boldwig's land. *Pickwick Papers*

WILKINS, DICK: Scrooge's fellow apprentice with old Fezziwig, who is shown by the Ghost of Christmas Past to Scrooge. He helps Scrooge put up the shutters of the warehouse on Christmas Eve and prepare the room for a dance. *A Christmas Carol*

WILKINS, MRS.: One of Mrs. Gamp's lady clients who Mrs. Gamp was afraid might have been 'took' before her time. Her husband was referred to as Young Wilkins. *Martin Chuzzlewit*

WILLET, JOE: Son of John Willet. He helps his father run the Maypole, but is kept down by parental control. He resents this treatment, and runs away and enlists in the Army, under the name of Tom Green. During the war in America he loses an arm at the siege of Savannah. He returns to England in time to fight the Gordon Rioters, and rescues Dolly Varden, with whom he has always been in love. He marries Dolly and they have a number of little Joes and Dollys. He inherits his father's money when the old man dies. *Barnaby Rudge*

WILLET, JOHN: Proprietor and owner of the Maypole Inn at Chigwell. During the Gordon Riots the inn is wrecked around him, and he never really recovers from the shock of that experience, nor to be reconciled to the fact that his son Joe has lost his arm at the 'Salwanners'. When he dies he leaves a considerable sum of money to Joe. *Barnaby Rudge*

WILLET, MRS. JOE: *see* Varden, Dolly

WILLIAM: Coachman who drives David Copperfield to London, when he goes there to 'look around him'. *David Copperfield*

Waiter at the inn at Yarmouth, where David waits for the coach to take him to London to school. He drinks David's glass of ale and eats a considerable part of his dinner, under the excuse of counteracting the effects of the ale. *David Copperfield*

The groom who was holding Sir Mulberry Hawk's horse when Nicholas attacked Sir Mulberry. *Nicholas Nickleby*

The waiter at the Saracen's Head in Snow Hill, London, who is told by Squeers to fill the mug of milk up to the top with lukewarm water to eke it out for the young pupils going to Dotheboys Hall, Yorkshire. *Nicholas Nickleby*

WILLIAM, SHINY: Deputy hostler at the Bull Inn, Rochester. He is told by the hostler to hand Mr. Pickwick 'the ribbons'. This is when Mr. Pickwick and his friends attempt to go to Manor Farm, for the first time. *Pickwick Papers*

WILLIAM, SWEET: Travelling showman. He comes to the Jolly Sandboys with other fairground people. *The Old Curiosity Shop*

WILLIAMS, WILLIAM: A customer at the Six Jolly Fellowship Porters. Abbey Potterson, the proprietress, tells him that he is due home. He takes his leave meekly with other customers in the tavern. *Our Mutual Friend*

WILLY: Brother of Little Nell's friend in the village, who had died. *The Old Curiosity Shop*

WINKLE, MRS.: *see* Allen, Arabella

WINKLE, NATHANIEL: Member of the Pickwick Club and one of Mr. Pickwick's companions on his travels. He is supposed to be an expert at various sports, but turns out to be quite the reverse. He is involved in many adventures including a challenge to a duel, a case of mistaken identity. He married Arabella Allen, whom he first met at the military tournament at Chatham and then at Manor Farm, Dingley Dell. *Pickwick Papers*

WINKLE, SENIOR, MR.: A wharfinger at Birmingham, and father of Nathaniel. Mr. Pickwick sees him to announce his son's marriage to Arabella Allen. The old gentleman receives this news coldly, but later travels to London and gives the couple his blessing when he meets Arabella. *Pickwick Papers*

WINKS: *see* Deputy

WISK, MISS: She becomes the fiancée of Mr. Quayle. Her mission was to show the world that woman's mission was man's mission. *Bleak House*

WITHERDEN, MR.: A notary to whom Mr. Abel Garland was articled. He is concerned with the final downfall of Sampson Brass. *The Old Curiosity Shop*

WITHERFIELD, MISS: Mr. Magnus comes to the Great White Horse, at Ipswich prepared to propose to her. Mr. Pickwick, however, loses his way in the hotel on the night of their arrival and gets into Miss Witherfield's room by mistake. When confronted with her in the morning there is a very awkward situation and thinking that Mr. Magnus and Mr. Pickwick will fight a duel, Miss Witherfield reports this to the Mayor. This results in the arrest of Mr. Pickwick and his friends. She is sometimes referred to as the lady in yellow curl-papers. *Pickwick Papers*

WITHERS: Mrs. Skewton's page—'a flushed page, who seemed to have in part outgrown and in part out-pushed his strength, for when he stood up he was tall, wan and thin'. *Dombey and Son*

WITTITERLY, HENRY: The husband of Mrs. Wittitterly who makes much of her supposed delicacy and poor health. *Nicholas Nickleby*

WITTITERLY, MRS. JULIA: A pale-faced lady who engages Kate Nickleby as her companion. *Nicholas Nickleby*

WOBBLER, MR.: In the Secretarial Department of the Circumlocution Office, who was having his lunch when Arthur Clennam calls to make an enquiry. He was spreading marmalade on bread with a paper-knife and answered Arthur Clennam with his mouth full. *Little Dorrit*

WOLF, MR.: A friend of Tigg Montague and a literary character, who is one of the guests at the dinner given by Montague to which Jonas Chuzzlewit is invited. He was said to have run a remarkably clever weekly paper. *Martin Chuzzlewit*

WOOD, JEMMY: Also of Gloucester. *See* Boffin, N.

WOODCOURT, ALLAN: A young doctor who attends Captain Hawdon, Miss Flite, and Jo, the crossing-sweeper. For a time he is a naval surgeon and he acts with great bravery during a shipwreck and looks after the survivors. He marries Esther Summerson. *Bleak House*

WOODCOURT, MRS.: Allan Woodcourt's mother—a Welsh lady who lays great stress on her ancestry. She therefore discourages Esther Summerson from thinking of her son as a suitor. Later she comes to appreciate Esther and withdraws her objection to the marriage. *Bleak House*

WOPSLE, MR.: A church clerk and friend of Pip's sister and Joe Gargery. He lives over his great-aunt's shop. Later he gives up the church and goes on the stage, under the pseudonym of Waldengarver, but he is not very successful. *Great Expectations*

WOPSLE'S GREAT AUNT, MR.: She kept a dame school which was attended by young Pip. 'A ridiculous old woman of limited means and unlimited infirmity, who used to go to sleep from six to seven every evening, in the society of youth who paid twopence per week each for the improving opportunity of seeing her do it.' Biddy was her assistant. *Great Expectations*

WRAYBURN, EUGENE: A barrister who is aimless and indolent. Friend of Mortimer Lightwood, a solicitor and attorney. Eugene refers to his father as M.R.F. (my respected father). His eldest brother was heir to the Family Embarrassments (called before company the Family Estates), his second brother was a 'pillar of the church', and his third brother appointed by M.R.F. to be a Circumnavigator—in the Navy, but he did not circumnavigate. It was settled that his youngest brother should have mechanical genius. Eugene accompanied Mortimer Lightwood to investigate a murder on the river and met Lizzie Hexam, the daughter of a riverside man who found the body, Gaffer Hexam. Eugene is attracted by her. She saves his life when he is nearly murdered by his rival in love—Bradley Headstone. Eugene later marries Lizzie Hexam. He is known to Rogue Riderhood, another riverside character, as 'T'other Governor'. *Our Mutual Friend*

WRAYBURN, MRS. EUGENE: *see* Hexam, Lizzie

WRAYBURN, SENIOR, MR.: Father of Eugene Wrayburn and referred to by Eugene as M.R.F. *Our Mutual Friend*

WREN, JENNY: *see* Cleaver, Fanny

WRYMUG, MRS.: Of Pleasant Place, Finsbury, whose name was down at an employment agency, as requiring a cook. *Nicholas Nickleby*

WUGSBY, JANE: One of Mrs. Colonel Wugsby's daughters who is reprimanded by her mother because she asked if she could dance with the youngest Mr. Crawley, whose father had eight hundred a year that died with him. The other Miss Wugsby, her sister, was praised for wanting to dance with Lord Mutanhed—immensely rich. *Pickwick Papers*

WUGSBY, MRS. COLONEL: Of an ancient and whist-like appearance. She was one of the whist party at the Assembly Rooms at Bath, in which Mr. Pickwick took part. *Pickwick Papers*

Y

YAWLER: An old schoolfellow of Traddles at Salem House—son of a professional man, with his nose on one side. Traddles began, with Yawler's assistance, to copy law writings and then made abstracts and so got into the law. *David Copperfield*

YOUNG BLIGHT: *see* Blight, Young

Z

ZEPHYR, THE: *see* Mivins, Mr.

Animals

BOXER: John Peerybingle the carrier's dog, who accompanies him on his rounds. 'His body all on one side, and his ears pricked up inquisitively, and that knob of a tail making the most of itself in the air.' *The Cricket on the Hearth*

BULLS-EYE: Bill Sikes' dog. A white shaggy dog, with his face scratched and torn in twenty different places. After the murder of Nancy, the dog tries to follow Sikes on his flight and the robber tries to drown him. The dog finally leads the mob to where Sikes is hiding, and when Sikes is accidentally hanged, is killed by a fall from the roof. *Oliver Twist*

CAPRICORN: Distinguished nephew of the prancing horse, driven by Bailey Junior, in the equipage belonging to Tigg Montague. *Martin Chuzzlewit*

CARLO: One of Jerry's troupe of performing dogs, the first one to have its name called out to eat. Little Nell and her grandfather meet them in the Jolly Sandboys. *The Old Curiosity Shop*

CAULIFLOWER: Distinguished brother of the prancing horse driven by Bailey Junior in the equipage belonging to Tigg Montague. *Martin Chuzzlewit*

DAPH: A pointer belonging to Sir Geoffrey Manning, on whose ground Mr. Wardle and the Pickwickians hold their shooting-party. *Pickwick Papers*

DICK: Tim Linkinwater's pet blackbird, which is blind. Linkinwater is clerk to the Cheeryble Brothers. *Nicholas Nickleby*

DIOGENES: The dog at Dr. Blimber's, of which Paul Dombey is fond. After Paul's death, Toots presents the dog to Florence Dombey in memory of her brother. 'A blundering, ill-favoured, clumsy, bullet-headed dog.' *Dombey and Son*

'EDDARD': The name of the donkey pulling the truck of the hoarse gentleman with a carrot for a whip, who gives Silas Wegg a lift to Boffin's Bower, when Wegg is going first to read to Mr. and Mrs. Boffin. *Our Mutual Friend*

FLITE'S BIRDS, MISS: Ashes, Cunning, Death, Despair, Dust, Folly, Gammon, Hope, Jargon, Joy, Life, Madness, Peace, Plunder, Precedent, Rags, Rest, Ruin, Sheepskin, Spinach, Want, Waste, Wigs, Words, Youth, plus Two Wards in Chancery added later. These are the captive birds which Miss Flite plans to release when the Jarndyce and Jarndyce case is completed. *Bleak House*

GRIP: A raven carried in a basket by Barnaby Rudge—his constant companion on all his wanderings. Grip talks a great deal and amuses all who see him. He finally lands in prison with his master. *Barnaby Rudge*

JANE, LADY: The large grey cat of Mr. Krook, the rag-dealer. *Bleak House*

JIP: Dora Spenlow's little dog. *David Copperfield*

JUNO: One of the pointers accompanying Mr. Wardle's shooting-party. *Pickwick Papers*

LION: Harry Gowan's dog. The dog distrusts Rigaud who is posing in Gowan's studio, and Rigaud poisons him. *Little Dorrit*

LOVELY: The dog referred to by the gentleman cleaning the gun in the Circumlocution Office. *Little Dorrit*

MERRYLEGS: The performing dog belonging to Signor Jupe, the clown in Sleary's Circus. *Hard Times*

PEDRO: One of Jerry's troupe of performing dogs seen by the grandfather and Little Nell in the Jolly Sandboys. He was a new dog and wore a cap over one eye and a gaudy coat trimmed with spangles. *The Old Curiosity Shop*

PINCHER AND NEPTUNE: Two watchdogs at Mrs. Maylie's house at Chertsey, which are sent to look for the robbers, and are recalled by a tremulous voice. *Oliver Twist*

PONTO: Mr. Jingle's very sagacious sporting dog which would not pass the notice—'Gamekeeper has orders to shoot all dogs found in his enclosure'. *Pickwick Papers*

WHISKER: The pony belonging to Mr. and Mrs. Garland, which pulls their trap. He is a very wilful animal and only Kit Nubbles appears to be able to manage him. Kit is engaged by Mr. Garland for this purpose. *The Old Curiosity Shop*

The Characters — Book by Book

Barnaby Rudge

Bleak House

Bleak House (cont.)

Bleak House (cont.)

Christmas Books

A CHRISTMAS CAROL

Christmas Books (cont.)

THE BATTLE OF LIFE (*cont.*)

Heathfield, Mrs. (*see* Jeddler, Grace)

Heathfield, Marion (*see* Jeddler, Marion)

Jeddler, Dr.

Jeddler, Grace

Jeddler, Marion

Jeddler, Martha

Martha, Aunt (*see* Jeddler, Martha)

Newcome, Clemency

Snitchey, Mr. Jonathan

Snitchey, Mrs.

Warden, Mr. Michael

Warden, Mrs. Michael (*see* Jeddler, Marion)

THE HAUNTED MAN

Denham, Edmund (*see* Longford, Edmund)

Dolph or 'Dolphus (*see* Tetterby, 'Dolphus)

Haunted Man, The (*see* Redlaw, Mr.)

Longford, Mr. Edmund

Moloch, Little (Sally Tetterby)

Redlaw, Mr.

Swidger, Junior, Charley

Swidger, George

Swidger, Mrs. Milly

Swidger, Philip

Swidger, William

Tetterby, Adolphus

Tetterby, 'Dolphus

Tetterby, Johnny

Tetterby, Mrs. Sophia

Tetterby, Sally (*see* Moloch, Little)

David Copperfield

David Copperfield (cont.)

David Copperfield (cont.)

Dombey and Son

Dombey and Son (cont.)

Dombey and Son (cont.)

Great Expectations

Great Expectations (cont.)

Hard Times

Hard Times (cont.)

Little Dorrit

Little Dorrit (cont.)

Martin Chuzzlewit

Martin Chuzzlewit (cont.)

Mystery of Edwin Drood, The

Mystery of Edwin Drood, The (cont.)

Nicholas Nickleby

222

Nicholas Nickleby (cont.)

Nicholas Nickleby (cont.)

Old Curiosity Shop, The

Old Curiosity Shop, The (cont.)

Oliver Twist (cont.)

Our Mutual Friend

Our Mutual Friend (cont.)

Our Mutual Friend (cont.)

Pickwick Papers

Pickwick Papers (cont.)

Pickwick Papers (cont.)

Pickwick Papers (cont.)

Tale of Two Cities, A